GORBACHEV'S NEW THINKING

GORBACHEV'S NEW THINKING
Prospects for Joint Ventures

Edited By
RONALD D. LIEBOWITZ

INTERNATIONAL INSTITUTE FOR ECONOMIC ADVANCEMENT

BALLINGER PUBLISHING COMPANY
Cambridge, Massachusetts
A Subsidiary of Harper & Row, Publishers, Inc.

International Standard Book Number: 0-88730-322-6

Library of Congress Catalog Card Number: 88-22229

Printed in the United States of America

Library of Congress Cataloging-in-Publication Data

Gorbachev's new thinking: prospects for joint ventures/edited by Ronald D. Liebowitz.

p.   cm.
Includes index.
ISBN 0-88730-322-6
1. Soviet Union—Economic policy—1986–   2. Soviet Union—Foreign economic relations   3. East-West trade (1945–   )   4. Joint ventures—Soviet Union.   5.Gorbachev, Mikhail Sergeevich, 1931–   .
I. Liebowitz, Ronald D.

HC336.26.G676   1988
338.8'8847—dc 19   88-22229   CIP

CONTENTS

LIST OF FIGURES

LIST OF TABLES

FOREWORD

The policy of *perestroika* (restructuring), centerpiece of General Secretary Mikhail Gorbachev's new thinking, invites economic, political, and social reform of staggering proportions. Indeed, we may be witnessing the advent of another Soviet revolution. A sagging economy appears to have convinced Soviet Party leaders who support new thinking that the Stalinist command economy is ill-suited to the enormously complex task of managing an increasingly mature, industrialized economy.[1]

Viewed from the West, from a market economy orientation, a set of incentives that propels market economy efficiency, growth, and technological development is missing from the official economy. The very nature of a centralized planning system, in which virtually every aspect of economic decisionmaking has been subject to absolute central control, is both throttling the Soviet economy and ineffectively allocating resources to satisfy peoples' material needs.

It was against this backdrop that Mikhail Gorbachev became General Secretary of the Communist Party of the Soviet Union (CPSU) in March 1985, and surprised the world with his call for Soviet radical reform on February 25, 1986. Is a second Soviet revolution imminent? Raymond E. Benson, a former United States Information Agency Foreign Service Officer stationed in Moscow for almost a decade, recently stated:

---

1. Ed. A. Hewett, *Reforming the Soviet Economy* (Brookings Institution, 1988), pp. 2-3.

I offer my view that recent events in the Soviet Union constitute nothing less than a sea change in the life of that enormous country. Neither we nor even they, and I include Gorbachev, know how it will all come out, what specific programs, reforms, and policies will rise to the top in this most yeasty period in Soviet life. They are, in fact, experimenting, and in doing so have forever changed the agenda for the discussion within the Soviet Union of domestic and foreign policy issues, and by the outside world as it considers the Soviet Union today. Moreover, the Soviet populace has been invited--more than that, exhorted--to participate. Thus, the vocabulary describing the social and economic and even legal problems of the day has been augmented, and the book of acceptable terms is now open for further editing. Now we have *glasnost, perestroika, demokratizatsia, kooperatsia, khozrashchet,* even *fermery,* and all are based on the vague concept, *novoye myshleniye,* at the core of which is supposed to be truth-seeking, telling it like it is, or, in Ranke's phrase, *wie es eigentlich gewesen ist,* like it was.[2]

Growing out of the International Institute for Economic Advancement's 1987 East-West conference on Gorbachev's New Thinking, organized by Middlebury College professors Ronald D. Liebowitz and Catherine Sokil, and held at Middlebury College's Bread Loaf Mountain Campus, this volume focuses on the economic dimensions of the Gorbachev revolution, particularly as they apply to possible new business activity between East and West. It is too early to make predictions about the success or failure of new thinking; however, it is already apparent that we are entering a new and unprecedented era of East-West economic relations. What do the reforms portend for business dealings with the East? Moreover, how much real reform is likely? How much decentralization of decisionmaking will or can occur, given the political constraints presented by Party interests? What is the business climate likely to be? Are the Soviets about to embrace closer interdependence by inviting a spate of joint ventures with the West?

The papers in this volume examine and seek answers to these questions from a variety of perspectives. That they do not all speak in one voice allows the compilation to contribute to our understanding of the range of possible outcomes, and as such should assist policymakers in formulating possible legislation, business people in assessing the potential for operating in East Bloc countries, and students of East-West relations in trying to gain a fuller

---

2. Raymond E. Benson, "Glasnost and the Soviet Media," Robert E. VanDeVelde Lecture Series, Middlebury College, 24 February 1988. Mr. Benson currently serves as Director of the American Collegiate Consortium for East-West Cultural and Academic Exchange, Middlebury College. *Khozrashchet* is a system of cost accounting that requires Soviet enterprises to maintain solvency through their own profits. *Fermery* (farmers) is a word that had been missing from the Soviet lexicon because of its bourgeois roots. *Novoye myshleniye* means "new thinking."

understanding of just what Gorbachev's startling proposals might augur for Soviet society and future East-West relations.

Suffice it to say that this volume simply would not exist without the able, energetic, and immeasureable contributions of two key people. Sally Evans managed to organize our conference so deftly that the organization was hardly visible. Everything simply flowed smoothly and flawlessly. Colleen Duncan, who arrived on the scene just as we were embarking on the volume's production, is largely responsible for the accuracy and readability of the volume. The Center would like to thank both for their skills and work on this project.

The International Institute for Economic Advancement seeks to promote a clearer and more complete understanding of international economic issues within and among the business, academic, and government communities. As such, the Institute and its research center, the Middlebury Center for Economic Studies, are dedicated to sponsoring and publishing policy-oriented research and seminars, and providing advice and consultation to policymakers on domestic and international economic policy. Annual conference series for each project provide sustained forums for diverse groups of academic and business researchers, and government representatives to examine, debate, and illuminate specific sets of issues. The Institute is privately funded, non-partisan, and not for profit.

We welcome ideas and opinions for better achieving our goals.

Michael P. Claudon
Managing Director
International Institute for Economic Advancement
Middlebury Center for Economic Studies
Middlebury College
Middlebury, VT 05753

INTRODUCTION

The emergence of Mikhail Gorbachev reflects a realization among members of the Communist Party elite that the march toward communism has gone awry and needs to be put back on course.[1] Indeed, problems that were once described by the Soviets as being inherent to the capitalist system--and absent in socialist societies--have begun to surface in the Soviet Union. Other developments, which appear to be a result of deteriorating economic, social, and environmental conditions, have been identified by both Soviet and western analysts and serve to underscore the need for change.

The challenges facing Mikhail Gorbachev since he assumed the leadership of the Communist Party of the Soviet Union (CPSU) in March of 1985 have been evident to many both inside and outside the USSR. The Soviet economic system has become encumbered and is unable to provide the quantity and quality of goods for its population at home and for its foreign policy objectives. A decade of stagnant or declining economic growth rates, and all the problems associated with a rigid system of economic management that has inhibited large scale technological innovation, have left the USSR a military superpower with a second-rate economy. Food shortages in many areas outside Moscow, Leningrad, and Kiev have been reported with greater frequency, and a host of other problems ranging from alcoholism to increases in crime are but some of the issues Gorbachev needs to address. While the severity of all these problems and their uniqueness to the Soviet Union may have been--and

1. Judging from the continual criticism directed at virtually all of Leonid Brezhnev's programs, along with the changing of all things named after the former leader, one must assume the present leadership feels the wrong turn was taken sometime during the second half of the Brezhnev years.

1

continue to be--exaggerated in the western press, there is no doubt that
Gorbachev recognizes the problems exist and need to be addressed, discussed,
and alleviated if the material well-being of the Soviet population is to improve
and the legitimacy of the Party and socialist system is to be maintained.

Recognizing these challenges is one thing, but meeting them, especially
those Gorbachev faces, is quite another. There is great skepticism as to
whether anybody, let alone the new General Secretary, has an effective agenda
for reform, and whether the system he is inheriting could even be reformed.
Needless to say, the changes that need to be introduced entail more than
tinkering with the system. However, because opposition to reform in the
Soviet Union has become institutionalized and comes from so many segments
of Soviet society, many in the West wonder whether any meaningful changes
are possible with anything less than a *complete* overhaul of the Soviet

economic and political system. Reform attempts since Stalin resulted more in
chaos than progress, as interest groups created and strengthened by the highly
centralized Soviet system prevented the full implementation of a meaningful
reform program. Despite failures of past Soviet leaders, Mikhail Gorbachev
has proposed a sweeping program of reforms intended to reverse his country's
economic and social stagnation. Although the blueprints for the program are
extensive, many of the prescriptions appear vague, some seem impossible
given institutional constraints, and many are likely to irk large segments of the
Soviet population. Although the reasons and needs for economic and social
reforms in the Soviet Union are many and are being spelled out each week in
both the Soviet and western press, one can reduce the Gorbachev task to the
following: maintain political control and stability while allowing the
decentralization of economic decisionmaking and greater flexibility for the
economic mechanism in order to encourage technological innovation and
greater incentive for workers.

The method by which Gorbachev intends to complete the aforementioned
task involves "restructuring" *(perestroika)* of the Soviet economy and society.
Calls--even exhortations--for greater openness and democratization, absent in
the Soviet Union since the 1920s, have unleashed discussion and at times
lively debate over issues previously discussed only in private. The new
openness of Soviet society is deemed necessary by Gorbachev if the ills of the
system are to be confronted and alleviated, but critics feel the airing of errors
and failures can only result in the diminution of political control by the
Communist Party--the institution most responsible for the problems now
under discussion. And, while the impetus for the Gorbachev reform program is
no doubt grounded in domestic issues, the potential impact of openness and
new thinking *(novoye myshleniye)* transcends Soviet borders and can indirectly

challenge Party control at home. The substance and style of Gorbachev's *perestroika* have already affected the domestic politics of the East European states (and will continue to do so), and the broad range of issues Gorbachev is proposing for international discussion under the rubric of *perestroika* will undoubtedly influence the domestic politics of West Europe and the United States, challenge the unity of the NATO alliance, and, of course, redefine Soviet-American relations.[2]

While few inside the Soviet Union argue with the need to improve the economy, the potential impact of the measures necessary for economic improvement generates apprehension, skepticism, and domestic opposition to the whole program. By transferring decisionmaking power from a highly centralized bureaucracy to decentralized managerial levels, the reform program threatens the power and jobs of a large and powerful interest group. But the bureaucrats are not alone in seeing their positions threatened or compromised. The rank and file, for whom the reforms are ultimately to bring a new era of material prosperity, wonder what will be sacrificed from the old system while the economy is in transition. While it is true the Soviet system has become ossified and in dire need of some reform, it must be recognized that it is also a system that has provided a substantial degree of security for the Soviet population, limited as it may appear to those in the West. If the new economic mechanism eliminates the long-established and *expected* subsidies for food, housing, and other necessities, why should it be embraced by the population?

In addition to these forms of opposition, regional interests threaten the implementation of the reform program. When Gorbachev calls for the more *efficient* use of investment funds, he is proposing an investment strategy that favors areas of higher capital and labor productivity. Because of historical and other factors, the western areas of the state, which are predominantly Russian and Slavic, would receive the lion's share of new capital at the expense of the lesser developed and therefore less efficient non-Slavic southern regions. Given the multinational character of the Soviet state, and the propensity for most ethnic groups to remain in their well-defined ethnic homelands, a policy that favors one region over another can be seen as one that favors one ethnic group over others. The "Nationalities Question," which Gorbachev recently called "the most fundamental, vital issue of [Soviet] society,"[3] could easily generate political instability that could curtail or even end the reform program. The

2. See Mikhail Gorbachev, *Perestroika: New Thinking For Our Country and the World* (New York: Harper & Row, 1987).

3. See Philip Taubman, "Gorbachev Urges Party to Update Communist Theory," *New York Times,* 19 February 1988, p. 1.

articulation of ethnic discontent, which before the advent of *glasnost* was prohibited and censored, has led to political uprisings in Kazakhstan, the Baltic Republics, and most recently in Armenia. Such events could have a snowballing effect throughout the multinational Soviet state and fuel the discontent among those opposed to the program and further threaten its success.

The International Institute for Economic Advancement convened a group of social scientists specializing in Soviet Studies and entrepreneurs who have established business relationships with the East to discuss the prospects for reform, the domestic limitations to Gorbachev's program, East and West European perspectives on the reforms, and the overall climate for increased East-West economic interaction. It is clear that a major goal of the openness, new thinking, and restructuring strategy developed by Gorbachev is to rationalize the changes deemed necessary for the Soviet economy's modernization, including increased trade and economic cooperation with the western, capitalist economies. While it is too early to provide details on the prospects for joint economic ventures, compensation contracts, or other forms of increased business relations, the ten essays compiled for this volume provide a foundation that allows one to assess the future climate for increased trade and economic agreements between East and West. Greater East-West economic interaction is a major item on the Gorbachev agenda, but several objective changes need to be made before meaningful exchanges can begin.

In the first chapter of the volume, Ralph S. Clem focuses on the social issues that served as an impetus for the Gorbachev reform program and represent some of his greatest challenges. The interrelated nature of the social, political, and economic dimensions of *perestroika* is highlighted by Clem, who sees the success of *perestroika* linked to the development of a new social contract between the leadership and the population based on the fundamentals of a meritocracy rather than the now outdated contract based on egalitarianism. Such a shift could ultimately lead to greater incentive and productivity, but it will inevitably lead to greater inequality and elitism, which may--at least initially--increase the chances of political instability. As Ed Hewett has pointed out, if *perestroika* proceeds smoothly in its initial stages without any signs of disaffected workers and consumers, we can assume nothing is really changing.[4] The very things restructuring must do will have to result in increased political or social tensions. Whether or not Gorbachev succeeds in forging a new social contract with the Soviet populace, Clem calls for objectivity in assessing the events of change.

---

4. See Ed A. Hewett, "Day No. 1 of Soviet Reforms," *New York Times*, 1 January 1988, p. 31.

Robert E. Leggett and Robert A. Kellogg trace the performance of the Soviet economy over the past two decades, and assess the potential impact of the Gorbachev program on its future performance. The two economists provide a summary of the proposed changes to be made as part of the reform program, and provide "best case-worst case" scenarios for the Soviet economy depending on how fully the major aspects of the reform program are implemented. Even if the reforms are implemented without a hitch, Leggett and Kellogg conclude that after initial improvements in the economy's performance, the long-term prognosis for the Soviet economy is not good; Soviet targets of 4 or 5 percent growth rates by the end of this century will not be met. The success of the program, however, will not be judged solely on the basis of output growth. As Leggett and Kellogg note, "The quality dimension will weigh heavily in how the shortfall between actual and planned growth is perceived."

Gertrude E. Schroeder provides another assessment of Gorbachev's economic reform package and outlines the changes the Soviet leader has thus far proposed. Schroeder analyzes recent Soviet documents and decrees and evaluates the changing role of central planning, the position of the firm, the balance of power between central and regional administrative bodies, prices and wages, the role of foreign trade, and private economic activity. Like Leggett and Kellogg, Schroeder is skeptical about Gorbachev's chances for attaining his stated goals. The long-term effects of a centrally managed socialist economy, according to Schroeder, may be too much to overcome--at least in the short term.

Lieutenant General William E. Odom and Wladyslaw W. Jermakowicz feel the underlying reasons for *perestroika* are more political than economic, and both are pessimistic about the chances for meaningful and successful reform. Odom offers the argument that it would be implausible to believe that Gorbachev and the Party could follow their stated goals on reform to their logical conclusion because to do so would challenge the foundations of democratic centralism. The true aim of the reforms, according to Odom, is to *revitalize* the old system, and he asserts that the Gorbachev strategy--built around the *glasnost, perestroika, novoye myshleniye* triad--can be traced back to Khrushchev and Stalin. Jermakowicz traces the history of economic reforms since World War II and combines data on the turnover rates among Party and Government elites with the timing of reform programs to arrive at a conclusion similar to Odom's. Jermakowicz sees the Gorbachev reform program as a continuation of the Andropov era, and doubts that Gorbachev can overcome conservative elements in the Party apparatus and bring meaningful change to the economic system. He sees the reforms as a way for the General Secretary to change Party personnel, and predicts that the reform program will cease when Gorbachev either fully defeats his more conservative opponents or loses the battle.

Three papers focus on the view of the Gorbachev program from outside the Soviet Union. Michael Kraus and John E. Parsons evaluate the perspectives of the Soviet Union's East European allies, and Gary G. Meyers addresses the West European view of greater Soviet-West economic cooperation. Kraus underscores the economic and political importance of East Europe to the Soviet reform agenda. The East European economies represent possible testing grounds for some of the economic reforms considered for the Soviet economy, though the structures and sizes of the economies make it impossible to draw clear comparisons. These economies fit into the Gorbachev reform scheme by way of their special trade relationships with the Soviet Union. As Kraus notes, Gorbachev is eager to have some of the Soviet reforms--especially those requiring better quality control and state-of-the-art technology--applied to the East European economies to ensure an improvement in the shoddy machinery the East Europeans have been exporting to Moscow. Politically, it is not clear how eager the aging and conservative leaders of the East European states are to accept the Gorbachev program, nor is it clear how much *glasnost* the Soviet leader wants to see introduced next door. Encouraging openness in societies that for years have permitted more freedom of expression than what is now allowed in the Soviet Union could lead to demands for greater political freedom. The anti-reform elements in Moscow need only see East European unrest or excessive demands to justify their desire to halt Soviet reforms.

John E. Parsons argues that increased economic interaction depends not only on new thinking in the East, but in the West as well. Parsons uses the experiences of the 1970s, the first period of significant East-West economic interaction, to assess the prospects for a second wave of extensive industrial cooperation agreements. While the rules of the game have obviously changed for the socialist states on account of new thinking, Parsons feels the West must reassess how it views greater trade with the socialist states. New thinking should not be limited to East Europe and the Soviet Union.

The West European perspective on significant economic interaction between East and West is provided by Gary G. Meyers. Meyers feels that, although the West Europeans in the past have been more willing than the Americans to conduct business with the Soviets, the new generation of West European leaders may very well be more cautious in its approach to new overtures from the Soviets for fear of misreading the true aims of *glasnost* and *perestroika*. While this may be true in the long term, Meyers feels the greatest barrier to expanded East-West trade relations will be the pressure exerted by conservative elements in the United States, which oppose increasing economic interaction with the Soviet Union regardless of the political climate in Europe and the United States.

The final two essays of the volume concentrate on the role of Siberia, with its enormous resource wealth, in promoting greater trade and joint economic activity with Pacific Basin states. Victor L. Mote examines the feasibility of the "eastern alternative"--developing Siberia in order to increase trade opportunities by marketing primary industrial and energy resources. Mote concludes that, although the massive Baikal-Amur Mainline railway (BAM) will be further developed, and there is vast wealth waiting to be exploited in the region, the costs of development, labor problems, competition, and "few prospects for payoffs within the next score of years," preclude the imminent development of the eastern regions' trade with the Pacific states.

Michael J. Bradshaw evaluates the Gorbachev reform program as it relates to the Far East and the Pacific Basin, and assesses the potential for increased Japanese involvement in the development of the Soviet Far East. He cites historical constraints to greater Soviet-Japanese economic interaction, but also sees other factors limiting economic cooperation in general and joint ventures in particular. Bradshaw cites the Soviet demand for majority ownership and the requirement that the chairperson of any joint venture be a Soviet citizen as examples of roadblocks to an agreement. Other factors, including the changing structure of Japanese imports, have reduced the likelihood for joint venture activity. And finally, even if Gorbachev is successful in restructuring the Soviet economy, Bradshaw concludes that his success may lead to a relative decline in the importance of resource-producing areas such as the Soviet Far East, limiting further the chances for increased Japanese-Soviet joint venture activity.

The overall sense of the conferees was perhaps more optimistic about the chances of Mikhail Gorbachev's leadership *improving* the Soviet economy and social conditions than in meeting fully all of the stated goals in his reform package. Perhaps more significant than the absolute success or failure of the reform program, however, are the long-term effects of *glasnost* and *demokratizatsia* on domestic politics inside the Soviet Union. Some argue that the longer these two aspects of the reform program are encouraged, the more difficult it will be to undo their effects. While this may or may not be true, Mikhail Gorbachev has already made a great impact on Soviet history, and despite the pessimistic view held by many at the Conference concerning the chances for a radical transformation of the Soviet economic mechanism, the consensus was, as Leggett and Kellogg wrote in this volume: "Judging by Gorbachev's personality and the advice he is getting, he can be counted on to move forward with his 'new economic mechanism' in the years ahead." While none of the participants at the conference envisioned the commencement of significant joint venture activity in the short term, there was agreement that, since greater trade with the capitalist states is necessary for the Soviet economy, the Soviets will have to reevaluate their trading position within the CMEA and with the West. Consequently, work has begun on coordinating the 1988 Middlebury Center for Economic Studies Conference at Middlebury, which will focus on CMEA-West trade issues, and continue the Institute's economic, political, and social examination of the Gorbachev reform program.

Ronald D. Liebowitz
Department of Geography
Middlebury Center for Economic Studies
Middlebury College
June 1988

1 PERESTROIKA: THE SOCIAL CONTEXT OF REFORM IN THE SOVIET UNION

Ralph S. Clem

In a remarkably brief period and in a dramatic manner largely unforeseen, the study of the Soviet Union has been transformed from a moribund subject into an exciting, revitalized field. As Seweryn Bialer put it, "The Soviet Union has become the most interesting country in the world."[1] The reason for this sudden and intense interest in the Soviet Union is, of course, the sweeping and perhaps profound set of reforms initiated by General Secretary Gorbachev and his political allies under the rubric *perestroika*. This movement, which encompasses political, economic, cultural, and social elements, has the potential for effecting changes in the Soviet system almost beyond imagination prior to Gorbachev's accession to power. It is, in short, ". . . a gigantic experiment touching virtually all fields of endeavor,"[2] ". . . an elaborate and far-flung program affecting Soviet society at a host of points."[3]

Before even attempting to answer the vital and obvious questions about the likelihood of success for *perestroika*, it is important first to inquire why such a radical departure from the past--fraught as it is with political risk--was deemed necessary, and, with those reasons in mind, to try to comprehend the program in all of its complexity. This is not a simple task, because the problems that prompted the Soviet leadership to implement "revolutionary" changes in the

1. Seweryn Bialer, "Inside Glasnost," *Atlantic Monthly,* 261 (2), pp. 65-72.
2. Ibid., p. 65.
3. George F. Kennan, "The Gorbachev Prospect," *New York Review,* 21 January 1988, pp. 3-7.

economic and social order are multifaceted, interconnected, and deeply rooted, and therefore are not amenable to simple solutions or ". . . timid, creeping reforms."[4]

The ultimate goal of *perestroika* is to reinvigorate the Soviet economy to break out of a long-term decline in its rate of economic growth. Indeed, many of the most important features of the program are essentially economic in nature and have been widely discussed in the Soviet Union and the West; price reforms, capital investment priorities, planning and administration of production, and technological improvements in industry are examples of economic issues that are receiving attention from reformers. But it is clear to the new Soviet leadership that much more than technical "tinkering" with the economy or even the introduction of efficiency and quality-oriented criteria for evaluating enterprises will be required to escape from the doldrums in which the Soviet Union is drifting.

Rather than limiting themselves to the purely economic realm, the *perestroichiki* see reform as incorporating aspects of Soviet society and culture as well, not that such changes are necessarily desirable in the abstract--although Gorbachev has characterized the program as a relegitimation of socialist ideals-- but because they are *required* for the attainment of economic goals. Thus, *perestroika* must take into account "the human factor" across the social, economic, and political dimensions to ". . . wake up those who have fallen asleep,"[5] which apparently means the majority of Soviet citizens.

In this chapter I will examine the social environment of *perestroika*, with an eye toward articulating the linkages between the political leadership, the society, and the economy. Certainly, most people would agree that there are linkages, but the trick is to specify the connections and the direction of causality to enable a meaningful analysis and to make guarded forecasts. In this regard the manner in which one approaches the study of the Soviet Union becomes an important issue in itself; epistemological questions to some degree shape the course and outcome of discussion. Thus, if one is predisposed to view the Soviet system in terms of the classic "totalitarian" model as articulated so lucidly by the late Leonard Schapiro, then social conditions are important only insofar as they impose constraints on the political leadership's plans (the ultimate *raison d'etre* of that leadership being simply and solely to keep itself in power). Schapiro summed up this line of thinking thus: ". . . if one ignores the totalitarian nature of Soviet power, and in particular the way in

---

4. Mikhail Gorbachev, *Perestroika: New Thinking for Our Country and the World* (New York: Harper & Row, 1987).

5. Ibid., p. 29.

which the ruling elite exercises power by ignoring, circumventing and manipulating all institutions, one is writing about a product of one's imagination, not the Soviet Union."[6] In the same vein, he stated that "another recent fashion which has developed in some writing about the Soviet Union is calling in aid the specialized jargon of sociological analysis and applying it to Soviet society, with the result that all perception of the real nature of that society is lost in a welter of meaningless technicalities--meaningless, that is, in the Soviet context, where the basic data for sociological analysis are absent."[7]

On the other hand, the "revisionist" or "interest group" or "reformism-conservatism" school, epitomized by scholars Jerry Hough and Stephen Cohen, takes into account what its practitioners perceive as constituencies within the system that are not necessarily passive or manipulated, but which may also exert pressure on the political leadership. As Cohen noted: "Authentic reformism and conservatism are always social as well as political . . . . In fact, there is every reason to think that virtually all the diverse trends in society . . . also exist inside the political officialdom, however subterraneanly."[8] In this light, society is not only acted upon but forces the political elite to respond to various interests, even though these interests may not be articulated overtly.

Another point about contemporary Sovietology needs to be made, and that concerns the tendency manifested in recent years by journalists and academicians to portray the Soviet Union as beset by crisis.[9] In this connection, I am reminded that in 1970 the late dissident Andrei Amalrik published a much-touted book entitled *Will the Soviet Union Survive until 1984?* Allowing for some rhetorical effect in that question, it is nevertheless instructive to reflect that although the answer is now clear in the affirmative, others continue this tradition of dire analysis and prediction of the decline of the Soviet system. Referring to them, Robert Lewis said: "From the current Western literature one derives the impression that here is a country characterized mainly by weaknesses and few strengths, and yet it appears to be quite stable.

6. Leonard Schapiro, "My Fifty Years of Social Science," *Russian Studies,* ed. Ellen Dahrendorf (New York: Viking, 1987), p. 22.

7. Ibid., p. 22.

8. Stephen F. Cohen, *Rethinking the Soviet Experience: Politics and History Since 1917* (New York: Oxford University Press, 1985), pp. 132-133.

9. See Marshall I. Goldman, *USSR in Crisis: The Failure of an Economic System* (New York: W.W. Norton and Company, 1983).

Such interpretations reveal more about the authors than about the Soviet Union and involve considerable wishful thinking."[10]

This is not to say that problems, perhaps even serious problems, do not exist within Soviet society. Clearly they do, and they are partly the reason *perestroika* is necessary. Ironically, even when Gorbachev addresses the pressing need for reform, improved relations with the West, or arms control, his statements are often viewed as an attempt at deception. In this regard, George F. Kennan stated:

> To suggest, as some Western commentators seem to do, that words and insights of this nature are brought forward only to deceive people in the West and to lull them into a sense of false security while Soviet forces prepare to attack them reveals a lack of understanding for the realities of Gorbachev's position that borders on the bizarre. Such words cut to the heart of established beliefs and policy. They represent a serious responsibility on the part of the statesman who puts them forward. To suppose that Gorbachev has all internal problems so beautifully solved that he can afford to play around irresponsibly, for the purpose of throwing sand in our eyes, with statements of this nature is to misjudge fundamentally the responsibilities he assumes in making them, and the priorities he has to bear in mind between the external and the internal effects of his words.[11]

It may be that the dominance of the totalitarian model as an analytical device together with a tendency to assume the worst about the Soviet Union and an unwillingness to accept declaratory policy from the Soviet leadership are the reasons why the Soviet Studies community in the West largely failed to anticipate and has yet to appreciate fully the pace, scope, and potential of the changes engendered by Gorbachev.[12] To approach the situation from a different

10. Robert A. Lewis, "The Universality of Demographic Processes in the USSR," *Geographical Studies on the USSR,* eds. George J. Demko and Roland J. Fuchs (Chicago: University of Chicago), Department of Geography, Research Paper No. 211, p. 114.

11. Kennan, "The Gorbachev Prospect," p. 6.

12. Consider the words of Marshall I. Goldman published in 1983: "Thus the regime still holds together more from inertia and fear than from momentum and hope. The sense of radical change and experiment has long since passed. Now there seems to be general agreement that even a minor change might trigger an uncontrollable avalanche." (*USSR in Crisis,* p. 70). Or, from a piece by the same author on the Op-Ed page of the *New York Times* ("Will Gorbachev be Brezhnev II?") shortly after Gorbachev was confirmed as General Secretary: "The rapidity of Mr. Gorbachev's appointment indicates he may be able to consolidate power sooner than expected. If he masters the system--rather than its mastering him--this may augur bold moves in domestic and foreign policy. Don't bet on it." By 1987, however, after many of Gorbachev's reforms were in place, Goldman sounded more optimistic: "But if anyone is to break the Soviet Union out if its trap, Gorbachev appears to be an excellent choice to do it . . . he moved quickly to consolidate his power. . . moreover, the sincerity of his desire to reform his country is beyond doubt . . . . Given his insight,

perspective, therefore, here we will examine the *perestroika* reforms as a response to social forces and conditions and as an attempt to correct or compensate for the negative and harness the positive aspects of those trends to facilitate economic measures designed to boost growth rates. As I see it, the three principal social areas that have a direct bearing on *perestroika* and are intended to be influenced thereby are labor force, ethnic, and health and aging issues, all of which are related and complex. Here I propose to describe these issues in the tangible or evidentiary sense and then to relate them to the reforms insofar as they are addressed by policy measures or public pronouncements. In conclusion, I will try to frame the overall question of the relationship between society and *perestroika* in terms of a new "social contract" between the Soviet citizenry and the political leadership.

LABOR FORCE

The fact that the Soviet economy has been facing a secular decline in the number of new entrants into the labor force has been evident for quite some time and has been detailed in both western and Soviet scholarship. To recapitulate the main points, owing to a long-term drop in fertility and intermittent demographic catastrophes, the rate of increase in the population of working age has decreased since the mid 1970s from about 2 percent per annum to a low of virtual stasis in the mid 1980s, followed by a projected slow increase to a level of approximately 1 percent per annum by the year 2000. Warren Eason summarized the consequences of this trend as follows: ". . . the transformation has been dramatic: from a country where labor policies and practices have reflected [an] abundance, to one where labor is 'scarce' and must be treated as such if economic performance is not to suffer."[13] Further difficulties arise from heavy military manpower requirements and from the lack of labor reserves in most rural areas and among women, both traditional sources of additional workers when the need has arisen in the past.

Compounding this problem is a significant interregional imbalance in the supply of labor created by geographical differentials in fertility. In short, virtually all growth in the labor force through the end of the century will occur in the southern tier of republics stretching from the Caucasus and across Central Asia and Kazakhstan. For example, Lewis estimated that between

enthusiasm, effort, and proselytizing style, he comes well equipped for the challenge." (*Gorbachev's Challenge*, p. 228).

13. Warren W. Eason, "Population and Labor Force," *Economics of Soviet Regions*, eds. I.S. Koropeckyj and Gertrude E. Schroeder (New York: Praeger, 1981), pp. 11-91.

1980 and 1990 almost three-quarters of the increase in the working age population will take place in these regions and, furthermore, most of that will be in rural areas.[14] As a result, Soviet planners are confronted by a spatial misalignment of most of the factors of production for an industrial economy: the developed infrastructure is largely in the west, the labor supply is mainly in the south, and natural resources are concentrated in the east. Allocating a larger share of investment to the labor surplus regions to use manpower *in situ* is not an attractive option as returns to capital in these areas are typically much lower than elsewhere.[15]

As daunting as these prospects may seem, they are not unique to the Soviet Union and may be amenable to at least partial solution through normal social processes and government policy initiatives. The slowdown in the growth in the number of workers might be offset by qualitative improvements in the Soviet labor force; indeed, educational attainment has risen dramatically in the past twenty years, to the point that about two-thirds of the population now has secondary level schooling. Of particular importance here is the huge projected expansion of vocational-technical education.[16] In the quantitative sense, labor force policy seems much more constrained, at least over the next twenty years, with the two main options involving a reduction in military manpower and an extension of retirement age and encouraging retirees to work at least part-time. The gravity of the former decision is obvious (but not without historical precedent), and in the latter it is already the case that many retirees continue to work. Finally, manpower will be redistributed as enterprises trim "stockpiled" labor from the wage rolls and a loss of job security and perhaps even unemployment forces displaced workers to seek new positions.[17]

To just touch on this next point, a higher level of labor productivity will in any event prove necessary for future economic growth, as has been stated in the political and academic literature in the Soviet Union and among western analysts. Greater labor discipline, involving a heightened sense of personal

14. Robert A. Lewis, "Regional Manpower Resources and Resource Development in the USSR: 1970-1990," *Soviet Natural Resources in the World Economy,* eds. Robert G. Jensen, Theodore Shabad, and Arthur W. Wright (Chicago: University of Chicago Press), pp. 72-96.

15. See Leslie Dienes, "Investment Priorities in Soviet Regions," *Annals of the Association of American Geographers,* 62 (4), pp. 437-454; and Ronald D. Liebowitz, "Soviet Investment Strategy: A Further Test of the 'Equalization Hypothesis,'" *Annals of the Association of American Geographers,* 77 (3), 1987, pp. 396-407.

16. Walter D. Connor, "Social Policy Under Gorbachev," *Problems of Communism,* 35, July-August, pp. 31-46.

17. V. Kostakov, "One Person Must Work Like Seven," *Sovetskaya kultura,* 4 January 1986, p. 3, translated in *Current Digest of the Soviet Press,* 38 (3), pp. 1-4.

responsibility and pride in workmanship, coupled with a decline in absenteeism, alcoholism, and corruption have been prominent features of the Gorbachev era, as has been the call for a reduction in labor turnover.[18] Other facets of the labor productivity issue, such as capitalization, wage increases, the availability of consumer goods, and a restructuring of authority in the workplace are clearly made more vital by the aggregate demographic trends.

As regards the geographical dimension of labor supply, it is possible that interregional migration may serve to balance the supply of and demand for manpower. It would be a gross understatement to characterize the debate over this point as contentious.[19] The majority of analysts view the prospects for such a migration on a large scale as unlikely, pointing to ethnic, cultural, and subtle economic factors as inhibiting an exodus from the south.[20] Others see this as essentially a question of timing; when conditions in the south are unfavorable enough to motivate people to move to areas of greater opportunity, then migration will occur regardless of the sociocultural obstacles.[21] Soviet government policy might influence this to some extent through more pronounced wage incentives in labor deficit regions and disincentives to remain in place.

THE ETHNIC FACTOR

The dramatic ethnic diversity of the Soviet population and the socioeconomic correlates thereof have prompted many observers to see this as a condition posing a serious threat to the stability of the system and its prospects for the future. Not surprisingly, ethnic plurality does lead to social and political problems in the Soviet Union, including discrimination and other forms of intolerance, some hostility on the part of minorities toward the majority and predominant Russians, as well as language, education, and employment disputes.[22]

---

18. Connor, "Social Policy Under Gorbachev," pp. 34-36.

19. See Michael Rywkin, "Central Asia and Soviet Manpower," *Problems of Communism,* 28, pp. 1-13, 1979.

20. See Murray Feshbach, "Prospects for Outmigration from Central Asia and Kazakhstan in the Next Decade," Joint Economic Committee of the U.S. Congress, *Soviet Economy in a Time of Change* (Washington: Government Printing Office, 1979), pp. 656-709.

21. See Robert A. Lewis, Richard H. Rowland, and Ralph S. Clem, *Nationality and Population Change in Russia and the USSR* (New York: Praeger, 1976).

22. Ralph S. Clem, "The Ethnic Dimension of the Soviet Union," *Contemporary Soviet Society,* eds. Jerry G. Pankhurst and Michael P. Sacks (New York: Praeger, 1980), pp. 11-62.

However, the ethnic factor in the Soviet context is usually portrayed in a more negative fashion and is seen as potentially more disruptive than similar situations elsewhere. Thus, although issues such as bilingualism and language rights are common to multiethnic societies, in the Soviet case the effort to establish Russian as a *lingua franca* is often seen as part of an effort to force the assimilation of non-Russian ethnic groups into an ethnic Russian linguistic and cultural norm. Another popular approach to this subject is to characterize the Soviet Union as ". . . the world's last empire."[23] Although the Russians were not the only people to create and hold a vast territorially contiguous state through military conquest and political domination, it is true that such scenarios can engender considerable resentment, resistance, and perhaps even rebellion against groups viewed as usurpers. With that in mind, Richard Pipes views the Soviet situation as one in which ". . . ethnic conflicts . . . assume the form of a battle of wits [wherein the non-Russians] . . . try to outsmart Moscow . . . [while] . . . there smolders resentment and, in some areas, hatred that can quickly explode into genocidal fury should the heavy hand of Russian authority weaken."[24]

Short of this catastrophic "genocidal fury," some tangible features of the ethnic dimension in Soviet society will no doubt influence the course of events politically, and, indirectly, economically in the Soviet Union in the future. Specifically, the much-publicized shifting population balance between the Russians and other European peoples of the Soviet Union and, on the other hand, the predominantly Muslim peoples of Central Asia (and some areas of the Caucasus) is a tendency that will gradually--and predictably--alter the ethnic composition of the Soviet populace.[25] Some of the consequences of this ethnodemographic shift are obvious and important: there will be a larger non-Russian component in the Soviet armed services and in the labor force (the regional aspect of the latter was discussed in the preceding section). However, the "crisis"[26] or "time bomb"[27] or "threat"[28] label that is often attached to this

23. See Richard Pipes, *Survival Is Not Enough: Soviet Realities and America's Future* (New York: Simon and Schuster, 1984); and *The Last Empire: Nationality and the Soviet Future,* ed. Robert Conquest (Stanford: Hoover Institution Press, 1986).

24. Pipes, *Survival Is Not Enough,* pp. 184-185.

25. Ralph S. Clem, "Ethnicity," *The Soviet Union Today: An Interpretive Guide,* ed. James Cracraft (Chicago: University of Chicago Press, 2nd Edition, 1988), pp. 303-314.

26. Herbert Meyer, "The Coming Soviet Ethnic Crisis," *Fortune,* 14 August 1978, p. 158.

27. *U.S. News and World Report,* "The Population Time Bomb that Kremlin Faces," 6 December 1982, p. 28.

28. Alexander Bennigsen and Marie Broxup, *The Islamic Threat to the Soviet States* (London: Croom Helm, 1983).

phenomenon is probably unwarranted, because such population trends occur slowly and are easily projected; this is certainly not a surprise to anyone, especially not to the Soviet political leadership. Clearly, plans might be made and policies developed to expand Russian language training for military recruits or those entering the civilian economy in critical, nationally integrated sectors. Ellen Jones, in considering the implications of ethnic plurality in the Soviet armed forces, reminded us that ". . . the USSR is by no means the only modern state whose military manpower management system must cope with ethnic, linguistic, and regional diversity among its troops."[29] The challenge to Soviet policymakers is to accommodate the interests of the ethnic minorities while maintaining the integrity of the state, a difficult but not impossible task.

As is true in other areas, it is premature to assess definitively the impact of *perestroika* on the ethnic situation, but we might at least be able to propose some possibilities. In his principal work on *perestroika,* Gorbachev devoted relatively little space to "the nationality question," portraying the issue in general thus:

> The Revolution and socialism have done away with national oppression and inequality, and ensured economic, intellectual and cultural progress for all nations and nationalities. Formerly backward nations have acquired an advanced industry, and a modern social structure. They have risen to the level of modern culture, although some of them previously did not even have alphabets of their own. Every unbiased person is bound to acknowledge the fact that our Party has carried out a tremendous amount of work and has transformed the situation.[30]

He went on to add that:

> All this does not mean, however, that national processes are problem-free. Contradictions are typical of any development, and they occur here as well. Regrettably, we used to stress our really considerable achievements in the solution of the nationality problem, and assessed the situation in high-flown terms. But this is real life with all its diversity and all its difficulties.[31]

The "contradictions" he refers to seem to be those which have troubled Soviet theorists and policymakers in the ethnic field since the inception of that state: how to reconcile integration with the development of ethnic

---

29. Ellen Jones, *Red Army and Society: A Sociology of the Soviet Military* (Boston: Allen and Unwin, 1985), p. xv.

30. Gorbachev, *Perestroika,* p. 118.

31. Ibid., pp. 118-119.

consciousness among the myriad minority groups while keeping "Great Russian chauvinism" at bay. The answer, in practice, has been to maintain a delicate balance between the needs of the center and the desires of the periphery through the operational medium of the ethnically federated Soviet state. Whereas the basic structure of the Soviet Union, created by Lenin in 1922, has endured these many years through extremely difficult times, there are some who see the entire thing as ready to come apart at the seams, as evidenced by titles such as *Decline of an Empire: The Soviet Socialist Republics in Revolt*.[32] Certainly, many features of the Soviet political system are not what they purport to be, and there is no doubt that genuine discontent exists among members of some ethnic groups because of their inclusion in the "fraternal socialist brotherhood of peoples." It is just as certain, however, that the republics are not "in revolt," and that over the decades a certain legitimacy has been attached to the Soviet federation, that most people at least acquiesce to its continuation, and that a non-Russian political elite has learned how to operate within that system to gain economic and social benefits for their constituents.[33]

The Gorbachev reforms are interesting in this context because they may threaten this *modus vivendi* in several ways. First, the sacking of Dinmukhamed Kunaev (the Party chief of Kazakhstan) and the subsequent disturbances in Alma Ata, and the recent disclosures of scandal in the Uzbek cotton industry, indicate that the anti-corruption drive might result in a curtailment in ethnic-based privilege and, if not carefully handled, the growth of anti-Russian or even anti-Soviet sentiment. Erosion of existing affirmative action policies favoring the minorities, as greater emphasis is placed on merit criteria in jobs and education, would also be viewed negatively by the non-Russians.[34] Secondly, the spread of *glasnost* to the ethnic groups has already led to nationalist demonstrations in the Baltic and Caucasian republics and to the surfacing of an incipient Russian nationalist movement. In the economic area, the decentralization of decisionmaking might lead to a reoccurrence of *mestnichestvo* (localism), the *bête noire* of Khrushchev's *sovnarkhozy* scheme. Likewise, if investment is allocated to regions without regard to the long-standing sensitivity to ethnic territorial development, some groups will lose ground and spatial socioeconomic inequalities would probably be exacerbated.[35]

32. Helene Carrere d'Encausse, *Decline of an Empire: The Soviet Socialist Republics in Revolt* (New York: Newsweek Books, 1979).

33. Teresa Rakowska-Harmstone, "The Dialectics of Nationalism in the USSR," *Problems of Communism*, 23 (3), 1974, pp. 1-13.

34. See Ellen Jones and Fred W. Grupp, "Modernisation and Ethnic Equalisation in the USSR," *Soviet Studies*, 36 (2), 1984, pp. 159-184.

35. Liebowitz, *Soviet Investment*, p. 405.

Finally, plans to allow workers to elect foremen and higher officials in enterprises could take on ethnic overtones if (as is often the case) the rank and file are drawn from minorities and the supervisory staff are Russians.

AGING AND HEALTH ISSUES

As is true in many developed states, the Soviet Union has been undergoing an aging process, a natural demographic consequence of declining fertility and continued low mortality. Estimates are that the population older than fifty-five years for women and sixty years for men will increase from about 15.5 percent of the total population in 1980 to between 18.2 and 19.0 percent in the year 2000.[36] Assuming that a retreat from the provisions of the pension laws of 1956 and 1965 is inadvisable politically and not morally acceptable and that the government continues to attempt to provide pensioners with a standard of living at least approaching the poverty level, the fiscal impact of the aging trend will be obvious.[37] Gorbachev has already indicated that his administration is committed to maintaining a safety net for the elderly, so there would seem to be little flexibility on this score.

The issue of the health of the Soviet population and resultant mortality levels in the Soviet Union has generated considerable interest and not a little hyperbole. Nick Eberstadt, for example, stated that: "From what I can make out, the USSR is indeed in the midst of a social and spiritual collapse the likes of which we in the West have never seen, and in fact can scarcely imagine."[38] Contrary to Eberstadt's belief, those in the West who lived through the Great Depression could say much about "social and spiritual collapse," but the real question is the extent to which the quality of life and health have deteriorated in the Soviet Union. Gorbachev has pointed to ". . . glaring shortcomings in our health services" and to the need ". . . for improving the country's public health services" as a part of the *perestroika* reforms.[39] There is little doubt--and Soviet authorities agree on this point--that inadequacies of the medical care delivery system, the impact of smoking and alcoholism, and possibly the effects of

36. Ward W. Kingkade, "Estimates and Projections of the Population of the USSR, 1979 to 2025," U.S. Bureau of the Census, *CIR Staff Paper No. 33*, 1987, p. 10.

37. Alastair McAuley, "Social Policy," *Soviet Policy for the 1980s,* eds. Archie Brown and Michael Kaser (Bloomington: Indiana University Press, 1982), pp. 146-169.

38. Nick Eberstadt, "The Soviet Union's Health Crisis," *Washington Inquirer,* 1 April 1983, p. 7; and Eberstadt, "The Health Crisis in the USSR," *New York Review,* 19 February 1981, pp. 23-31.

39. Gorbachev, *Perestroika,* pp. 21, 100.

pollution are serious concerns that need to be addressed by public health officials and the medical establishment. To what extent mortality has actually risen in the Soviet Union in the past ten to fifteen years is, however, highly problematic and subject to differing interpretation.[40] The principal reason for uncertainty is that the purported increase in mortality may well be spurious, in that it is to some degree attributable to technical factors associated with the collection of death statistics; improvements in mortality reporting may have led to an "artificial" rise in death rates--especially infant mortality rates--because a higher percentage of deaths is now captured by the registration system than before.[41] In any case, the trends in mortality were not of great magnitude and are probably within the range of error of the data; for example, life expectancy at birth for men declined from sixty-four years in 1971-1972 to a temporary low of sixty-two in 1978-1979, but has now risen back to sixty-four in the most recent data (which are for the second half of 1985 and first half of 1986).[42] Further, some common sense about comparing mortality data over time or between countries is probably in order. Eberstadt claimed that ". . . by the late 1950s the average Soviet citizen could expect to live 68.7 years; longer than his American counterpart . . .," and that by 1981 "there is not a single country in all of Europe, in fact, in which lives are so short, or babies' death rates so high--not even impoverished, half-civilized Albania."[43] The possibility of either of these statements being correct is, in my opinion, quite remote, and suggests that mortality levels in the Soviet Union were understated in the 1950s and are more accurate today, and the idea that life expectancy in Albania exceeds that of the Soviet Union is ridiculous and owes to a pronounced under-reporting of deaths in the former.

Gorbachev has addressed the need to make improvements in health care and to raise wages for the health professions, which might bring about further positive developments. In light of the ambiguities of mortality data, it would

40. See Christopher Davis and Murray Feshbach, *Rising Infant Mortality in the USSR in the 1970's*, U.S. Bureau of the Census, series p-95, no. 74, 1980; Murray Feshbach, "Social Maintenance in the USSR: Demographic Morass," *Washington Quarterly,* Summer 1982, pp. 92-98; Ellen Jones and Fred W. Grupp, "Infant Mortality Trends in the Soviet Union," *Population and Development Review,* 9 (2) 1983, pp. 213-246; and Albert Szymanski, "On the Uses of Disinformation to Legitimize the Revival of the Cold War: Health in the U.S.S.R.," *Science and Society,* 45 (4) 1982, pp. 453-474.

41. Jones and Grupp, "Infant Mortality Trends."

42. "USSR, Tsentral'noye Statisticheskoye Upravleniye," *Narodnoye Khozyaystvo SSSR v 1985g* (Moscow: Finansy i Statistika, 1986), p. 547.

43. Eberstadt, "The Health Crisis," p. 23.

seem prudent to downplay the crisis implications of health and mortality in the Soviet Union while continuing to be mindful of problems in these areas.

CONCLUSIONS

In attempting to assess the relevance of the foregoing to the larger question of *perestroika*, it is fruitful to consider the concept of "social contract" as put forth by Peter Hauslohner.[44]   He argued that ". . . the degree of social and political order observed in the Soviet Union . . . must be due to volunteered (rather than coerced) compliance and, more particularly, a result of the high stability, high-security, egalitarian, and libertarian elements of an otherwise austere and illiberal social policy."[45] The problem confronting Gorbachev, Hauslohner goes on to suggest, is that ". . . [the] bargain between the regime and society has now come undone."[46] Its undoing he attributes to the mutually negative influence of the old social order (which stifled initiative and productivity) and the economic slowdown which it at least partly created; as the system's ability to provide the minimally acceptable level of goods and services was threatened, the existing social contract between society and the political leadership became invalid. Gorbachev, in explaining why *perestroika* is necessary, confirmed this scenario, and stated:

> . . . [a] broad and frank analysis of the situation that has developed in our society by the middle of the eighties . . . [made it] . . . particularly clear . . . [that] the country began to lose momentum . . . [with] a kind of "braking mechanism" affecting social and economic development . . .[47]

Furthermore, "parasitical attitudes were on the rise, the prestige of conscientious and high-quality labor began to diminish, and a 'wage leveling' mentality was becoming widespread."[48]

At least some of the pressure put on the old social contract was generated by long-term changes in the composition of Soviet society. The change from a predominantly rural, agrarian, and uneducated population to an overwhelmingly urban, industrial, and increasingly professional society with much higher levels

---

44. See Peter Hauslohner, "Gorbachev's Social Contract," *Soviet Economy,* 3 (1), 1987, pp. 54-89.

45. Ibid., pp. 57-58.

46. Ibid., p. 60; see also Jerry F. Hough, "Gorbachev's Strategy," *Foreign Affairs,* 65 (1), 1985, pp. 33-55; and Seweryn Bialer, "Inside Glasnost," *Atlantic Monthly,* 261 (2), 1988, pp. 65-72.

47. Gorbachev, *Perestroika,* pp. 17-19.

48. Ibid., p. 20.

of educational attainment has fundamentally altered the manner in which the political elite must relate to the citizenry.[49] As Pipes stated, ". . . it is quite obvious . . . that it [the Soviet political leadership] must respond to the pressure of changing conditions brought about by such independent factors as the emergence of a large, well-educated technical intelligentsia, demographic developments, and a change in mood of the young generation."[50] Accordingly, concepts derived from other than the Soviet experience--such as Lerner's idea of "rising expectations" and Gurr's theory on "relative deprivation"--now make considerable sense in the Soviet context.

If *perestroika* is to succeed, a very significant change in the social contract must be implemented, a change toward a meritocracy and away from egalitarianism. Almost certainly the byproducts of this "to each according to his work" ethic will include greater socioeconomic inequality and elitism and considerably less of the all-embracing security to which Soviet citizens have become accustomed. During this long transitional period, stresses on the system may be more evident as the government rationalizes (raises) prices and reduces subsidies, as the private sector expands in services, and if deliveries of consumer goods fail to meet expectations. An appeal to workers to substitute "socialist morality" for material goods in an environment of tighter labor discipline clearly creates the danger of alienating the population and undercutting the very support on which *perestroika* depends.[51]

As such policies and events continue to unfold during this pivotal period in Soviet history, those of us concerned with trying to understand the Soviet Union must take care to see Gorbachev's moves in the economy and in attempting to redefine the social basis of legitimacy as objectively as possible. Viewing these changes through single-issue lenses or in comparison with other ideologically and developmentally different cases runs the risk of not seeing a critically important forest through less important trees.

49. Blair A. Ruble, "The Social Dimensions of Perestroika," *Soviet Economy,* 3 (2), pp. 171-185.

50. Richard Pipes, "Can the Soviet Union Reform?" *Foreign Affairs,* 53 (1), 1984, p. 48.

51. Alfred Evans, Jr., "The Decline of Developed Socialism? Some Trends in Recent Soviet Ideology," *Soviet Studies,* 38 (1), 1983, pp. 1-23.

2 THE SOVIET UNION: AN ECONOMY IN TRANSITION AND ITS PROSPECTS FOR ECONOMIC GROWTH

Robert E. Leggett and Robert L. Kellogg

This paper discusses General Secretary Gorbachev's economic program for revitalizing the Soviet economy, assesses the performance of the economy thus far under Gorbachev, and evaluates prospects for economic growth in the Soviet Union to the year 2000. A large-scale, macroeconomic model is used to analyze Soviet growth prospects. Because of the considerable uncertainty regarding the ultimate success of Gorbachev's modernization program and reform package, and the long timeframe of the projection, a single "most likely" forecast cannot be made. Instead, we developed three scenarios to reflect different degrees of success. The results of these simulations provide insights into what is possible and illustrate the dynamics involved when an economy administered by central planners for nearly seventy years attempts to change its method of operation.

When Gorbachev was appointed General Secretary in March 1985, the Soviet leadership faced an array of problems that was more complex than at any time in the postwar era:

The views and analyses expressed in this paper are those of the authors alone and do not necessarily represent judgments of the U.S. Government. Thanks are due to Gertrude E. Schroeder, University of Virginia, Charlottesville, Virginia, and to James Noren and F. Douglas Whitehouse, Central Intelligence Agency, McLean, Virginia, for helpful comments on earlier versions of the paper and the underlying research.

1. The Soviet Union was beset by political malaise extending back to the final years of the Brezhnev period.
2. Economic stagnation in much of East Europe, political unrest in Poland, and "counterrevolution" in Afghanistan, Angola, Ethiopia, and Mozambique threatened to undermine the stability of the Soviet empire and increase the cost of its maintenance.
3. The Reagan defense build-up and NATO's modernization of its conventional and theater nuclear forces threatened military gains of the 1970s.
4. The Soviet Union's status as a role model for economic development was being more openly called into question by some developing countries.

Perhaps most important, however, domestic economic growth had slowed.[1] Soviet per capita GNP growth in 1985 was less than half the United States', below most western countries', and even trailed some East European countries' growth (Figure 2-1).

Indeed, the Soviets faced a broad spectrum of economic problems. Civilian industrial facilities were, to a large extent, old and technologically obsolete. The rapid advances in computers, transistors, and integrated circuit microchips in the past decade, which led to the mass production of high-tech products in most developed countries (what Marshall Goldman calls the Third Industrial Revolution), had not been well assimilated in the Soviet Union nor diffused effectively throughout the economy.[2] Labor productivity in the Soviet Union lagged behind that in the West.[3] At the same time, improvements in living standards tapered off as a result of the economy's declining growth rate, which caused popular discontent to grow, and this was accompanied by rising crime rates, alcohol and drug abuse, declining worker morale, and a further decline in labor productivity. Simply put, the formula for economic growth that propelled the Soviet Union to world power status--a massive infusion of labor and capital--no longer seemed to be working. The highly centralized system of planning and management, in fact, seemingly had become overwhelmed by the increasing size and complexity of the economy.

The combination of these adverse events probably convinced a divided

1. Annual Soviet economy GNP growth rates (1982 prices) as calculated by the CIA were: 5.0 percent, 1966-1970; 3.0 percent, 1971-1975; 2.3 percent, 1976-1980; and 1.9 percent, 1981-1985.
2. Marshall I. Goldman, *Gorbachev's Challenge* (New York: W.W. Norton and Company, 1987), pp. 86-117.
3. In a recent study, Bergson showed that output per worker in socialist countries in 1975 was about 30 percent below that in western mixed-economy countries. See Abram Bergson, "Comparative Productivity: The USSR, Eastern Europe, and the West," *American Economic Review*, June 1987, pp. 342-357.

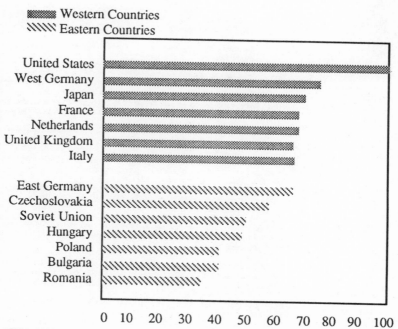

Figure 2-1. *Relative Per Capita GDP, 1985*

Index: USA = 100

Politburo--still dominated by holdovers from the Brezhnev era--that the economy was the state's most serious challenge, and that a younger, more aggressive General Secretary was needed to deal with its problems. The Politburo chose Mikhail Gorbachev, who quickly set forth the most comprehensive program to deal with Soviet economic problems in decades (Table 2-1). Indeed, the Soviet Union's ability to improve living conditions at home, to compete in world markets, and to keep up with the United States militarily will depend on the success of his policies.

CHARTING A COURSE

The Gorbachev Politburo, at least in its first months, was probably united more by a sense that new policies were needed than by agreement on what the

Table 2-1. *Chronology of Events During Gorbachev's Rule*

CPSU Conference on Scientific and Technical Progress June 1985	Defined a new investment policy Modernization plans for machine-building branch of industry focusing on high-tech sectors presented Developed plans for improving domestic R&D and integrating it more effectively at production level Spelled out vague outline of economic reform: price reform, financial, autonomy, increased use of collectives
Plenum of Central Committee and Session of Supreme Soviet	Draft plan for 1986-1990 and guidelines to year 2000 announced 5 percent average annual growth rate during 1986-2000 called for: 3.5 percent annual rate of growth during second half of decade and rates in excess of 5 percent annually during 1990s
27th Party Congress of CPSU Feb.-March 1986	Draft guidelines for economic and social development of USSR for 1986-1990 and for period ending in 2000 published Gorbachev criticized policies of Brezhnev regime and called for "honest and frank" assessment of recent policies, "radical economic reforms," more "flexible" prices, and greater decentralization
Plenary Session of CPSU and Meeting of Supreme Soviet June 1986	Gorbachev criticized bureaucracy for moving too slowly in replenishing social and economic programs Ryzkhov reviewed economic targets contained in guidelines, raising some, such as goal for capital investment, and specified high end of original ranges for others. Also called for 80 to 85 percent of machinery to be up to world standards by 1990
Central Committee Conference August 1986	Conference called to discuss technical standards, quality, and competitiveness of machinery and equipment produced in USSR. Singled out for criticism sectors not producing up to world standards, including pivotal machine tool and tool-building industries Slow progress made in improving scientific technology base of new machinery products criticized Goals set for producing only state-of-the-art equipment in 1991-1995; 80 to 85 percent of equipment is to be up to world standards by end of 12th FYP Called for careful review and planning of production of new machinery and for formulation of indicator of technical standard of output produced
Plenum of Central Committee and Session of Supreme Soviet November 1986	Plan and budget for 1987 approved. Although sparse in detail, plan indicated no let-up in Gorbachev's modernization drive
Central Committee Plenum January 1987	Gorbachev called for multiple candidates and secret ballots in elections of Party officials at republic level and below Party conference in 1988 to revise election procedures called for
Central Committee Plenum on Economic Reform June 1987	Promoted three Party secretaries to full Politburo membership and passed resolution outlining procedure for electing delegates to upcoming Congress Approved document called Basic Provisions for Fundamentally Reorganizing Economic Management, laying out official blueprint and time schedule for "new economic mechanism." (Eleven documents detailing changes in major areas of economy also approved but not published) Adopted new Law on the State Enterprise designed to expand decisionmaking powers and force enterprises to be financially responsible for own activities
Publication of Decrees on Economic Reform August 1987	Decrees approved at June 1987 Plenum published. Decrees deal with following subjects: planning, statistics, science and technology, supply, finance, banking and credit, reorganization of branch ministries and departments, republic ministries and departments, price formation, labor and social affairs, and Council of Ministries

policies should be. To its credit, the new regime focused quickly on the most troublesome problem areas, suggesting that Gorbachev had at least a vague game plan before he became General Secretary. The new leader immediately surrounded himself with a select group of advisors. Economist Abel Aganbegyan, for instance, was brought from his post in Novosibirsk to serve Gorbachev in Moscow, and Nikolai Ryzhkov, who shared Gorbachev's views on the need for economic change, was elevated to the important position of Chairman of the Council of Ministers. The buzz words *uskoreniye* (acceleration) and *perestroika* (restructuring) quickly became symbols of a new program for economic revitalization. Gorbachev ordered revisions in the 1986-1990 Plan and the Plan to the year 2000, remanding these documents to the State Planning Committee (GOSPLAN) for revision on at least three occasions prior to the Twenty-Seventh Party Congress of February 1986. Goals for economic growth were ultimately raised to 4 percent per year for the second half of the 1980s, and to 5 percent per year during the 1990s. These targets are optimistic given the recent trend of slower and generally decreasing growth rates.

The Initial Steps

Upon assuming office, Gorbachev instituted measures to give the economy a quick shot in the arm and to buy time to work out specific, long-term solutions. Increases in production from the following initiatives constitute what Gorbachev refers to as the "human factor."[4]

1. Reviving the so-called labor discipline campaign Andropov initiated, but which floundered somewhat under Chernenko. The program was instituted to cut down on violations of the rules such as taking time out of the work day to shop, to enforce tighter discipline in management, and to punish corruption.

---

4. According to Abel Aganbegyan, writing in the Soviet labor newspaper *Trud* in 1981, one-half of the decline in growth of labor productivity that occurred in 1976-1980 compared to 1971-1975 was due to "people's attitudes toward their work." Andropov recovered some of the earlier momentum with the initiation of a tough discipline campaign in 1982; labor productivity rose by 3.2 percent in industry in 1983, in part because slackers were forced to actually be on the job during the time they were counted as being there. Gorbachev's labor force initiatives, together with his direct appeal to workers, may elicit a greater effort by many who might otherwise merely put in their time.

2. Instituting a vigorous anti-alcohol campaign to curtail alcohol abuse and reduce the consequent loss in worker productivity, estimated by the Soviets as 10 percent or more.
3. Replacing prominent personnel with younger, more innovative, and more competent officials and managers.[5]

Investment Strategy

The new regime first established a capital modernization program. Gorbachev quickly revised the course of Soviet investment policy. The new policy requires a renewal of capital stock through a combination of high rates of investment and increased rates of retirement for both plants and equipment. The plan calls for:

1. Total capital investment to increase by about 5 percent annually during 1986-1990 compared to 3.5 percent per annum during 1981-1985 (Figure 2-2).[6]
2. The share of investment allocated for the retooling of existing facilities to rise from 37 percent of state "productive" investment in 1985 to 50 percent in 1990 (Table 2-2).
3. Retirement rates for capital assets, historically very low compared to western standards, to almost double during 1986-1990.

Because the existing stock of fixed capital is so large, its renewal will take time. Indeed, Soviet planners are not counting on modernization efforts to have a large impact on economic growth until the end of this five-year planning period. Nonetheless, industrial modernization will ultimately determine the Soviet Union's ability to compete economically and militarily with the West in the years ahead.[7]

5. Within the first nine months, for example, numerous economic ministers and Central Committee department chiefs had been replaced and there was an extensive turnover among regional party First Secretaries. Soon thereafter, such key officials as the chairperson of the State Price Committee and the head of GOSPLAN were dismissed.
6. Planned investment growth in 1987 apparently has been revised upward, indicating that the rate of growth for the Twelfth Five-Year Plan may be even higher.
7. For a more in-depth discussion of Moscow's investment policy, see Robert E. Leggett, "Soviet Investment Policy: The Key to Gorbachev's Program for Revitalizing the Soviet Economy," *Gorbachev's Economic Plans,* Joint Economic Committee of the U.S. Congress, 23 November 1987, and James Noren "Soviet Investment Strategy Under Gorbachev," presented at the Eighteenth National Convention of the American Association for the Advancement of Slavic Studies, New Orleans, November 1986.

Figure 2-2. *USSR: Growth of Fixed Capital Investment*
(Average Annual Percentage Rates of Growth)

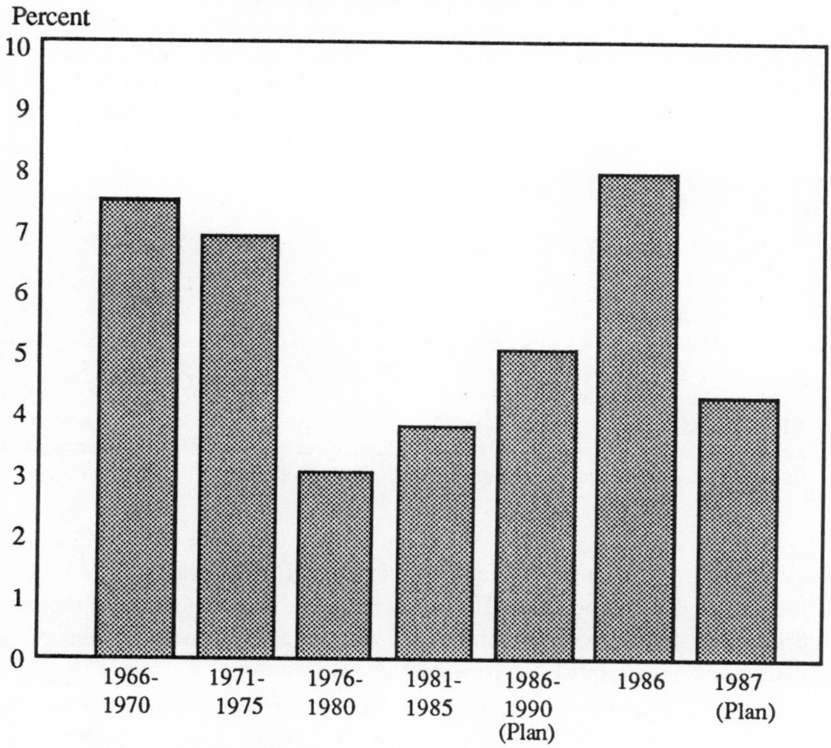

Percent

An Emphasis on Quality

Soviet leaders have asserted that, although higher investment rates represent the quantitative dimension of the modernization effort, the qualitative dimension is more important.[8] By this they mean that the returns on investment depend

8. A number of recent statements from Soviet officials indicate that the success of Gorbachev's program will be judged not only on the quantity of production as measured by GNP growth rates, but also on the *quality* of production. For example, in March of 1987, Soviet Politburo member Lev Zaykov, speaking to the Czech Central Committee about engineering (machinery) production said, "But growth as such is not the most important thing. The policy of the development of engineering is above all a policy of its far-reaching qualitative modernization." L.I. Abalkin wrote in *Mirovaya ekonomika i mezhdunarodnye otnosheniya,* no. 4, April 1987, "It is entirely wrong to identify acceleration with economic growth rates. An increase in rates is only part, and not even the main part, of this strategy. These rates are in fact a purely quantitative index, which does not always reflect the depth of structural and qualitative transformations . . . . The main point is the shift to a new quality of economic growth."

Table 2-2. USSR: State Capital Investment in Reconstruction, Expansion,
and New Construction[a] (Billions of Rubles--1984 Prices)

Investment	1981-1985		1986-90 (Plan)	
	Value	Rate[b]	Value	Rate[b]
Reconstruction of Existing Enterprises	144.3	7.0	232	11[c]
Expansion of Existing Enterprises	103.0	-0.4	n/a	n/a
New Construction	153.6	3.0	n/a	n/a

a. Values for 1980-1985 are taken from *Narodnoe Khozyaystvo*, 1985, p. 52.
b. Average annual rate of growth.
c. Estimated. Ryzhkov stated in his June 1986 speech to the Supreme Soviet that investment to renovate existing enterprises would total 232 billion rubles in 1986-1990. This equates to about an 11 percent average annual rate of growth during this period.

heavily on the efficiency and technological level of the plant and equipment being installed. Gorbachev clearly realizes that the Soviet system of managing and planning the economy inhibits innovation and technological change, and the structural constraints must be removed.

The leadership's immediate approach has been to institute programs to force the production of better products, while working out a system of incentives to encourage innovation. Such innovation is to be generated by the self-interest of participants in the production and research and development cycles, rather than by decree from the center. In January 1987, Gorbachev also introduced an ambitious quality control program, known as State Acceptance, that enforces higher standards and improves the quality of production in several sectors of the economy. The program includes 1,500 industrial enterprises that are responsible for roughly 15 percent of all industrial output and nearly one-third of the production of the critical machine-building sector. As of January 1988, nearly 2,300 factories were to be covered by the program. State Acceptance augments existing plant quality control forces with an independent staff of state-appointed inspectors who have the final authority over matters of quality at the plant. The program is similar to, and may have been modeled after, the quality control program used by the military for many years to ensure quality of defense goods. Over the long haul the new system is only the first step in an uphill battle against poor quality production in Soviet industry. It can only ensure that products meet some acceptable level of quality, and, as currently designed, State Acceptance cannot tackle the issue of advancing technology to western levels.

The regime is relying--at least in the short term--on what might be called "administered technical progress" to sustain a higher rate of innovation and technological change. Government controls over the design and approval of new equipment and investment products have been tightened. In practice, this translates into more internal technical review of new product designs to ensure they incorporate the best available technology. Tougher targets have also been set for the introduction of new products, especially in the machine-building sector. At the June 1986 meeting of the Supreme Soviet, Ryzhkov called for 80 to 95 percent of the most important kinds of machinery produced in the USSR to meet world standards by 1990. Optimistic goals for the production of computers, new machine tools, robotics, and other advanced equipment, were included in the 1986-1990 Plan. To reach these goals, the civilian machine-building industries responsible for manufacturing this equipment are being upgraded. Investment in these industries is planned to increase by 80 percent during 1986-1990, and the rate of retiring old plant and equipment in the machine-building sector is scheduled to increase from just over 2 percent in 1985 to about 10 percent in 1990 (Table 2-3). A Bureau of Machine Building has been created under the Council of Ministers to coordinate and manage the activities of the eleven civilian machine-building industries. Meanwhile, in the science sector, the Academy of Sciences has been directed to set up new departments to support the development of more modern machinery and equipment.

Changing the Economic Structure

Most of Gorbachev's efforts during his first two years as General Secretary were directed at making the existing economic structure work better rather than changing the system itself. Behind the scenes, however, Gorbachev and his advisors have been working on a "new economic mechanism" designed to move the Soviet economy into the modern world. Gorbachev is searching for a combination of organizational changes and economic levers that will permit the center to maintain overall economic control *and* encourage enterprises and research and development institutions to be more innovative and creative. This, he hopes, will lead to the production of higher quality products and a faster rate of technological change in industry.

Table 2-3. *USSR: Gross Fixed Investment in Civilian*
Machine-Building Industries

Investment	1981-1985	1986-1990 (Plan)
Billion 1984 Rubles	31	56[a]
Percentage Change Over Preceding Five-Year Period	n/a	80
Share of Total Industrial Investment	10.3[a]	21[a]

a. Estimated. See Robert E. Leggett, "Soviet Investment Policy: The Key to Gorbachev's Program for Revitalizing the Soviet Economy," *Gorbachev's Economic Plans,* Joint Economic Committee of the U.S. Congress, 23 November 1987, pp. 236-256.

The initial stage of this effort was Gorbachev's call for a "radical reform" of the management of the economy at the Party Congress in March 1986. This dramatic proposal was the first made by a Soviet official in years. A high-level commission was appointed to act as a clearinghouse for new initiatives and to manage the reform process. A freer and more open public discussion of the problems of the Soviet economy and their potential remedies has also been encouraged. Articles have appeared in leading Soviet journals--including the Party journal, *Kommunist.* Some of the articles have been very critical of the Soviet system and recommend solutions ranging from reinstating Lenin's New Economic Policy of the 1920s (NEP) to adopting a system of markets, prices, and profits to allocate resources.[9] In the months following the March 1986 Party Congress, Gorbachev escalated his rhetoric, comparing the reform to a "revolution" and describing it as a turning point in Soviet history.

Meanwhile, the details of his economic reform program were still being developed. A special session of the Central Committee and Supreme Soviet was held last June to discuss and approve the "new economic mechanism."

9. One of the most interesting articles published thus far appeared in the June 1987 issue of *Novyy mir.* In the article, the author characterizes the Soviet economy as having been "ruled for too long by decree instead of the ruble" and as being "a shortage economy, unbalanced in virtually every point, in many respects uncontrollable . . . scarcely susceptible to planning . . . and which still does not accept scientific and technical progress." According to the author, Moscow's economic woes can be solved only through "economically accountable socialism" and the development of the market itself. Among the solutions offered: making enterprises dependent directly on profits and making the ruble into a convertible currency. Nikolai Shmelev, "Advances and Profits," *Novyy mir,* June 1987, pp. 142-158.

Eleven draft decrees and a guideline document entitled "The Main Provisions of the Fundamental Restructuring of Economic Management," which detailed changes in major aspects of the economy, were ratified. A new Law on the State Enterprise that codifies enterprises' rights and gives them legal protection from bureaucratic muddling was also adopted. These provisions--together with decrees on overhauling the wage and salary structure, reorganizing foreign trade, increasing enterprise autonomy, and sanctioning expansions of private economic activity and producers cooperatives--offer an official blueprint and some schedules for implementing Gorbachev's program. The "new economic mechanism" is supposed to be almost fully operational by 1991, the start of the Thirteenth Five-Year Plan. Endorsement of these wide-ranging initiatives, together with the addition at the Plenum of three full members to the Politburo (Table 2-4), gives Gorbachev both an approved agenda and a stronger political base to move ahead with his program.

The package of reforms already in place, or in the process of being worked out, is impressive (Table 2-5). It provides for changes in the economic system that most western experts previously thought would never be seriously considered by Soviet leaders. Nevertheless, past reforms in the USSR and East Europe have looked promising when announced, only to have bureaucratic resistance gut or at least significantly weaken them.[10] The most difficult phase of the reform campaign still lies ahead. Remaining challenges include:

1. Establishing a system of prices that will provide acceptable signals to enterprises.
2. Managing the transition to greater reliance on wholesale trade instead of centrally directed deliveries.
3. Designing new credit-financial institutions.
4. Fending off stiff resistance from bureaucrats whose jobs, status, power, and privileges are threatened and, ironically, from segments of the Soviet population who see the reforms violating their "implicit social contract."
5. Addressing issues of unemployment, inflation, and the emergence of widening divisions within Soviet society. These are thorny issues that go to the heart of socialism.

---

10. The Hungarian economy, for example, has been undergoing systemic change over the last thirty years. Still, the scope of these reforms may be far less than many westerners think. According to Janos Kornai, a prominent Hungarian economist and member of the Hungarian Academy of Sciences, the Hungarian economy is a "symbiosis of a state sector under indirect bureaucratic control and a nonstate sector, market oriented but operating under strong bureaucratic restrictions." See Janos Kornai, "The Hungarian Reform Process: Visions, Hope and Reality," *Journal of Economic Literature*, December 1986, p. 1715.

Table 2-4. New Politburo Lineup

Full Members	Age	Current Position
Mikhail Gorbachev	56	General Secretary
Viktor Chebrikov[a]	64	KGB Chairman
Andrei Gromyko	77	Chairman, Supreme Soviet
Yegor Ligachev[a]	66	Party Secretary for Ideology, Cadres
Viktor Nikonov[a]	58	Party Secretary for Agriculture
Nikolai Ryzhkov[a]	57	Premier
Vladimir Shcherbitsky	69	Ukrainian First Secretary
Eduard Shevardnadze[a]	59	Foreign Minister
Nikolai Slyunkov	58	Party Secretary for General Economics
Mikhail Solomentsev	73	Chairman, Party Control Committee
Vitali Vorotnikov	61	Premier, Russian Republic
Aleksandr Yakovlev[a]	63	Party Secretary for Ideology, Propaganda Culture
Lev Zaykov[a]	64	Party Secretary for Defense Industry, General Economics

Candidate Members	Age	Current Position
Pyotr Demichev	69	First Deputy Chairman, Supreme Soviet
Vladimir Dolgikh	62	Party Secretary for Energy, Heavy Industry
Yuri Maslyukov[a]	50	Chairman, State Planning Committee
Georgi Razumovsky[a]	52	Central Committee Secretary, Personnel
Yuri Solovyev[a]	61	Leningrad Oblast First Secretary
Nikolai Talyzin[a]	58	First Deputy Premier
Dmitry Yazov[a]	63	Defense Minister

a. Officials selected under Gorbachev

Table 2-5. Gorbachev's Reform Initiatives

Category	Objective	Limitations
Enterprise Economy	To allow enterprises to make more day-to-day decisions with less interference from the ministries	Enterprises still receive a fairly detailed set of production targets. Their decisionmaking is further "guided" by performance indicators, assigned supplies, controls on investment, wage norms, and administered prices
Wholesale Trade	To reduce central controls over the distribution of enterprise supplies and to expand use of contracts among enterprises	There is no specific timetable for shift to wholesale trade and no guarantee reforms will eventually allow enterprises to choose their suppliers freely. For the present, enterprises will only be able to influence marginally the quality of goods they receive
Self-Financing	To allow enterprises to keep a larger share of their profits, which can be used for operating expenses and investment	Enterprises will have difficulty obtaining investment supplies because of centralized supply system. Many firms do not earn enough profits to be self-supporting. There is no provision for redistribution of capital funds to more "efficient" enterprises
Bankruptcy	To allow liquidation of enterprises that operate at a loss	Current price system is designed to enable average enterprise to earn a profit. Given an administered price system and success indicators not necessarily reflecting efficiency, basis for making judgments about liquidation is uncertain
Wages	To create pay differentials and a closer relationship between workers' pay and amount and quality of work they produce	Pay increases will depend on enterprises' ability to finance them from funds related to productivity increases. Wage "normatives" will be set by superior organs
Agriculture	To increase self-financing, give farms greater control over disposal of their product, and encourage workers' interest in final harvest results	These goals continue to conflict with irrational price system for farm products and industrial outputs, high procurement targets, and centralized allocation of natural resources
Private Activity	To increase incentives for individual, family, and small business groups	These are cautious regulations--much more restrictive than those enacted in East Europe. Participation is limited, for example, to housewives, students, pensioners, and state employees working in their free time
Foreign Trade	To allow a limited number of enterprises to conduct trade directly with foreign partners and promote joint ventures with western firms	Central control remains tight over most foreign trade, and firms participating in joint ventures are insulated from rest of economy

Figure 2-3. USSR: Economic Performance under Gorbachev and his Predecessors

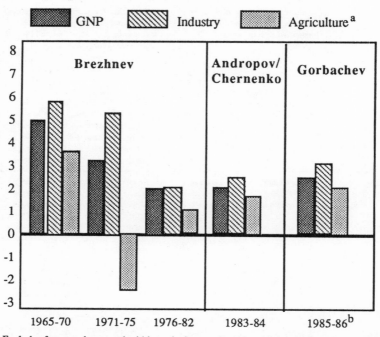

a. Excludes farm products used within agriculture and purchases by agriculture from other sectors.
b. Preliminary.

PERFORMANCE SO FAR UNDER GORBACHEV

The performance of the Soviet economy has improved somewhat under Gorbachev (Figure 2-3). During his first year as General Secretary, Soviet GNP increased by about 1.5 percent, and industrial output increased by nearly 3 percent--both roughly the same as in the previous two years. The pace of non-farm output growth improved after Gorbachev took over in March and, the final quarter of the year, industry was growing at a rate close to 3.5 percent per year.[11]

---

11. A record of the performance of the Soviet economy in 1985 is spelled out in detail in "The Soviet Economy Under a New Leader," a paper presented by the Central Intelligence Agency and the Defense Intelligence Agency for submission to the Subcommittee on National Security Economics of the Joint Economic Committee, U.S. Congress, July 1986.

The first full year of Gorbachev's stewardship (1986) was a relatively good period for the Soviet economy. GNP grew at its fastest rate in a decade--about 4 percent--and non-farm GNP increased slightly more than 3 percent. Industrial growth was the highest in nearly a decade, although momentum slowed as the year progressed. Agricultural production reached a new high; the grain harvest was the fourth largest on record. In the consumer area, supplies of many quality goods increased and additions to the housing stock were the largest in two decades.[12]

Economic growth for 1987 was less than 1 percent. Industrial production was only about 1.5 percent higher than in the previous year, and agricultural production declined by about 3 percent. The Soviet economy was hit hard in early 1987 by severe winter weather, and a number of new measures introduced by the regime--State Acceptance, experiments in self-finance, and the expansion of new managerial practices throughout industry--precipitated unexpected disruptions.[13]

It is difficult to assess how much of the improvement during the past two years is due to Gorbachev and his policies. Clearly, policies initiated by previous regimes have been responsible for some, if not most, of the improvement that has occurred. Brezhnev and Andropov relaxed the five-year plan constraints on new fixed investment imposed by the "intensive growth" philosophy, removing some of the bottlenecks that had earlier plagued the economy. Andropov initiated the campaign to enforce tighter discipline in the workplace, and the turnaround in Soviet agriculture coincided with the implementation of Brezhnev's food program in 1982. Weather has also been a major factor. The break in the weather shortly after Gorbachev came to power-- the winter of 1984-1985 was the coldest in the Soviet Union in twenty years-- helped unclog the transportation network and get supplies and finished goods moving to the factories and markets. Better weather also helped the Soviet Union produce a record agricultural harvest in 1986--a major factor behind the marked increase in GNP growth that year.

Gorbachev's image as a decisive, take-charge leader and his no-nonsense attitude have probably helped boost public morale and improve worker productivity. The fruits of his reform initiatives and modernization program

---

12. The performance of the Soviet economy in 1986 is analyzed in *Gorbachev's Modernization Program: A Status Report*, a paper prepared by the CIA and DIA for the Subcommittee on National Security Economics of the Joint Economic Committee, U.S. Congress, 19 March 1987.

13. An experiment in industrial management was launched under Yuri Andropov in January 1984 and ordered into effect industry-wide by Gorbachev in January 1987. It reduces the number of enterprise performance indicators, increases rewards and penalties for fulfilling and not meeting plan targets, and gives the enterprises greater control over investment funds and material rewards for the workforce.

will not be evident for a few more years. Nevertheless, Gorbachev can take credit for beginning the *uskoreniye* of the national economy, which he established as a primary national objective.

PROSPECTS FOR FUTURE ECONOMIC GROWTH

Inherent Limitations to Growth

Gorbachev's initiatives, if fully implemented, have the potential to improve the future performance of the Soviet economy. Unfortunately for Gorbachev, a number of inherent problems will limit the impact of his "new economic mechanism." These limitations have been at least partly responsible for the gradual decline in growth rates in the Soviet Union and show no sign of easing. They include:

1. The annual number of new entrants to the work force during the second half of the 1980s will be the lowest in decades because of lower birth rates in the 1960s,[14] an increase in the number of workers reaching retirement age, and rising mortality rates among males in the twenty-five to forty-four age range.[15] In fact, the working age population of the European republics of the Soviet Union is actually declining and will continue to do so through 1995.
2. The quality of the labor force is deficient by modern standards. They lack, at present, a large pool of skilled workers, such as computer technicians, necessary to operate a modern economy.
3. The cost of producing energy, particularly oil, is skyrocketing as the Soviet Union continues to adjust to the transition from an era of cheap, abundant energy to one of more expensive, less accessible fuels.
4. Other natural resources, such as iron ore, coal, lumber, and nonmetallic minerals, continue to be of lower quality and more costly to obtain.
5. The transportation network, particularly the railroads, is strained to capacity.[16] The Soviets will need to expand it substantially if transportation

---

14. See Clem, this volume.

15. Unpublished projections of the civilian labor force in the Soviet Union were obtained from the U.S. Department of Commerce, Bureau of the Census, Center for International Research.

16. Holland Hunter and Vladimir Kontorovich, "Transport Pressures and Potentials," *Gorbachev's Economic Plans,* Joint Economic Committee of the U.S. Congress, 23 November 1987, pp. 382-396.

bottlenecks that contributed to the 1976-1982 industrial slowdown are to be avoided.

Material, labor, and possibly energy constraints are likely to continue into the next decade, limiting the economic gains that can be achieved. The regional imbalance of the labor supply, potentially the most serious of growth-limiting factors, is outside the planners' control. Resource bottlenecks could be alleviated through input substitution and major technological breakthroughs, but such developments are not likely to occur rapidly or often. The impending transport constraint could be avoided if resources are diverted from the modernization drive to expand the carrying capacity of the railroads, but this would require cutting investment allocations to other sectors critical to the modernization drive, and does not appear to be in the offing.

Projecting Economic Growth

There is no easy way to evaluate the complex array of factors that will influence the performance of the Soviet economy in the years ahead. In an effort to assess how much improvement can be expected, we constructed a macroeconomic model of the Soviet economy. The model is designed to project the *real* growth of Soviet GNP, measured in constant, factor-cost prices.[17] It is a supply-side model that projects GNP by estimating net output according to the historical relationship between capital and labor inputs and output (see Appendix A).

Extrapolating Along Past Trends--The Baseline Case. A baseline case was designed to simulate what the economy would be like from now until the turn of the century if Gorbachev had chosen to do nothing but adjust the allocation of investment, that is, adopt a business-as-usual approach. Capital modernization and human factor policies are not taken into account. It is further assumed that productivity trends since Andropov continue, and that energy, raw materials, transportation, and other such constraints become no worse. Other assumptions used in projecting the baseline (for example, setting

17. The principal conceptual difference between GNP and Soviet reported national income is the latter's exclusion of: (1) the non-material portion of most personal services as well as services provided by the government (for example, health, education, housing, personal transportation and communications, recreation and personal care, government administration, credit and insurance, research and development, and military personnel costs), and (2) depreciation on fixed capital. For a discussion of the methodology for constructing national economic accounts for the Soviet Union along western lines, see *USSR: Measures of Economic Growth and Development, 1950-80*, Joint Economic Committee of the U.S. Congress, 8 December 1982.

model parameters and values for exogenous variables) were made by simply extending the trends for recent years (usually 1981-1985) into the future. In light of recent developments in the Soviet Union, this scenario is clearly too stark, but it does indicate what might happen if Gorbachev's program is aborted, or if political rhetoric begets no real economic change.[18]

Under these conditions, the model predicts that GNP would grow approximately 2.3 percent per year for the period 1986-1990 (compared to 1.9 percent in 1981-1985) and would then drop to 1.5 percent per year in the 1990s, assuming average weather (Table 2-6). When the uncertainties of weather are factored into the analysis, the most likely range for average growth per year is 1.8 to 2.7 percent for 1986-1990, and 1.3 to 1.7 percent for the 1990s.[19] Furthermore, the level of technology would remain much the same, and the same mix of goods would be produced with little improvement in quality. For 1986-1990, the outcome can best be described as "growth without progress," but would lead to growth below 2 percent during the 1990s and result in a widening of the technology gap between the Soviet Union and the West.

The Impact of Gorbachev's Program

Gorbachev's modernization and reform programs are intended to alter the business-as-usual growth approach to the economy. If his initiatives are to work, they must elicit profound changes in the long-standing relationships between inputs (capital and labor) and outputs. Such changes in the production technologies of any economy, including western economies, cannot be accomplished without adjustment costs. The faster the pace of the trans- formation, the greater the adjustment costs. Moreover, the costs of adjustment are likely to be especially severe in centrally planned economies, because they lack market mechanisms for adjusting supplies to changing demands.[20]

Soviet history provides examples of the costs of abrupt shifts in government policies. In the latter half of the 1950s and early 1960s, Nikita

18. At present, there is every indication that Gorbachev's program will be fully implemented. In a speech delivered to a conference of the Party Central Committee in July 1987, Gorbachev criticized the civil machine-building industry for insufficient progress in raising the technological level of machinery, declaring that "no retreat is possible" and demanding that Soviet machinery achieve the highest "world standards" in less than seven years.

19. The most-likely range means there is a 10 percent chance growth could be below the lower limit of the range and a 10 percent chance it could exceed the upper limit of the range.

20. In fact, one could argue that one reason for bureaucratic resistance to change in centrally planned economies is the risk that change will move the production frontier inward. There are no automatic mechanisms to prevent such an occurrence.

Khrushchev pushed through major changes on a broad front: the "Virgin Lands" and other campaigns in agriculture; a crash program to develop the chemical industry; a sharp change in the composition of military production; a drastic change in investment policy; and major reorganizations of the administrative bureaucracy. The substantial expansion of cultivated land, especially for corn, had little payoff in the long run. The crash program in the chemical industries, based largely on imported plant and equipment, produced a good deal of waste and deprived other industries of vital investment funds. The shift to a regionally based system for managing the economy's industrial and construction sectors interrupted the flow of supplies to enterprises, and the frequent reorganizations created discord within the bureaucracy and confusion for the enterprises. In 1964, Khrushchev was removed from power. Another example of the effects of sudden changes in government policies on the economy--especially investment plans--was the slowdown in industrial growth that occurred during Brezhnev's rule in the late 1970s and early 1980s.[21]

Gorbachev is pushing for change on numerous fronts simultaneously, and his modernization drive, like Khrushchev's, will likely result in production setbacks in the short run as the economy adjusts to the changes.[22] Some problems have already developed, including:

1. The State Acceptance program has disrupted production and the supply network because poor quality goods are being rejected. According to the Soviet press, new inspectors rejected 10 to 20 percent of products submitted in the initial stages of the program.
2. The wage reform has already met resistance, especially--and predictably--by those who have been most adversely affected.
3. The new financial requirements in industry have caused confusion and impeded production in several ministries.

Perhaps the most disruptive element of Gorbachev's program will be the sudden reallocation of investment funds to the production of machinery, leaving other important sectors in short supply. There is evidence already that the planned increase in investment is too great for the economy to absorb

---

21. Gertrude E. Schroeder, "The Slowdown in Soviet Industry, 1976-1982," *Soviet Economy* vol. 1, January-March 1985, pp. 42-74.

22. In his June 26, 1987, Plenum speech, Gorbachev acknowledged that there had already been some disruption resulting from "restructuring" when he said, ". . . in the first months of the year, grave errors were committed which led to disruptions in many areas of the economy. Both the Politburo and the government had to take urgent measures to rectify the situation. Even though the situation is returning to normal, considerable damage has nevertheless been done."

effectively. In 1986, for example, the actual growth rate of investment in civilian machine-building was 17 percent, compared to the planned rate of 30 percent. Moreover, complaints about the quality of the new equipment have increased and become more evident.

To capture the impact of Gorbachev's program on economic growth, features were incorporated into the model to distinguish between the productivity of new and old capital equipment (embodied technological change), to account for human factor effects by allowing increases in the work effort, and to account for disruptions in economic activity as the economy adjusts to the new production technologies and the "new economic mechanism."

Using the macroeconomic model, we are able to evaluate the effects on growth of alternative judgments about Gorbachev's program. Two scenarios are developed--a best-case scenario and a worst-case scenario.[23] Both project growth under the assumption that Gorbachev's plan is vigorously implemented during the next four to six years, changing long-standing economic mechanisms and practices. These changes are assumed to be disruptive in the short run, but over the longer term, higher returns to new capital and an increase in the effectiveness and productivity of the labor force in the 1990s would be achieved. In these simulations, we account for the possibility of increases in worker effort (human factor effects), capital modernization, and reform initiatives implemented prior to the June Plenum, such as self-financing, wage reform, and organizational changes. Our model simulations exclude, however, more radical reform measures such as market-determined prices and a significant reduction in central planning.

Best-Case Scenario. The extent and duration of the temporary disruption period are difficult to project; they depend on how fast the changes are implemented. For the purposes of this study, adjustment costs were modeled by approximating the value of foregone production during the first two years of the 1976-1982 period of declining industrial growth rates. The sectors affected are industry, construction, and agriculture. Basing the adjustment cost on historical precedent provides some assurance that the assumption is realistic. It was assumed that adjustment costs would begin in 1987, peak in 1989-1991, and, in the best-case scenario, the economy would recover completely by 1993.[24] In exchange for this "sacrifice" for the period 1987-1992, the return to

----

23. Both scenarios incorporate actual economic performance for 1986.

24. The intensity of the short-run growth slump is determined in the model by the variable "SLUMP." A SLUMP value of 1 indicates that the adjustment costs are equivalent to the average annual downward shift in the production function intercept during the 1976-1982 growth slowdown period. A value of 2 following a value of 1 indicates that the downward slide in the intercept would continue for one period. For the best-case scenario, SLUMP was set equal to .5 in 1987, 1 in

capital for the 1990s was increased 25 percent above the pre-Gorbachev trend in the machine-building sector, where the modernization program is most sharply focused, and increased 15 percent in other sectors. In addition, human factor effects were assumed to increase the work effort of the labor force by 4 percent in the 1990s in response to increased availability of better consumer goods, housing, and an upbeat atmosphere in the workplace.

Using these assumptions, the model results indicate that economic growth during 1986-1990 would be below the rates of recent years, but would then increase in the 1990s to rates similar to those in the early 1970s. Assuming average weather, average annual GNP growth for 1986-1990 would be 1.9 percent and then increase to 2.9 percent in the 1990s (Table 2-6). GNP growth slightly above 3 percent per year is possible in the 1990s if favorable weather prevails. In industry, average annual growth in the 1990s would be more than twice as high as industrial growth during the 1986-1990 planning period. More important, the goods produced during the 1990s should be of higher quality, greater diversity, and they should more closely meet consumer and producer expectations.

Worst-Case Scenario. This scenario repeats the previous one through the 1986-1990 period, but postulates that Gorbachev's programs, while implemented, will fail to raise technology to a higher level. Economic disruptions occur, but there is no recovery from the 1987-1990 slump, and consequently no payoff in the form of higher factor productivity in the 1990s. This situation could arise, for example, if new programs further disrupt economic mechanisms, moving production technologies to a less efficient level, with more red tape instead of less. Political turmoil and frequent changes in objectives could contribute to the growth slump. In addition, it is assumed that bottlenecks will worsen, possibly because of capacity constraints in transportation and energy production, or due to an increased drain on resources by the military. Some gains in human factors and return to capital are postulated (equal to those in the 1986-1990 period in the previous scenario), but no additional gains are assumed to occur in the 1990s.

In this scenario the model indicates that the average annual growth rate for GNP during 1986-1990 would be the same as in the previous scenario--1.9 percent assuming average weather. However, even lower growth rates would follow in the 1990s--1.6 percent per year--which is approximately equivalent to the performance under the baseline case. The product mix and quality of goods

1988, 2 in 1989-1991, 1 again in 1992 (simulating a partial recovery), and 0 after 1992 (simulating a complete recovery). For the worst-case scenario, SLUMP followed the same pattern through 1991, but remained at 2 until the year 2000 (simulating a permanent disruption).

Table 2-6. Simulations of Soviet Economic Performance to the Year 2000
Average Annual Rates of Growth (Percent)[a]

Scenario	1986-1990	1991-2000	1986-2000
Total GNP[b]			
Baseline Case	**2.3**	**1.5**	**1.8**
	(1.8 - 2.7)	(1.3 - 1.7)	(1.6 - 1.9)
Best-Case	**1.9**	**2.9**	**2.6**
	(1.4 - 2.3)	(2.7 - 3.1)	(2.4 - 2.7)
Worst-Case	**1.9**	**1.6**	**1.7**
	(1.4 - 2.3)	(1.4 - 1.8)	(1.6 - 1.8)
Industry			
Baseline Case	2.9	2.7	2.8
Best-Case	2.3	5.5	4.4
Worst-Case	2.3	2.9	2.7

a. Growth rates for 1986-1990 use 1985 as a base, and growth rates for 1991-2000 use the estimated value for *1990* as a base. Actual results for 1986 are factored into the analysis.
b. The point estimate (boldface) assumes "average weather." A most-likely range, in parentheses, was derived by incorporating the uncertainties of weather into the analysis. The most-likely range means there is a 10 percent chance GNP could exceed the upper limit of the range and a 10 percent chance it could be below the lower limit of the range. The base used to calculate the growth rate range for 1991-2000 was the estimated *median* value for 1990.

would increase only slightly. Gorbachev's overall attempts to modernize the Soviet economy would fail, as reflected by continuation of low growth throughout the 1990s.

Can Radical Reform Lead to Higher Growth?

What are Soviet growth prospects if the more radical changes called for at the June Plenum are fully implemented? That is, what would be the impact on the growth of the economy if the Soviets allowed prices to be determined by market forces, abolished or substantially reduced central planning, and decentralized investment decisionmaking? Would such "radical" measures enhance or hinder prospects for economic growth?

In our judgment, changes of such massive proportions would be so disruptive to the Soviet system that there would be an initial period of recession, which could last for several years in some sectors, such as industry.

Other sectors, such as services and agriculture, might rebound from the slump relatively quickly and perhaps exhibit sharply increased growth rates for a few years. We believe that as the economy reaches a new equilibrium, however, overall growth would once again slow, perhaps to present levels. A number of factors would be at work. First, in a demand-driven economic system, which these reforms would produce, growth would not be limited by the ability to produce as much as by the ability to consume. Thus, growth would depend to a large extent on Soviet society's ability to generate wealth. Second, the more open economy, with its currency tied to that of other countries, would be affected more by external economic factors than is currently the case. Defense spending would continue to place a heavy burden on the economy, taking investment from the civilian sector. Finally, the inherent problems discussed above, such as the slow growth of the work force and rising resource costs, will remain and work to limit increases in growth. At the same time, Soviet leaders would be confronted with additional new problems, such as unprecedented inflation as prices suddenly adjust to reflect relative scarcity, which could curtail their enthusiasm for reform.

SUMMARY AND CONCLUSIONS

There are, of course, possibilities for Soviet economic growth other than those presented above. Gains from the modernization drive may be more or less than assumed; the costs of adjustment associated with those gains may vary, and factors outside the control of Moscow could change unpredictably. Annual rates of GNP growth could vary nearly a full percentage point during 1986-1990 and by nearly a half percentage point in the 1990s depending on weather alone. The performance of the economy, moreover, will depend not only on the specific nature of reforms, but also on *how* they are implemented. It is also unclear if the regime is willing or able to sustain the modernization drive when faced with the inevitable short-term reductions in growth that are a consequence of a successful restructuring.

These simulations suggest that Soviet growth goals of 4 to 5 percent per year through the end of the century, measured in real terms, will not be achieved. If Gorbachev's program is not fully implemented, short-term prospects for growth would closely reflect those in recent years, roughly 2 percent per year. If his program is vigorously implemented, short-term prospects for growth would almost certainly be lower than 2 percent, but if successful, growth in the 1990s could potentially approach the relatively high rates of the early 1970s (about 3 percent per year), which would still fall short of Soviet plans. Finally, if Gorbachev's program is implemented more slowly than first planned, perhaps in reaction to unacceptable high adjustment costs and associated low growth rates, gains from modernization would be stretched out over a longer period of time, resulting in overall growth rates somewhere between those estimated for the best-case and worst-case scenarios. What is more difficult to assess is the potential impact of more "radical" reform measures. As mentioned above, such changes have not been factored into our models.

Most western scholars on the Soviet economy are skeptical that Gorbachev can dramatically reform the Soviet economy; they doubt he can increase efficiency markedly and make the Soviet Union a world leader in technology. According to Dr. Gertrude E. Schroeder, a western expert on economic reform in the Soviet Union, " . . . the reforms do not go nearly far enough to create a market environment . . . . It leaves the pillars of socialist state economic administration permanently in place . . . "[25] In his recent book, Soviet specialist Marshall Goldman is pessimistic about whether conditions in the Soviet Union lend themselves to that state becoming a member of the "high tech" club. ". . . there is no doubt the Soviet Union will have a difficult time catching up to the rest of the high-technology world. Indeed, its strengths seem to be in the opposite direction."[26] According to Goldman, "If reforming the Chinese and Hungarian economies is comparable to turning around an ocean-going tanker, reforming the Soviet economy is analogous to turning around a dock that is firmly anchored to the shore."[27] Nonetheless, what one of Gorbachev's economic advisors calls a "third wave" of reforms is already under study. Judging by Gorbachev's personality and the advice he is getting, he can be counted on to move forward with his "new economic mechanism" in coming years.

It is important to point out that Gorbachev's program will not be judged a on the basis of output growth alone. The quality dimension will weigh heavily in how the shortfall between actual and planned growth is perceived. Particularly important will be indications that real technological progress is being made. In the last June Plenum report, Gorbachev implied that growth was not the relevant measure of progress, but rather that the gains from restructuring should be "assessed in terms of end results and the extent to which social needs are satisfied." While it is clear from this political rhetoric that quality of output will be an important indicator of success, what is not clear is how much of a growth reduction can or will be tolerated in exchange for gains in quality.

25. See Schroeder, this volume.
26. Marshall I. Goldman, *Gorbachev's Challenge*, p. 115.
27. Ibid., p. 228.

While we cannot predict with confidence whether Gorbachev's program will succeed, some real progress is bound to occur, particularly if meaningful economic reforms can be implemented and sustained without an accompanying political upheaval. But, because movement in the direction of reform will be painful and risky for many in the leadership and bureaucracy, real progress is likely to be slow.

APPENDIX A: A SUMMARY OF THE MACRO-ECONOMIC MODEL

The model estimates future GNP by aggregating net output forecasts for each of twelve Soviet economy sectors.[28] The forecasts are based on Cobb-Douglas production functions modified to allow for capital-embodied technological progress. Embodied technological progress is incorporated into the model in two ways, depending on the sector of the economy. For all sectors except agriculture, services, housing, and the electric power branch of industry, the capital elasticity for new capital is set higher than that for old capital, thus making new capital more productive.[29] In the agriculture, services, and electric power sectors, where increases in the quality of capital might occur--resulting in greater output per unit of new capital--but where new, improved technologies are not expected, the new capital input is multiplied by a "capital productivity factor" to simulate an increase in quality without an accompanying change in the technology of production. The function used for housing was not a legitimate production relationship (capital stock is converted to output using a simple ratio), so modernization features were not incorporated into the function.

Generalized equations for the two forms of the production functions are:

1. $Q = a(t)[K_o^\beta (HF*L_o)^{1-\beta} + K_{n1}^\emptyset (HF*L_{n1})^{1-\emptyset} + K_{n2}^\partial (HF*L_{n2})^{1-\partial}]$, and

2. $Q = a(t)[K_o^\beta (HF*L_o)^{1-\beta} + (KPF_1*K_{n1})^\beta (HF*L_{n1})^{1-\beta} + (KPF_2*K_{n2})^\beta (HF*L_{n2})^{1-\beta}]$,

where Q = value-added output (constant prices)

K_o = capital stock of vintage prior to 1986 ("old" capital)

K_{n1} = capital stock of 1986-1990 vintage

K_{n2} = capital stock of 1991-2000 vintage

L_o = labor input *required* by "old" capital

---

28. The twelve sectors are transportation and communications, construction, agriculture, services (less housing), housing, domestic trade (including an "other" category), machine building, chemicals, fuels, electric power, consumer goods (including light industry and food processing), and industrial materials (including ferrous metals, nonferrous metals, forest products, construction materials and other branches of industry).

29. The capital elasticity is an estimate of the percentage change in output that results when capital is increased 1 percent, holding the labor input constant. Increasing the capital elasticity implies more than just an increase in the quality of capital--it implies a fundamental change in the nature of the capital (such as automation). The improved production technology embodied in the new capital in turn implies a reduction in the contribution of labor relative to that of capital in the production process (that is, capital substitutes for labor). This approach seemed to be most in keeping with the spirit of restructuring proposed by Gorbachev.

L_{n1} = labor *required* for the 1991-2000 vintage capital
L_{n2} = labor available for the 1991-2000 vintage capital
a(t) = intercept term and adjustment cost factor
ß = capital elasticity for "old" capital
ø = capital elasticity for 1986-1990 vintage capital
∂ = capital elasticity for 1991-2000 vintage capital
HF = "Human Factor" multiplier
KPF_1 = capital productivity factor for 1986-1990 vintage capital
KPF_2 = capital productivity factor for 1991-2000 vintage capital

In both methods, the productivity of old capital is constrained to that observed in the recent past. That is, the capital elasticity parameter for old capital, ß, was estimated using historical data and thus reflects actual returns to capital during the recent past. The labor requirement for capital stock of vintage prior to 1986 is set equal to the labor demand reported in 1985, thereby providing old capital with the same labor resources it had received in the past. The remaining labor resources are made available to new capital.

The production function for agriculture differs from equation 2 in two ways: (1) weather is included in the function, and (2) the labor input is not disaggregated and allocated according to the capital vintage. Weather effects are modeled by expanding the intercept term--a(t)--to include relevant weather variables. Labor was not disaggregated as done for other sectors because labor in agriculture is much more fungible than in other sectors, making it impractical to allocate a portion of the agricultural labor force exclusively to new capital. Gains in productivity from higher quality farm machinery and equipment were incorporated into the capital productivity factor. The resulting production function for agriculture is:

3. $$Q = a_1(W)\, a(t)\, (K_o + KPF_1*K_{n1} + KPF_2 * K_{n2})^\beta\, (HF*L)^{1-\beta}$$

where $a_1(W)$ is the adjustment function for weather[30]

The model also allows for productivity gains originating from "human factors" by multiplying labor by a "human factor" multiplier, HF. Human factor effects were modeled for labor allocated to both old and new capital. Human factor effects modeled by HF are those that result from the regime's ef-

---

30. The production function for agriculture estimates net agricultural output, which excludes intra-agricultural use of farm products but does not make an adjustment for purchases by agriculture from other sectors. Net agricultural output must be converted to value-added units by subtracting intersectoral inputs before making the GNP calculation.

forts to institute better management and planning, the discipline and anti-alcoholism campaigns, and improved labor incentives. For example, setting HF=1.10 implies that the productive utility--or efficiency--of existing labor resources will be 10 percent greater than the average productive utility observed during the recent past. In simple terms, labor will "work 10 percent harder."

Changes in the production technologies of an economy cannot be accomplished without adjustment costs, and the faster the pace of the transformation, the greater they will be. To model these expected adjustment costs, the intercept term was expanded to a function of time--a(t)--to permit downward shifts in the production function during the transition period, as follows:

4. $\quad a(t) = e^{(a_0 - a_1 SLUMP)}$,

where $\quad$ SLUMP is a variable that simulates the intensity of the adjustment costs, a_0 is a scaling parameter, and a_1 is the adjustment costs parameter for each sector

With these production functions, output for each sector can be projected by forecasts of labor and capital.

Forecasting Labor

A projection of the Soviet labor force to the year 2000 has been made by the Center for International Research. In the model, this labor force projection is converted to a projection of total employment, which is then allocated among sectors of the economy according to investment priorities and the historical relationship between investment allocations and the employment increment.

5. $\quad L = L_{-1} + \mu_1 \mu_2 \Delta M$,

where $\quad$ L = labor in man-hours allocated to a particular sector
ΔM = the increment of new workers entering the civilian economy
$\mu 1$ = parameter converting number of workers to man-hours
$\mu 2$ = share of new workers allocated to a particular sector as a function of the capital investment share, determined by multiplying the investment share by the historical ratio of the share of new workers to the investment share during the recent past (1981-1985)

Within each sector, labor required by "old" capital (L_0) is set by multiplying the amount of "old" capital by the inverse of the capital-labor ratio in 1985.

Additional labor from increases in the overall labor supply (ΔM) and from labor displaced by retirement of old capital is allocated to new capital. Equations for L_n and L_o are:

6. $L_o = wK_o$, and

7. $L_n = L - L_o$,

where   w is the inverse of the 1985 capital-labor ratio

Forecasting Capital

Values for new capital are generated by accumulating commissionings beginning in 1986.[31] Future values for "old" capital are generated by subtracting retirements from the value of the "old" capital stock from the previous period. The equations are:

8. $K_n = K_{n-1} + C$, and

9. $K_o = K_{o-1} - R$,

where   K = value of capital stock at the end of the year
           R = retirements of capital stock, and
           C = commissionings

Retirements are calculated by multiplying the total capital stock at the beginning of the year by the planned retirement rate. Commissionings are generated from new fixed investment, which in turn is generated by output from the machine-building and construction sectors.[32] Total new fixed investment is distributed among sectors of the economy exogenously, typically according to published Soviet plans.

---

31. Commissionings are gross additions to capital; they include: the value of new enterprises buildings, and installations completed and put in service; the value of all types of equipment put into service; the value of additional production tools; the value of additions to perennial plantings; the cost of work to irrigate and drain land; and other outlays augmenting the value of fixed assets.

32. Commissionings are generated as a weighted average of new fixed investment for the current year and for up to three previous years. Total new fixed investment is calculated by adding machinery imports to the output from the machine-building and construction sectors, and subtracting the amount of machinery, equipment, buildings, and structures allocated for export, capital repair, consumer durables and military procurement. Capital repair is estimated using an equation that relates previous capital repair costs to the size of the capital stock. Other end-uses for machinery, equipment, buildings, and structures are set exogenously.

3 GORBACHEV'S ECONOMIC REFORMS

Gertrude E. Schroeder

By his own admission, Mikhail Gorbachev inherited an economy in a mess.[1] Growth rates had fallen sharply since 1970 in the economy as a whole and in the long-favored industrial sector. The overall productivity of resources used in the economy had declined markedly, and the technological level of the capital stock was backward compared to the capitalist West. Soviet manufactures were largely unsalable there, and domestic purchasers perennially complained of their quality. The rate of improvement in living standards slowed to a crawl, and random shortages, black markets, and queues pervaded. A kind of malaise seemed to beset the populace, manifested in reduced work effort, widespread alcoholism, rampant corruption, and a burgeoning underground economy. Such a state of affairs, highly unflattering to Soviet socialism's image abroad, also threatened the Soviet Union's status as a superpower and the legitimacy of its political system. Gorbachev vowed to turn the situation around, mapped out a strategy for doing so, and proceeded to implement it with vigor.

This paper, presented at the symposium, is the Prepared Statement submitted for the Hearings on Gorbachev's Economic Reforms, conducted by the Subcommittee on National Security Economics of the Joint Economic Committee of the U.S. Congress, 14 September 1987. The text appears in the published *Hearings*. The author has supplied documentation and some updated information in footnotes. An expanded version of the Prepared Statement appears in *Soviet Economy*, vol. 3, no. 3, 1987, pp. 219-241.
1. For an overview of the economic problems inherited by General Secretary Gorbachev see: Gertrude E. Schroeder, *Soviet Economic Problems: System vs. Progress* (London: CRCE, 1987).

GOALS AND STRATEGY

Gorbachev's goals and his strategy[2] for achieving them are vividly expressed in three Russian words that have become rallying cries and buzz words--*uskoreniye* (acceleration), *intensifikatsiya* (intensification or an upsurge in efficiency), and *perestroika* (restructuring). Above all, acceleration applies to growth rates for the economy and all major sectors. The goals are outlined in the Twelfth Five-Year Plan adopted in June 1986 and in the specific plans for 1986 and 1987. Growth of GNP is slated to be about 4 percent annually during 1986-1990, double that during 1976-1985, and then to rise to somewhat over 5 percent during the 1990s, thus returning to growth rates of the 1960s. Similarly, industrial growth during 1986-1990 is targeted to reach more than double that in the preceding decade and even higher during the 1990s. Gains in agricultural output in 1986-1990 are to be triple those of the preceding fifteen years. Investment growth is to accelerate and exceed that of consumption. Consequently, only a modest gain in living standards is planned for this five-year plan, but they should improve at a much faster clip in the 1990s, resulting in an overall gain of 60 to 80 percent in real income per capita, the Soviet official measure of changes in living standards.

A critical part of Gorbachev's turnaround strategy is his investment program designed to modernize the industrial sector in a hurry.[3] Not only is the growth of investment to be accelerated, but priorities are to be altered in major ways. The bulk of investment is to go toward reconstructing and reequipping existing plants, rather than building new ones. In support of the drive to modernize the nation's antiquated capital stock, the plans call for nearly doubling retirement rates and replacing over one-third of the total capital stock by 1990. This gigantic task is to be made possible by an increase of 80 percent in the amount of investment directed to the civilian machinery industries, compared to a gain of perhaps 20 percent in the preceding five years. With this investment, machinery industries are to double the growth rate of output and radically upgrade their quality and technological level. By 1990, 90 percent of all machinery is supposed to meet "world standards," compared to about 20 percent now.

2. For a more detailed treatment see: *The Soviet Economy Under a New Leader,* a joint CIA/DIA paper prepared for submission to the Subcommittee on Economic Resources, Competitiveness, and Security Economics of the Joint Economic Committee, U.S. Congress, August 1986.

3. For a more detailed treatment see: *Gorbachev's Modernization Program: A Status Report,* paper prepared by CIA and DIA for the Subcommittee on National Security Economics of the Joint Economic Committee, U.S. Congress, August 1987.

The planned accelerated growth across the board is supposed to result from an upsurge in the efficiency with which labor and capital are used. Indeed, without such a breakthrough, sustained accelerated growth is impossible. Demographic factors limit the growth of the labor force to about 0.5 percent per year, and the capital stock will grow more slowly than previously because of past and present investment policies and planned accelerated retirement of old capital. To achieve the economic growth rate targeted for 1986-1990, the labor productivity growth will have to double, and the rate of improvement in the productivity of all resources will have to return to levels not experienced since the 1950s. The strategy demands large gains across the board in the technical quality of all manufactures and a radical upgrading of the modernity of their design.

To generate the accelerated economic growth that he deems essential and the boost in efficiency that is required, Gorbachev has launched a vigorous and multifaceted campaign to "restructure" Soviet society. He wants to alter fundamentally the thinking and behavior of workers and managers, to transform them into disciplined employees who appear at work on time and sober, put in a full day's work, take personal responsibility for the quantity and quality of the product, and are innovative in seeking ways to produce more and better products with fewer resources. To effect this change, Gorbachev has called for "radical economic reforms" to alter the basic parameters of the "economic mechanism," that is, economic organization and incentives aiming their productive enterprises and employees in the desired directions.[4] In his two and a half years of tenure, he has acted vigorously to further the restructuring, giving many speeches filled with exhortations and a series of actions to implement his economic reforms. Gorbachev has characterized this program as "radical," "revolutionary," and rooted in the principle of "more socialism, more democracy."

On June 30, 1987, the Supreme Soviet approved by decree a package of measures designed to alter the ways by which the Soviet economy is managed.[5] These measures were set forth in a document approved a few days earlier at a plenum of the Central Committee of the Communist Party of the Soviet Union (CPSU). The document, entitled "Basic Provisions for Fundamentally Reorganizing Economic Management,"[6] was supplemented by eleven

---

4. Gorbachev's programs for "restructuring" the economy and society (*perestroika*) are set forth in his speeches at the Twenty-Seventh Party Congress of the CPSU in February 1986 (*Pravda*, 26 February 1986) and at the Plenum of the Central Committee of the CPSU in June 1987 (*Pravda*, 26 June 1987).

5. *Pravda*, 1 July 1987.

6. *Pravda*, 27 June 1987.

documents not yet available.[7] The Supreme Soviet also adopted a new Law on the State Enterprise that forms a key part of the reform package.[8] Also included are the decrees adopted in 1986 mandating an overhaul of the entire wage and salary system, reorganizing the conduct of foreign trade, expanding the responsibilities of the regional authorities, and sanctioning expansion of the scope of economic activity by private individuals and producer cooperatives, as well as actions taken during 1985 and 1986 to reform agriculture and to establish new bureaucracies and reorganize old ones. As a whole, this program provides the present official blueprint and time schedules for implementing a "new economic mechanism" that is supposed to be almost fully operational by the start of the Thirteenth Five-Year Plan in 1991.

DESCRIPTION OF THE REFORM PACKAGE

Role of Central Planning

The Basic Provisions stress that the economy will continue to be centrally planned and managed as "a unified national economic complex" directed toward carrying out the Party's economic policies. These policies will be embodied in a fifteen-year plan that sets goals and priorities and outlines a program for implementing them. This plan, which is to contain specific targets for the fifteen-year period, is to be the basis for detailed formulation of the plan for the initial five-year period, with a breakdown by years. As now, this plan will be prepared by the State Planning Committee (GOSPLAN) and sent down to union republic Councils of Ministers and to ministries. These bodies, in term, send initial planning data to firms, on the basis of which they work out and ratify their own five-year and annual plans.

The firms receive:

1. "Non-binding control figures" that specify value of output, total profits, foreign currency receipts, and "major indicators of scientific and technical

---

7. Subsequently, ten of the eleven documents were published as decrees (dated July 17, 1987) of the Central Committee of the CPSU and the Council of Ministers: *O korennoi perestroike upravleniya ekonomiki: sbornik dokumentov* (Moscow: Gospolitizdat, 1987). These decrees concern: the State Planning Committee; the State Committee for Material-Technical Supply; the State Committee for Science and Technology; finance; statistics; price formation; rights and responsibilities of regional administrative bodies; the ministries; and the State Committee for Labor and Social Problems. Although the decrees provide much more detail, they do not alter any of the parameters of the reform packages laid out in the Basic Provisions.

8. *Pravda*, 1 July 1987.

progress and social development," a list to be fixed by the Council of Ministers.

2. A mandatory bill of state orders for output that includes commissionings of facilities financed by state centralized investment and products essential for fulfilling priority state tasks for "social development, scientific-technical progress, defense, and deliveries of farm products."

3. Limits, which include normatives according to a list approved by the Council of Ministers, regulating such matters as growth of total wages and the allocation of profits among various kinds of taxes and funds.

Position of the Firm

The Law on the State Enterprise fixed the intended status of the firm under the reforms in a fair amount of detail. The law took effect January 1, 1988, and firms are to be put under its full provisions gradually during 1988 and 1989. Firms, which are founded and liquidated by superior bodies, remain under state ownership and formally subordinate to government agencies.

The firm now "independently" works out and approves its five-year and annual plans, based on control figures, mandatory state orders, limits, economic normatives, and contracts with customers. The Law states, "The enterprise is obligated to strictly observe plan discipline and meet plans and contractual obligations in full." It states further, "Fulfillment of orders and contracts serves as the most important criterion for evaluating the activities of the enterprise and providing material rewards for its employees."

The reform documents require the firm "as a rule" to finance all its current and capital expenditures from its sales revenues and other internally generated funds--a condition labeled "full economic accountability and self-finance." Furthering Gorbachev's call for "more democracy," the Law provides for organizing elected enterprise Labor Councils and for election of key personnel. Work collectives are supposed to set up Councils and elect leaders during 1987-1988. The Law supposedly greatly expands the decisionmaking authority of the firm by providing that it "is entitled to make on its own initiative any decisions provided that they do not run counter to existing legislation." The Law endows the firm with "rights whose observance is guaranteed by the state" and provides means by which the firm may obtain redress if superior organs violate such rights. Finally, the Law explicitly provides for liquidating and declaring bankrupt firms that persistently show losses. Displaced workers are to be given severance pay and helped to find new jobs.

Role of Central and Regional Administrative Bodies

Gorbachev's recipe for managerial reform includes an idea often advocated by Brezhnev--setting up super-ministerial bodies to oversee groups of related economic activities. Six such bodies were set up during 1985 and 1986.[9]

The Plenum documents make clear the intent to carry out a major shakeup of the central and regional bureaucracies, revising their functions, reorganizing their structures, and cutting their staffs. According to Premier Ryzhkov, this is to take place during 1987-1988. GOSPLAN, whose staff is to be reorganized to deemphasize sectoral subdivisions, is supposed to concentrate on long-range strategic planning and development of techniques for managing the economy through "economic methods"--long-term plans and normatives, finance, prices, and credit. More specifically, GOSPLAN is supposed to coordinate the work of all central bodies dealing with the economy, work out five- and fifteen-year plans and transmit them to executants, and determine the composition of state orders. The State Committee for Science and Technology is to be reorganized to carry out its main functions of working out state programs for development of science and technology, specifying and monitoring the relevant state orders, and guiding the work of intersectoral scientific and technical complexes, whose role is to be expanded.

The number of ministries is to be reduced and they are to be reorganized to eliminate sectoral subbranches (*glavki*) and to cut staffs.[10]   In place of the *glavki*, the new scheme is to have "several thousand" large associations and enterprises directly subordinated to all-union ministries; this is to be accomplished by the end of 1988 by accelerating the ongoing process of amalgamating enterprises into production and science-production associations and creating large new groupings called "state production associations," which integrate entities engaged in all phases of the research-production-marketing chain. While supposedly being relieved of the functions of day to day control over firms, the ministries are still given enormous responsibility. According to the Basic Provisions, the ministry "is responsible to the nation for satisfying demand for the branch's product, preventing disproportions, ensuring that the product meets world technical and quality standards, and working out and implementing branch scientific and technical programs." As now, it is to serve as an intermediate level in the planning process and monitor the performance of subordinate firms, including monopoly behavior.

---

9. A seventh "super-ministry"--for the chemicals and forest products complex--was set up in late 1987.

10. In late 1987, four machinery ministries were merged into two, and another was abolished.

The Basic Provisions and a decree of July 1986[11] convey the intent to accord the republic Councils of Ministers and their subordinate bodies, notably the local Soviets, a greater role and responsibility for regional economies, especially those aspects relating to the welfare of local populations. These bodies, too, are supposed to be reorganized to improve administration; thus, "production-economic departments" are to be set up under local Soviets and other regional bodies.

Supply System

The Basic Provisions call for a "decisive transition from centralized allocation of material resources and the attachment of users to producers to wholesale trade in the means of production," to be completed in four to five years. Only "particularly scarce" goods will continue to be rationed, which includes raw materials required to fulfill mandatory state orders. Wholesale trade, which is to become the main form of supply, is to take the form of "free" purchase and sale under direct contracts between the parties or with wholesale organizations, and with manufacturers' direct outlets. The Law on the State Enterprise indicates that regional units of the State Committee for Material-Technical Supply (GOSSNAB) are to play the major role in supply. A Council of Ministers decree adopted July 17, 1987,[12] instructs GOSSNAB to increase the share of wholesale trade in total sales to 60 percent by 1990 and to complete the transfer by 1992, when it is supposed to cover 75-80 percent of goods passing through that network, according to GOSSNAB's chairperson.[13]

Prices and Wages

The Basic Provisions call for a "radical" reform of prices to be completed by 1990, so that the new prices can be used in developing the 1991-1995 plan. Unlike its predecessors, this reform is to encompass all forms of prices-- wholesale, procurement, and retail prices and rates, with changes in the various sets of prices to be interconnected. Centrally set prices, the share of which is to be "sharply reduced," are to be determined as part of five-year plan formulation and fixed on the basis of "socially necessary expenses of production and sale, utility, quality, and effective demand." They are to cover the costs of

---

11. *Sobraniye postanovlenniy pravitelstva SSSR*, no. 27, 1986.
12. *Pravda*, 18 July 1987.
13. Foreign Broadcasting Information Service, *Daily Report*, Soviet Union, 12 August 1987.

environmental protection and take into account the charges for natural resources, capital, and labor, which enterprises will now be required to pay. More specifically, prices of fuels and raw materials are to be raised sharply, so as to ensure normal profitability for those branches. Contract prices, limit prices, and those set by enterprises are to become more common and are to be set on the same basic principles as state-set prices. Those principles and procedures are to be laid down and all prices closely monitored by state organs, presumably the State Committee for Prices.

The sensitive issue of revising retail prices to conform to the new pricing formula is addressed by calling for a broad public discussion of the price reforms and by stating that changes in retail prices "not only must not reduce living standards of workers, but also must raise them for some groups and more fully promote social justice." At present, some foods and services are heavily subsidized, now costing the state budget 73 billion rubles.[14] Alcohol, clothing, many durables, and luxury goods are heavily taxed.

An essential ingredient of the reform package is a major overhaul of the wage and salary structure, to be carried out branch by branch and firm by firm during 1987-1990, whenever they are able to finance the higher wages by cutting the workforce or making other economies.[15] The intent of this sweeping reform is to raise the role of job rates in workers' earnings, make bonuses harder to get and more closely dependent on the efficiency and quality of performance of both the worker and the firm, tighten work norms, and contribute to more general objectives of enforcing self-finance, eradicating "wage-leveling," and encouraging work effort and acquisition of skills.

Agricultural Reform

Besides endorsing the 1982 Food Program, Gorbachev has spelled out a recipe for agricultural reform in two major decrees. The first one, adopted in November 1985,[16] established the State Committee for the Agro-Industrial Complex (GOSAGROPROM), a super-ministry to manage the production, marketing, and processing of farm products. It was formed as a merger of five ministries and a state committee, but agencies in charge of grain procurement and land reclamation remain independent. This reorganization also was intended to strengthen the position of the regional agricultural production associations

14. This figure was given by Gorbachev in his speech to the June Plenum, *Pravda*, 26 June 1987.

15. *Sobraniye postanovlenniy pravitelstva SSSR*, no. 34, 1986.

16. *Pravda*, 23 November 1985.

(RAPOs) that had been organized as part of the 1982 Food Program. The second decree, adopted in March 1986, was directed toward increasing the autonomy of farms and improving incentives.[17] The principal provisions of this complex and ambiguous decree are to permit farms to sell at market prices a larger share of production, to introduce measures to market farm products more flexibly, to extend to farms many of the arrangements now being applied in the industrial sector (such as normative planning and self-finance), and to endorse widespread use of collective contracts.

The Basic Provisions and the Law on the State Enterprise apply in general to agriculture. Although there are few specific references to that sector in these documents, Gorbachev addressed agricultural matters at some length in a speech to the June Plenum, stating that the measures already effected had created the potential for a breakthrough in farm output. He strongly endorsed the use of collective contracts, especially brigades using intensive technology and family groups. In a later speech, he stated that agriculture would be the subject of a future plenum.

Foreign Trade

Gorbachev's reform package includes an overhaul of the system for conducting foreign trade.[18] The relevant decree:

1. Established the State Foreign Economic Commission as a super-ministry overseeing all facets of foreign economic activity.
2. Reorganized the Ministry of Foreign Trade to end its monopoly over trade by transferring some of its foreign trade associations to the jurisdiction of ministries and other central bodies.
3. Granted the right as of January 1, 1987, to twenty ministries and other bodies and seventy selected enterprises to engage directly in importing and exporting activity with appropriate units in foreign countries.
4. Provided for establishing foreign currency funds in exporting enterprises and associations that can be used independently to finance imports of machinery and equipment.
5. Gave firms extensive rights to engage in joint projects with firms in CMEA countries.

17. *Pravda*, 29 March 1986.
18. *Sobraniye postanovlenniy pravitelstva SSSR*, no. 33, 1986.

6. Sanctioned joint ventures with firms in capitalist countries. Regulations were then issued detailing procedures for carrying out such joint projects.
7. Called for implementing a stage-by-stage convertibility of the ruble, starting with the CMEA trading system.

Private and Cooperative Economic Activity

Documents from the June Plenum strongly endorsed measures adopted in 1986 that aimed to expand the role of producer cooperatives and private individuals in the economy, particularly in the provision of consumer goods and services. A law adopted by the Supreme Soviet in November 1986 spelled out the permissible endeavors (only a few new kinds) and the groups that are to be encouraged to engage in them (state employees only outside working hours, pensioners, homemakers, and the handicapped).[19] The law took effect May 1, 1987, along with revisions in the income tax that lowered the extremely high tax rates on income from private work. In August 1986, the Politburo approved the "Basic Principles for Development of Cooperative Forms of Production" (not yet published), which specify that producer cooperatives are to be organized on a voluntary basis "with the participation of ministries, departments, and local Soviets." Subsequently, the Council of Ministers promulgated Model Charters for experimental cooperatives to be engaged in the collection and processing of waste materials and for producing consumer goods and services. The decree on expanding the rights of local Soviets adopted in June 1986 gives regional and local government bodies the major role in developing and regulating cooperatives and private businesses.

EVALUATION OF THE REFORMS

The Total Package

Taken as a whole, the package of reform measures already in place or set *en train* by Gorbachev in his first two and a half years of tenure is impressive. Embracing nearly every major aspect and sector of the economy, its scope is much more sweeping than that of the 1965 reform package, which focused on the industrial sector.

---

19. *Pravda*, 21 November 1986.

But one is hard-pressed to visualize the kind of economic system that the framers of this package intend to introduce. Certainly, its overall design is not that required to install a system of market socialism or of worker self-management as those terms are usually understood. It borrows bits and pieces from the various reforms taking place in East European countries. Despite allusions to creating autonomous, self-managed business firms, the reforms do not go nearly far enough to create a market environment, nor do they allow workers to make key decisions that determine the outcomes of the firm's activity. The reforms leave the pillars of socialist state economic administration prominently in place--state ownership, central planning (albeit changed in form and reduced in detail), numerous administrative agencies supervising business firms, rationing of many materials and investment goods, state control over price-setting, and enterprise incentives still oriented toward plans and output targets and biased toward dealing with administrative superiors rather than following the signals from markets. Moreover, the package, as spelled out in formal decrees as well as in the speeches of the leadership, is riddled with inconsistencies and contradictions that will create serious problems in the process of implementation, especially because Gorbachev is a person in a hurry. This reform, far more than its predecessors, imposes a staggering set of tasks on the central bureaucracies and on the producing units to be accomplished in the next three years. At a meeting on July 17, 1987, the Council of Ministers excoriated one and all for not moving fast enough on all fronts and imposed some specific tasks and deadlines. At the same time, both bureaucracies and enterprises are under continual pressure to meet the demanding targets set by the plans for 1987 and 1986-1990.

The schedule for imposing conditions of full self-reliance on the enterprises is potentially the most disruptive facet of the reforms. In 1987, those rules of the game affected all firms in five industrial ministries and thirty-seven entities in various others; together they represent about 20 percent of total industrial output and 16 percent of employment.[20] According to Premier Ryzhkov, self-financed enterprises will account for 60 percent of industrial output in 1988, when the new conditions will also apply to branches of transportation and a number of other sectors.[21] The new rules already are creating difficulties for many firms, according to press accounts.[22]

20. *Pravda*, 14 July 1987.
21. *Pravda*, 30 June 1987.
22. The evidence is provided in numerous press articles during 1987, most notably in *Ekonomicheskaya gazeta* and *Sotsialisticheskaya industriya*.

KEY COMPONENTS OF THE PACKAGE

Central Planning and Management

The policy statements and specific provisions of the reform program make it clear that strong central management of the economy is being retained. They display the traditional conviction that economic development--the composition of output and the direction of investment--as well as the broad content and direction of scientific and technological progress must be managed by the center. The framework of mandatory, "stable" five-year plans is retained, along with new and old government bodies to guide and monitor their outcomes. New forms of central management--"non-binding" control figures, state orders, and long-term, stable normatives--replace the familiar categories. These instruments, along with prices and interest rates, are now to be the means by which the state controls the behavior of its enterprises. That the center is to slough off a mass of detail is of secondary importance.

Position of the Firm

The business firm remains subordinate to government agencies, which are to eschew "petty tutelage," while ensuring the sector's output goals are met and the firm behaves "properly." Absence of "petty tutelage," if it eventuates, may reduce the managers' frustration, but ministerial micromanagement, which many people are prone to blame for all sorts of malfunctions, has been a minor factor in the past difficulties of the economy in any case. On the contrary, under the new arrangements the firm is likely to eagerly receive ministerial aid, particularly in respect to the functioning of the assorted normatives, which undoubtedly will provide a fertile field for bargaining. While being pushed to "freely" negotiate contracts for much of its output with customers and for the requisite raw materials and capital goods with suppliers in a framework of competition, the firm will find the tissue (information and infrastructure) needed to support competitive sales and purchases is almost totally lacking. Portions of its product and raw materials will have rigid state-set prices as now, and the prices it may set or negotiate are subject to methodological guidelines and strict state monitoring. The manager's bonus depends on meeting (planned) contracts for output, as well as on indicators for several other aspects of performance. Finally, the new deal provides the firm with still another participant in decisionmaking and monitoring--the Labor Council--and subjects its key managers to the elective process. Because all of this does not fundamentally alter the real position of the firm in the economic process, its behavior is unlikely to change much either; it is likely to remain risk-averse and center-oriented.

Although the reform's vision of autonomous, self-financing, socialist business firms threatened with bankruptcy for failure conveys an aura of markets and competition, it is, in fact, an artificial accounting construct, both under present Soviet conditions and under those created by the reforms. Because prices of products and material inputs do not reflect the economic tradeoffs (scarcities), the derivative accounting categories of sales, costs, profits, and returns on capital can be misleading. Managerial decisions based on them may not result in efficient mixes of inputs and outputs, profits do not indicate relative efficiencies of firms, and failure to earn profits and thus go bankrupt does not necessarily mean the firm was inefficient. The belief that large gains in efficiency will accrue from enforcing self-finance under such conditions is a grand illusion.

Supply

Along with its call for a "resolute" shift of the bulk of purchases and sales of intermediate and capital goods from central rationing to wholesale trade between competing buyers and sellers, the Basic Provisions accord GOSSNAB a key role in the process. Faced with the need to nail down through contracts their "independently" planned sales and purchases, firms in the near term can be expected to scramble to keep existing arrangements and tie up new ones. These arrangements, by and large, are likely to form the basis of the Thirteenth Five-Year Plan for the contracts on which the firms are required to base their plans. All this will create much confusion and also make for rigidity, not the flexibility that is needed.

Prices

The extent to which prices reflect supply and demand is the key to the success of any market-oriented reform. But the principles on which state-fixed prices and contractual prices are to be set are the same as used now--essentially average cost-based in the case of wholesale and procurement prices. The requirement that they remain stable for five years for state-set prices and be embodied in planned contracts in the case of contract prices preserves the rigidities now prevailing. Hence, prices will be little better guides to efficient choice than now. Moreover, widespread use of contract prices will be inflationary, unless hard budget constraints are imposed on both parties, something the reforms do not really do. Clearly, the government intends to monitor such prices closely, requiring it to peer into the detailed books of individual firms. Finally, the declared intent to link the three sets of prices--wholesale, procurement, and retail--involves coming to grips with a major political-economic policy dilemma of what to do about the existing huge subsidies on food and some services for consumers and the large subsidies on machinery and fertilizer sold to farms. We shall have to wait and see what political will can be mustered.

The planned overhaul of the wage and bonus system could be highly disruptive. Unlike its predecessor in the early 1960s, which offered a tempting carrot in the form of a substantial reduction in the work week (from forty-six to forty-one hours), the current wage reform offers no carrot to the rank and file workers. Although their base rates will be increased, their work norms will be tightened accordingly, and they will bear the brunt of layoffs, pressure to redefine and combine jobs, and demands to work second and third shifts. Meanwhile, earnings of white-collar workers will increase sharply. Will blue-collar workers, long nurtured on egalitarian values, regard those developments as fair, even though they are economically justified to correct the present unduly narrow differentials that blunt incentives?

Because the wage overhaul is being carried out piecemeal and firm by firm, both among sectors and within sectors, the potential for creating inequitable differences in wages and in the provision of amenities is great. This potential arises because of the highly uneven conditions under which Soviet enterprises operate that stem from factors over which they have little or no control. The playing field is unequal and in a fundamental sense unfair. Meanwhile, workers and managers alike will have to cope with the new rules for workplace democracy. Whether either group will find virtue in the new environment remains to be seen.

SOME TENTATIVE CONCLUSIONS

The reform programs adopted thus far under Gorbachev are a set of half-measures that retain the pillars of the traditional system. Even if the measures now outlined are fully implemented, as is now clearly intended, they do not go nearly far enough to accomplish Gorbachev's goal of creating a self-regulating, technologically dynamic "economic mechanism," one capable of rapidly closing the gap with the West. Those goals will be frustrated by the approach to pricing, a failure to take steps to create capital markets, and the large dose of central administration that is retained. Even when the reforms are fully in place (1991), they will constitute a hybrid system that is neither fish nor fowl and that is likely to require further reforms.

Meanwhile, the reforms, being introduced piecemeal, impose so many changes and encompass so much of the economy as to risk serious disruptions in the production process; in fact, disruptions did occur in 1987. Some sectors and parts of sectors will be operating under old procedures and others under new procedures, which are being phased in and worked out on the run, so to speak. The key agencies that must issue the necessary documents and monitor the process will be undergoing reorganizations and staff reductions. The risk is heightened by the unremitting pressure (as of now) to increase production, improve product quality, and proceed rapidly with plant modernization. The leadership has recognized that the next few years will be difficult. How it will react if growth rates tumble is a matter of speculation. The pressure for production could be relaxed and/or the reform timetable stretched out. Conceivably, the leadership could introduce a really radical reform, as Lenin did in 1921 with the New Economic Policy (NEP), which quickly introduced large doses of private enterprise and markets in the economy. Alternatively, it could continue to liberalize the present semi-market scheme, taking the reforms in directions now being pursued in Poland and Hungary. Or adjustments could be made that would preserve the essentials of the status quo into the Thirteenth Five-Year Plan period and beyond. Gorbachev has already shown that when his "reforms" are not eliciting the desired outcomes fast enough, he will resort to the traditional administrative methods. Recent decrees mandating state inspection of output, multiple shifts, and inventory reductions are cases in point.

This somber judgment on Gorbachev's reform package does not mean that it has no redeeming features. It moves in the right direction--toward decentralizing and marketizing the economy. If private and cooperative activity gains strong momentum, it will improve the lot of consumers to some degree. The somewhat greater leeway given factories and farms to dispose of above-plan output and unneeded inputs will work mainly to that same end. Some paring of government staffs and forced redistribution of labor, which is likely, will facilitate adjustment to slow growth in the labor force. Relatively higher wages for skilled and efficient workers should improve incentives. Some gains in efficiency could result from all of this. But Gorbachev aspires to have a Japanese miracle-type production system in place in the Soviet Union of the 1990s. His reform package as now laid out is not nearly radical enough to bring that about.

The short-run costs of implementing Gorbachev's present reform package will be high and the benefits few and slow to come. These costs will be manifested in disruptions in production, in slowed real gains in the quality of machines and of consumer goods, in a chaotic and unfair structure of wages, and in rising economic pressures for reversion to old and familiar ways. The central bureaucracies will be eager to intervene and alleviate the problems. Enterprise managers will seek relief from the confusion and uncertainties of their new environment. Rank and file workers will not like the erosion of the "social contract" with their rulers (low work effort in return for economic security and political quiescence) when the benefits are hard to see. Local Party units will find restructuring extremely painful, especially since they will be blamed for its shortcomings.

Even if Gorbachev manages to prevent backsliding and succeeds in pushing the present programs in more liberal directions (toward the Hungarian model), he is likely to be disappointed with the results, as the Hungarians have been. There, substantial economic reforms over twenty years have yet to produce significant gains in economic efficiency and growth. Decades of a centrally managed socialist economy leave formidable legacies in terms of people's outlook and attitudes and in terms of the state of the economy's physical assets. Much time will be required to overcome such legacies. Ultimately, Gorbachev and other would-be reformers are going to find they cannot enjoy the benefits, which they seek, of a private enterprise market economy without creating one with all its attendant blemishes. Experience, as well as theory, has yet to show that any species of halfway house will do the trick.

4 HOW FAR CAN ECONOMIC AND SOCIAL REFORM GO IN THE SOVIET UNION?

William E. Odom

If Mikhail Gorbachev is the radical reformer his Soviet and western admirers portray him to be, he is a Marxist without a model. The changes he is widely credited with espousing in Soviet economic management cannot succeed without simultaneously undermining the power of the political party he heads and the empire it rules.

Conceivably, effective decentralization of the Soviet Union's economy could bring the efficiency and strength of a free market to the Soviet Union and hence to its standing as a world power. The process, however, would require economic and political dislocations so extensive they would challenge the survival of communist power in the Soviet Union and perhaps the internal cohesion of the multinational state itself.

Whatever else he is, Gorbachev is not suicidal. And a closer look at his battle plan and slogans suggests that he is heading not a revolution, but an administrative purge. It is a tactic Soviet leaders have used successfully before, and, with the cooperation of western trading partners, it may indeed release new energies and spur a period of new growth. But because Gorbachev has recruited the Soviet intelligentsia as both allies and advance guard of his campaign, he has raised hopes of systemic change he cannot afford to satisfy. Whatever the economic results of his efforts, he is sowing the seeds for a fresh harvest of alienation between the most imaginative and restless of his subjects and their future rulers.

A few years ago, only the most serious specialists and scholars devoted to the study of Russian and Soviet affairs speculated about the prospects of internal reform in the Soviet Union. Today, western policymakers in government and business, journalists, commentators, and the public at large are interested in the incessant Soviet discussion of imminent domestic reforms. Although the change is largely attributable to General Secretary Gorbachev, the new course in the Politburo of the Communist Party of the Soviet Union (CPSU) was actually initiated under one of his predecessors, Yuri Andropov, temporarily set aside by Konstantin Chernenko, and reasserted by Gorbachev. Western observers tended accurately to dismiss Andropov as a phony "liberal," but they underestimated his commitment to dramatic change in the Soviet Union. His anti-corruption and anti-alcoholism campaigns, however, did not signal so clearly the extent of the intended transformation as Gorbachev's *glasnost* (speaking out publicly), *perestroika* (restructuring), and *novoye myshleniye* (new thinking).[1] The Party slogans have prompted unprecedented public criticism and debate about the present state of the Soviet economy and Party leadership. At the same time, the turnover in senior Party leadership has been greater than at any time since the early 1960s.[2] Because these are not ordinary events in the Soviet Union, the question of economic and social reform has to be taken seriously and urgently if we in the West are to comprehend the contemporary course of Soviet political and economic affairs.

The question, however, is fraught with ambiguities and potential confusion. The greatest ambiguity is found in the word "reform." Reform for what purpose? In pursuit of whose aims? Whose goals? Whose preferences should a "restructured" economy serve? Central planners' preferences? Consumers' preferences? All consumers or special groups? In short, Whose reform? Gorbachev has not made clear his answers to these questions; nor has the Central Committee promulgated a directive that gives a definition of what the Party leadership intends. We are left with speeches, proposals, some new laws, and articles, some official, some circulated as *samizdat*, from which to infer the intent under the slogans *glasnost*, *perestroika*, and *novoye myshleniye*.

From these sources, westerners (as well as Soviet citizens) draw different inferences about the aims and methods of reform, some of them incompatible. This is not surprising. If one takes Tatyana Zaslavskaya's criticism of the

1. *Glasnost* literally is the substantive from the verb *glasit*, meaning "to say," and as a noun connotes speaking out publicly, being heard. *Perestroika*, meaning "restructuring," is less ambiguous in translation but has a more complex connotation in Russian. *Novoye myshleniye* translates literally as "new thinking," a responsibility Gorbachev places on the Party- and state-leading cadres for abandoning their old work style in favor of a new effective style.

2. Thane Gustafson and Dawn Mann, "Andropov's First Year," *Problems of Communism*, 35, May-June 1986, pp. 1-18, provides excellent data on this turnover.

Soviet economy as the starting point for defining the policy for *perestroika*, dramatic and systemic reform is to be expected.[3] Zaslavskaya's tie to Abel Aganbegyan, and Aganbegyan's own views, reportedly shared by Gorbachev, promote this radical inference. When we read blistering criticism of the unreliability of economic accounting data, we are encouraged to believe that someone at the Politburo level recognizes the information logjam created by central planning and centrally determined prices.[4] A very recent essay by Nikolai Shmelev removes any doubt about the inadequacies of the system. Shmelev declares that all the pricing decisions since the late 1920s are a "terrible legacy" that must be ended if any prospect of success in the present reform is to be realized.[5] The implication of these and many other articles is that minor repairs in the present economic system will not suffice; systemic change is imperative.

When Gorbachev chides the leadership of the State Planning Committee (GOSPLAN) and the State Committee for Material-Technical Supply (GOSSNAB),[6] it seems that he endorses sweeping changes. All the more so when he goes on to insist that, "We urgently need a fundamental breakthrough on the theoretical front, based on the aggregate facts of social life, on a scientific foundation of goals and perspectives of our movement."[7] This call from above for a new, comprehensive economic theory sounds like proof that Aganbegyan, Zaslavskaya, and others, are succeeding in convincing Gorbachev and the Politburo that economic progress cannot occur without free play of market forces to set prices based on supply and demand.

The trumpet of reform, however, is not giving so clear a sound. As we read further, we find that Gorbachev wants a theoretical advance like the one Marx achieved from his examination of the Paris Commune, and Lenin's advances in the first years of Soviet rule. There is no hint of Adam Smith, David Ricardo, or any other classical liberals who might have inspired the Aganbegyan school of Soviet economists to hold the marketplace in such high esteem as a means of overcoming the stagnant bureaucracies in charge of Soviet central planning.

On the contrary, the tone of Gorbachev's June Plenum Report is reminiscent of Lenin calling for worker discipline and Stalin's lectures, "The Fundamentals of Leninism." Gorbachev envisions *perestroika* occurring in

---

3. T. Zaslavskaya, "Doklad o neobkhodimosti bolee uglublennogo izucheniia v SSSR sotsial'novo mekhanizma razvitiia ekonomiki," *Arkhiv Samizdata, Radio Liberty*, AS No 5042, 26 August 1987.

4. Vasilii Selyunin and Grigori Khanin, "Lukavaya tsifra," *Novyy mir*, no. 2, February 1987, pp. 181-201.

5. Nikolai Shmelev, "Advances and Debts," *Novyy mir*, no. 6, June 1987, pp. 142-158.

6. *Pravda*, 26 June 1987.

7. Ibid.

several "waves." This is only the first one demanded by the "masses." It is not to be achieved quickly but through a "long-term policy." "The Soviet people understand that the attainment of the many goals of *perestroika* demand a long time."[8] Yet they are anxious to see progress. Gorbachev reports that the "toilers" with whom he spoke in one town asked, "When will the *perestroika* reach us?" The republic, *oblast* (regional), and local officials accompanying Gorbachev were directed to draw the proper lessons from such questions and move ahead with restructuring. The "waves" of *perestroika* in the Gorbachev image are stimulated from below. The June Plenum Report emphasizes this role for the masses again and again. How do they generate a "wave" of reform? Through *glasnost* apparently, through openly voicing their complaints about the present state of affairs, through making their criticisms and desires publicly known.

Who is to respond to these demands from below? Market forces? Entrepreneurs? Hardly! Gorbachev places the tasks squarely on the economic bureaucracy. Moreover, he even asserts a stronger role for the Central Committee Secretariat of the CPSU (CC CPSU): "In this new circumstance, the departments of the CC CPSU are called to act in a new way, having a much deeper influence on the state of affairs in republic, *krai* (territorial), and *oblast* (regional) Party organizations, ensuring control over the execution of the decisions of the CC CPSU."[9] In discussing the need for modernization of the Soviet machine-building industry, Gorbachev calls for more aggressive ministerial action in designing a large-scale program and driving it through from the top. This is not the rhetoric of decentralization. It sounds more like the language of the leadership in the First Five-Year Plan in the late 1920s than it does of a voice for systemic change.

A vagueness characterizes Gorbachev's image of the completion of *perestroika*. Indeed, while it is difficult to discern where he believes he is going, it is easier to glean his proposed method for getting there. *Glasnost* is the impulse for movement. It comes from the "masses." It expresses the whole people's interests. *Perestroika* is the response. It comes from the Party's central organs, which must develop *novoye myshleniye*, that is, new thinking about how to make the system work better--new programs to overcome the old shortcomings. Whether the "quantity," or extent, of restructuring will bring a "qualitative" change in the system of the kind suggested by *glasnost* voices such as Zaslavskaya's is a question that ought to

---

8. Ibid.
9. Ibid.

occur to Gorbachev, schooled as he is in the laws of dialectical materialism. Perhaps he will soon give us his answer, but to date he has not.

We are faced, therefore, with two questions, not one. How far can economic and social reform go if the aim is a qualitative change, giving consumer preferences the major role in driving economic allocations? And, how far can such reform go if the allocation system remains centralized, essentially driven by "planners' preferences"? Such a sharp dichotomy may seem overdrawn. Indeed, reality usually does not break so neatly into the analytical categories of economic and political theorists, but that fuzziness does not diminish the utility of tidy categories for analysis. Rather, it suggests that one must be careful to apply these categories where they are conceptually appropriate. The experience of all Soviet-style centrally planned economies, in the many failed efforts at reform, suggests the choices may indeed be a sharp dichotomy.[10] Is there a halfway house between central planning and a market economy that allows the planners to grossly ignore consumer demands as expressed in scarcity prices? The ruling Social Democrats in West Europe have long ago made large theoretical and political concessions to the marketplace at the expense of central planning. Can modern Bolsheviks gain the advantage of the marketplace without paying the same price?

Gorbachev's call for change, in any event, offers the opportunity for many uncompelling alternatives to be presented, and we can be sure that several alternative development policies for the Soviet Union articulated by revolutionaries before 1917 and by parties and factions after 1917 will surface anew, finding contemporary proponents for the "might have beens" of history. Some will be reminded of the New Economic Policy (NEP) of the 1920s. Some will argue that Bukharin offered a way to industrialize Russia without ending the NEP.

Surviving Mensheviks, or their heirs, may feel vindicated in their original conviction that Russia could not skip over a lengthy period of capitalist development. The spate of open criticism of the central planning and pricing system appearing in the Soviet press today seems to prove their point. Others will look at the last decades of the Tsarist regime and find renewed interest in the ideas of the Constitutional Democrats. Constitutionalism, a greater role for private property, but yet a strong state led by like-minded liberals, brooking no breakaway by non-Russian national regions--these ideas appeal to some Soviet emigres who reject Marxism outright, and possibly to some of the economists in the Soviet Union who so ably indict the present state planning

---

10. See Jan Prybyla, *Market and Plan Under Socialism* (Stanford: Hoover Institution Press, 1987).

system. We may even conceivably hear from rejuvenated Social Revolutionaries about populism and agrarian socialism. Nor should we overlook the possibilities for "national socialism." Variants of fascism were appearing in Russia in the last years of the empire--for example, the Black Hundreds and *Pamyat,* an organization in Moscow ostensibly dedicated to preserving the Russian past, sound remarkably like that earlier line, one that took Russian nationalism as its spirit and blamed the Jews, Free Masons, and others, for contaminating Russian culture. Its economic program, if it can be said to have one, is anti-capitalist.[11] The alternatives advanced for economic development in the Soviet Union over the past century and a half are numerous. The chances that any or most of them will be seriously considered today are small if one examines the first question, the prospect for qualitative change in the Soviet economic system.

The analytical procedure for this examination requires three steps: (1) we must describe the features of the Soviet economic system that prevent it from functioning efficiently, (2) we must state criteria--objective conditions--that must be met in order for us to determine that systemic change has indeed occurred, and (3) we must anticipate the forces and pressures that systemic change would bring to bear on the economy and the political system. They will give us some idea of the risks Gorbachev would face if he chose to implement systemic change.

THE NATURE OF THE SOVIET ECONOMIC PROBLEM

The essence of Leninism is the primacy of the political over the economic. Lenin's quarrel with Russian trade unions at the turn of the century revealed this vividly. "The heresy of economism," as he called it, was the willingness of Russian Social Democrats to support the trade unions in getting better economic conditions for workers while ignoring, often even subordinating, the workers' revolutionary consciousness, that is, their determination to overthrow the existing political system. Better wages were nothing without political revolution.

The same spirit of Leninism is apparent in the essay "What is to Be Done?" Lenin demands a Party that can lead a revolution, not one that predicts a revolution and then sits back and waits for it. Certainly, revolution in Russia

---

11. See my "Soviet Politics and the Dustbin of History," *Studies in Comparative Communism,* IX, Spring/Summer 1976, pp. 187-208, for more on the "might have beens" of Soviet history.

was inevitable in the view of all Marxists, but Leninists believed they could make it come earlier by political action as the vanguard of the revolutionary classes. "Democratic centralism," Lenin's maxim for the Party, really meant Party dictatorship. The Party elite, specifically the Central Committee, would make the choices. One can debate if Lenin would have gone as far as Stalin in centralizing economic choice-making, but it is difficult to dispute the Leninist spirit of a system that places the Party elite in charge of all economic decisionmaking.

That is the essence of the Soviet economic system. It was designed to reduce to a minimum the impact of market forces on the allocation and the use of the factors of production. Land and capital were brought almost wholly under central control. Labor proved more difficult to manage centrally. Trotski's "labor armies" were short-lived, but the requirement for a passport to live in an urban area provided an administrative mechanism for slowing the flight of labor from the collective farms. Private farm plots, of course, are one case of land left in the free market. Otherwise, land remains in either state or "cooperative" or collective hands, which the state is able to direct for production, price, and exchange. All industrial enterprises are under state control. The state tells each enterprise what to produce, where to get its supplies, and to whom and at what price to deliver its produce.

For any economy to operate, two functions must be performed. The first is a designation of authority over the factors of production. Who controls what land, labor, and capital? The concepts of private property and a currency medium of exchange provide a solution to the authority function in western economies. The second function is the supply of information about what productive activity to undertake with the factors at one's disposal. Market-determined prices generally perform the information function in western economies, even in those where the public sector is quite large. Government directed programs--both defense and welfare--are exceptions, to be sure, but they are executed with the advantage of considerable market pricing knowledge, reflecting both domestic and international market demand. Billions of market exchanges contribute to the information and authority functions. Distortions, obstructions, and the like, disturb the efficient execution of these functions, but that is not our subject; rather, it is to note how these functions are performed in the Soviet economy.

The simple answer is that they are performed administratively by a central planning organ that acts on the authority of the CPSU. In other words, the center must specify in every sector of the economy who has what authority over what land, labor, and capital. Deeds and private ownership are disallowed. State administrative fiat allocates such authority and directs its use. The financial plan of a firm is not the determinant of authority and action. Rather, the production plan is. The financial plan is designed to make the production plan work. One does not seek a bigger budget to get more resources in the Soviet system; one seeks a bigger plan, one that requires more supplies and resources to execute. The finances will follow administratively.

Ponder for a moment the administrative task of compiling annually plans for every enterprise in the Soviet Union and ensuring that they are mutually consistent. The information-handling requirement for GOSPLAN is staggering. Prices are of little help because they have become little more than accounting devices, not a source of information about scarcity and demand. This task, however, is only the first of a number of insurmountable tasks facing central planners. Suppose by some miracle GOSPLAN worked out a mutually consistent plan and got the economy to implement it accurately, a most unlikely event. How is new factor productivity introduced by technological change reflected in these prices? In a context of dynamic growth, where new technology and new products appear in great numbers, these previously rational planned prices become the source of planning confusion and dysfunction. At present, new prices are determined by commissions that try to apply the "labor theory of value." These commissions do not have the slightest chance of keeping up with, much less providing, information on pricing that would allow efficient central allocations of capital.

The most incredible thing about the Soviet economic system is that it works at all. The informal procedures and illegal activities it gives rise to are legion; without them the Soviet economy would probably collapse. If there is a key to understanding why the system succeeds in some respect, the answer is probably found in central control of priorities for the supply of resources. GOSSNAB can give some sectors priority. All others must do with what is left--usually not much, the wrong things, and of poor quality. The military and certain technical sectors do reasonably well because they enjoy top priority. The military is especially distinctive because it has a system of "military representatives," *voyenpredy,* which puts it in a buyer's position, unlike all other sectors. The *voyenpredy* watch every step of production for quality control and do not accept products that fail to meet their standards. All other sectors in the factors market and retail markets must take what they are delivered, quality and kind notwithstanding.

As the Soviet economy has grown, the absurdity of the situation has grown. So, too, has the opportunity for illegal and irregular transactions, a phenomenon usually called the "second economy." The second economy in a sense keeps the system moving, but it also allocates resources quite at odds with the planners' preferences at the center. Cycle after cycle of plan preparation and issuance of production goals has been accompanied by intense pressures on firms from above to meet goals. Short on resources, confronted with irrational and inadequate allocation of supplies, managers have devised more and more ingenious ways of creating the impression, but not the reality, of plan fulfillment. The history of Soviet economic development has been a struggle between the preferences of the central planners (that is, the desires of the Party leadership) and the unsatisfactory response to those preferences by management at lower levels.

In Stalin's day, periodic blood purges of the Party quickened the sense of formal responsiveness. Successful cheating occurred, sometimes on a fairly large scale, but purges and transfer of Party cadres tended to break up the informal cliques that allocated for their own, not planners', interests. Under Khrushchev, blood purges ceased, but administrative turnover of cadres and frequent economic and Party reorganization were used as substitute means of struggle against localism.

Under Brezhnev, cadre stability became the rule. Reorganization was tried less frequently. The consequences were quite predictable. Informal techniques of cheating the center became more numerous, more sophisticated, and greater in their overall significance for plan fulfillment. What had once been a system conspicuous for its ability to massively direct resources from one sector to another, to limit consumption, to keep investment high, and to generate structural change desired by the Party elite now has become a lethargic bureaucratic structure presiding over local cliques that easily deceive the center and prevent major shifts in allocations.

In many cases, these local cliques have become mixed with national minority interests. Republics get their fair share of new construction, factories, and so on, even if the state planning aims may suffer as a result.[12]

This is the situation Gorbachev faces today. Increasing stagnation, inefficiency, and size of the planning task confront him at a time when rapid changes in technology are causing great structural changes in other industrial economies.

12. Konstantin Simis, *USSR: The Corrupt Society* (New York: Simon and Schuster, 1982), is an excellent first-hand account of ways in which local and regional leaders cheat the center. Walter D. Connor, "Social Policy under Gorbachev," *Problems of Communism*, 35, July-August 1986, pp. 31-46, provides good insight into recent social and economic dynamics confronting the center. Abram Bergson, "Toward a New Growth Model," *Problems of Communism*, 22, March-April 1973, pp. 1-9, offers one of the best early assessments of troubles confronting the Soviet economy. Nikolai Shmelev's "Advances and Debts," is the best Soviet assessment of the overall predicament of the Soviet economy and the gross dysfunctions it imposes.

CRITERIA FOR SYSTEMIC CHANGE

Let us presume for a moment that the Politburo wants systemic change that promises dynamic growth, exploitation of new technologies, increasing factor productivity, and renewal of the aging capital infrastructure. Let us also set aside the question, "Whose preferences--planners' or consumers'?" by answering it, "Anybody's preferences, if that means dynamic growth and recapitalization."

The system's weakness clearly lies in the way that it handles the two functions--authority over factors of production and information about how to use those factors. The information overload at the center is attested to by many witnesses in the Soviet press today. Western analysts have known it for a long time. Talk about increased incentives for managers and workers means little until the administrative approach to authority and information is largely abandoned.

What, then, is the alternative? Market forces. Systemic change must begin with a major relaxation of central planning and central price formation. How much is "major" relaxation? Enough to provide "relative scarcity" information about most of the factors of production. That means a lot; it means that the market sector must have greater influence than the planned sector. It cannot be a marginal relaxation, and it probably must be sufficient to make the ruble a convertible currency. Our first criterion, therefore, is a major shift to market pricing and allocation, a shift that lets the market exceed central planning in its impact on aggregate economic activity and creates valid scarcity information in prices of most goods and services.

Such a shift to a market economy is not possible without a free flow of information in the media, in banking, and in science and technology. Censorship as it has been exercised in the Soviet Union--and continues to be even under *glasnost*--makes such an information flow impossible. Vast amounts of such information are now considered state secrets. The criticality of censorship as an impediment to market activity became clear to the reformers in Prague in 1968. Once they started down the road to genuine relaxation of central planning, once they took systemic economic reform seriously, they found they had to suspend most censorship. Our second criterion, therefore, is the free flow of information to a degree required for effective market activity, not only domestic economic activity but also international trade. Without it, domestic economic activity cannot be based on competitive prices, and the ruble is unlikely to become convertible.

Finally, Party authority, not only at the center but particularly at local levels, blocks effective market activity. The role of the Party in economic affairs has always been supreme--the leading role in all social affairs, as every

General Secretary likes to remind Soviet citizens. The Party has always been above the law. In fact, one recent western study of the role of law in the Soviet Union concludes that it primarily serves to help the Party discipline society, to get society to do what the Party dictates.[13] The Party, however, is not constrained by law if it chooses not to be.

From the western viewpoint, where law is generally accepted as a limit on political authority, where law guarantees individual rights, where law is proscriptive--anything not forbidden is permitted--the Soviet view of law is the converse. It takes "prescription" as its premise: Do what the law dictates; all else is forbidden. Perhaps this judgment is overstated, but not by much. The tradition long antedates Soviet power. The crown was never subject to legal restraints in Russia, although the October Manifesto came close to imposing limits in 1905. The deeply embedded spirit of law as prescriptive is captured by Anton Chekhov in his story "Sergeant Prishibeyev," when the retired sergeant is explaining at his own trial how he dispersed a crowd of villagers. "By what full right have the people gathered here? I ask, 'Why?' Is it said in the law that people should gather like herds of horses? . . . . Where is it written in the law that people are given their will?" To be sure, law after the Great Reforms in the 1860s took on a large role in regulating economic affairs. Private property in the western sense came to have meaning, and a merchant or landowner could be sure that his authority over land and capital was generally protected by law. Not so, of course, in the Soviet Union. No legal claim, especially on property, is above Party power, the power of the Revolution.

Our third criterion, then, is that legal rights over the factors of production, particularly land and capital, must be assured. Local Party authorities cannot be allowed arbitrary interference in how a factory manager uses or allocates his resources. Otherwise, the "authority function" for market activity is confused and made uncertain as it relates to seeking economic efficiency. Economic decisionmakers cannot be sure about what resources they have or how long they will have them. Contracts must be enforceable. Individuals and firms, including state firms, must be accountable before tort law, and the Party must be restricted to appropriation of capital and land only through legally established means such as taxes and eminent domain.

These three criteria suggest fundamental change, change that would mark a break not only with Soviet tradition, but also with traditions that have deep Russian imperial roots. Anything less, however, is unlikely to address the

13. Olimpiad S. Ioffe and Peter B. Maggs, "The Soviet System: A Legal Analysis," *National Council for Soviet and East European Research*, no. 800-21, October 1986.

fundamental economic predicament in the Soviet Union. And some of the rhetoric from Soviet policy and specialist circles does suggest basic change.

THE IMPLICATIONS OF SYSTEMIC CHANGE

Schumpeter's idea of capitalism as a dynamic and revolutionary force, perhaps more distinctive for its destructive effects precisely because it thrives on innovation, certainly springs to mind when one contemplates letting market forces drive the Soviet economy. Growth and gains in efficiency are unlikely to be the first consequences. Perhaps the most frightening consequence for the Party leadership would be the loss of political power to nonparty groups, especially regional and national minority groups. Already, in the name of *glasnost,* some ethnic groups and regions have raised the issue of their sovereignty. Keeping the union of nationalities together under such new political and legal conditions could prove a great challenge indeed, requiring larger military and police power. The spectre of losing political control would probably make the expected economic gains too risky to seek through systemic change. Let us set political concerns aside for the moment, nevertheless, and turn to the likely economic behavior.

Initially, at least, it is the small-scale enterprises that would most likely prosper. Their managers could more quickly adapt to market demands. The scale of change they would require should be more manageable. The scale and proximity of markets they would supply should be smaller, taxing the information-gathering capacity of management less. Such efficiency, however, has its limits. Gorbachev, concerned about agriculture in his June Plenum Report, noted that bringing people more in line with the production they want would lead to many small operations, too small to make modern technology attractive or usable. The same disadvantage, of course, is likely to afflict much of industry. Shmelev, in his call for systemic change, recognizes this problem for industry but insists that it is a price worth paying. We already have examples in East Europe, including Yugoslavia, where modest economic reforms have led to large factories being left idle, factories celebrated only a few years earlier as monuments on the road to socialism. Now they are monuments to Party incompetence in economic development.

The concomitant consequence of small-scale enterprises is the one Gorbachev recognized in agriculture: new technology will be unattractive, if not impossible, to apply on a small scale. Rather than taking advantage of new families of technology that are revolutionizing western economies, "restructured" Soviet firms could well prove more resistant to such advances than the present state-run large firms and industrial branches. To be sure, there would be exceptions, and in time the trend could reverse, but initial resistance is almost certain to predominate.

Wide unemployment is also likely to accompany the decline of the inefficient firms. Hidden unemployment already exists in the form of poorly used manpower and labor padding. Trying to make a profit, managers surely would also try to cut labor costs. The results will inexorably include large labor layoffs.

Two more adverse developments in the labor market are likely. Economic restructuring will require radical shifts of labor in a society where immobility has been the prevailing tendency. Will Muslims from Central Asia readily move to Russia and the Ukraine to find work? They and many other ethnic, social, and religious groups are likely to resist movement. At the same time, quality of labor will become a larger problem. Market activity will require new skills. While labor may be available, it will not have the requisite skills for the most abundant jobs. Although the technical-cultural level of the labor force has long been a problem, mass literacy and elementary education have dramatically changed the nature of the labor force as compared to pre-WW II. Nonetheless, automation, greater introduction of western production technology based on computers, will require a significant additional improvement in labor training and basic education.

Another potentially troubling aspect of labor mobility is the migration from rural to urban areas. The Soviet leadership, of course, has controlled the urbanization process through internal passport requirements, moderating the flow at manageable levels. Although the old pressure has been reduced by a major demographic shift to the cities over seventy years, a free market agricultural economy might still push villagers toward urban employment. That would certainly be the case if technology introduced in farming has the intended effect of greatly improving productivity. Surplus labor would accumulate in the countryside. Depending on when and at what rate this occurred, the problem could prove manageable, even desirable, if industry eventually restructures under market forces and begins to prosper, requiring more labor.

The present white-collar workforce in the Soviet Union is primarily composed of bureaucrats and production engineers. Production-oriented skills will be all the more in demand if a market economy is allowed in the industrial sectors. Planners and clerks in the planning and management hierarchies--the economic ministries, GOSPLAN, GOSSNAB, and the Central Statistical Agency--will have no jobs; their roles will go away. At the same time, the need for a new white-collar and professional class will become critical. Skills for marketing specialists, sales representatives, advertisers, and sales researchers are not widely needed or taught in the centrally planned Soviet economy. A systemic change, however, would put them in high demand, yet there is no educational infrastructure to train them.

The same would be true of management skills for directors of firms competing in a market environment. The old Soviet manager, his "bookkeeper," his other colleagues in the management system--Party official, "special section" (KGB), trade union chief--are not the kind of people who will easily make the shift to market economy requirements at the firm level.

Another similar problem confronts the financial sector. Banks and those who look after the "financial plans" would face a wholly new kind of task. Financial accounting and planning in the Soviet Union do not drive decisions about resource allocations. They follow production planning, making sure money relations expressed in contracts and labor costs are coordinated with the requirements of the production plans.

As market forces came into play, those in the financial sector would have to fill the key role in major capital allocations. Their investment decisions would become the determinants of production planning, not vice versa. Investment banking is an alien activity in the Soviet Union, yet financial institutions would have to take on that function. Gorbachev spoke at the June Plenum about the major modernization effort required in the machine-building sector and the ministries' importance in coordinating and leading the effort. For the market to undermine the process, financial institutions--not the ministries-- would be key in raising and loaning capital.

A sense of the intractability of this financial planning problem for an economy trying to shift from a dominant state planning role to a market system has been evident in Egypt during the last decade. An American consultant to the Egyptian government told the author in considerable detail of the extent to which many Egyptian officials seem to have internalized Soviet planning techniques. Whether they did not like the anticipated consequences of market-oriented analysis for investment decisions or simply could not understand such analysis, they resisted it strongly after having agreed in principle to accept it. Again and again he confronted *non sequitur* reactions to analyses concerned with market forces and scarcity prices as the Egyptian officials resorted to concepts of "material balances" and similar Soviet categories. We can only assume that the problem in the Soviet Union would be many times more difficult. Gorbachev's new thinking, if it means this kind of change, will indeed take a long time.

Another adverse development most likely to confront a shift to a market system is inflation. A great deal of pent-up inflation already exists. Letting consumer demand drive production, of course, would create initially a large demand at the very time of transition when production is likely to fall. The old Bolshevik description of this phenomenon during NEP, a "goods famine," would be particularly appropriate once again. The Party's reaction to it at that time was fright. A Soviet market economy might be maintained isolated from the world economy, but that does not appear to be Gorbachev's intent. On the contrary, the new laws for joint ventures with western entrepreneurs suggest that he believes more, not less, economic interaction with the West is necessary.

What are the likely consequences of expanding economic dealings with the West? Traditionally, students of economic development have told us that developing countries should borrow from advanced economies to import modern technology for industrialization and should try to pay off the loans with exports of their commodity sectors--agricultural and mineral. The Soviet Union has historically adopted this approach, especially with the export of grain, oil, furs, timbers, minerals, and other such products. Today, however, commodity prices have fallen in relation to industrial prices, and few show convincing signs of climbing back to former levels. Much of the large Third World debt is evidence of this new phenomenon.

The Soviet Union has been unable to avoid all the effects of this "uncoupling" of industrial and commodity prices.[14] Its hard currency reserves have dropped as oil prices have dropped. At the same time, the Soviet Union has long ceased to be an agricultural exporter of significance and has become dependent on large grain imports. The present world economy, therefore, is not likely to treat the Soviet Union kindly if it enters--or opens its doors--to world market forces. There never was much prospect for large mutually beneficial East-West trade, even in the heyday of the early 1970s. Today the prospect is dim indeed.

Many more purely economic disorders and pressures could be listed, but the above set should suffice to illustrate the magnitude and variety of forces a shift to a market system would unleash. It might be possible, given a sustained and broad political consensus behind such a move, to schedule some of the change so that all the disorders do not occur in full force simultaneously. In other words, in spite of the dysfunctions, a strong economic argument could be made for the shift in any event. The price would be worth paying for the future efficiency advantages of equilibrium of market forces achieved after several years of serious disequilibria. Shmelev, who shows a full awareness of most

---

14. See Peter Drucker, "The Changed World Economy," *Foreign Affairs*, 64, Spring 1986, pp. 768-791, for the concept of "uncoupling" of this relationship.

of the probable disequilibria, comes down firmly on the side of accepting them. Other consequences are perhaps more serious in the minds of Soviet leadership, because a sustained and broad political consensus would not be easy to maintain. The most fundamental consequence would be the inherent shift of political power. The Party, especially its elite, the *nomenklatura*, would be, by and large, disenfranchised.

The present system allows, or ensures, that, for the most part, the *nomenklatura's* "preferences" drive economic activity. They have preferred heavy industry, military consumption, and a privileged system of consumer product distribution for their own restricted circles. They have preferred this in the face of great inefficiencies, even economic stagnation. They have preferred the political stability the central control of economy affords in a highly fragmented polity, one in which national minorities and dissatisfied social groups create strong centrifugal forces. They have preferred the control the present political system affords over client states, especially in East Europe. They must now be assessing some of the possible consequences of letting market forces loose where command economies have ruled.

There has always been concern in Moscow about centrifugal political forces among the national minorities. A shift of the rule of law would give some of those minorities the legal option, under the Constitution of the Soviet Union, to secede, to leave the union. As the Baltic republics had more economic success in market circumstances, why should they not seek to go their own political way? Why would the republics of the Caucasus not do the same? In the present system, inefficient though it is, Party elites from several of these republics have learned to take advantage of the central planning structure and its flaws.[15] One of the curious developments under Brezhnev was the allegiance of minority national bureaucratic elites to Soviet rule. The pressure for national separatism comes almost entirely from the small set of national literary intelligentsia, from writers and artists interested in cultural identity. They pose little political threat to Moscow, although they are an irritant the Party does not neglect. The effect of market forces might well bring an alliance of these politically feckless groups with the more powerful political and economic *apparatchiki* in the Baltics and the Caucasus, and possibly in the Ukraine and the Central Asian republics. Victor Shlapentokh, a Soviet emigre sociologist, has already noticed the incipient fragmentation along national lines that Gorbachev will have trouble controlling.[16] Minority nationalities as well as

15. See Simis, *The Corrupt Soviet Society,* for examples of the corruption among minority national elites and the stake they developed in the system under Brezhnev.
16. See his manuscript, "An End of Affirmative Action in Russia?" Unpublished, 16 April 1987.

Russians are showing an uncharacteristic articulateness on ethnic issues. Centrifugal forces along national and ethnic lines, it seems, are already increasing without a major shift to a market economy.

Another development that is bound to confront the leadership will concern the large allocations traditionally granted the military. In the long run, an economy restructured systemically to respond to market forces should provide a better scientific and technical base for military production. In the short run, however, consumer demand would make it impossible for the regime to continue the old priority for military spending. In the past, the Party has been able to cut the military sharply. From 1921-1923, a radical reduction of the Red Army occurred, forced by the Party and resisted by many of the rank and file military who did not want to return to the village. After World War II, Stalin forced another large cut in manpower in the military. Those were special circumstances--the army was exhausted and needed new and modern equipment. The military leadership could agree with the Party that sacrificing contemporary military power for greater future military power made sense.

Perhaps that could be done again, but the circumstances are different today. A large modern force is extant. Military commitments are large. Would not a dramatic cut carry unacceptable risks? Could the Warsaw Pact states be kept under control with a large reduction in Soviet standing forces? Real savings from the military sector would not come from the strategic forces and advanced weapons production sectors. Rather, the major resources, unproductive resources, are in the large ground forces, air defense forces, and naval forces. Current arms control negotiations do not address these categories. They concern the high technology categories, those sectors which the military industrial support has made the most modern part of the Soviet economy.

The "military question" has always figured centrally in Soviet policy-- economic, social and political. It remains no less central today, and in many respects it is more difficult to answer differently today than in the past, even if the economy seems to warrant a different answer. Military "demand" on the economy has probably done more to promote modernization than any other factor, and central planning has been the key to this progress. Dismantling central planning would not only raise the question of military security risks but also the issue of whether the advanced military-industrial sector would stagnate and slip backwards. The facile argument that military spending hurts economic growth in all economies is simply not borne out in the Soviet experience or in the case of many other states. In some cases it seems to hurt; in others, economic growth and high rates of military spending have gone hand in hand.

Finally, the regional political elite, the Party and economic *apparatchiki*, would risk major disenfranchisement in the face of market forces being unleashed in the Soviet Union. How would they react? Certainly they would not surrender their privileges quietly. A strong and consolidated super-elite--the Politburo, the Central Committee apparatus, and the KGB--would have to contain them and defeat them politically. Such conquest is not unprecedented. Stalin defeated them in the 1920s and 1930s, but his aim in those instances was centralization of economic controls, not decentralization. We cannot say, *a priori,* that such a major disenfranchisement of the bureaucracy is impossible. In fact, it would be essential if reform is to succeed. But we can say that it would involve a fundamental political revolution imposed from above.

Gorbachev's effort to build a coalition in support of his program for *perestroika* is instructive on this point. He has drawn much of the intelligentsia into an alliance. He has encouraged them to express compelling arguments for dramatic change, to demonstrate that an economic crisis is at hand, one that cannot be overcome with old ways of thinking. He has even gone far in trying to gain support from the western press and opinionmakers for *perestroika,* an unprecedented step for a General Secretary. Heretofore, Soviet dissidents have drawn on western opinion to support their cause against the regime. Today, we are witnessing the curious spectacle of Gorbachev appropriating their gambit in his own struggle against the entrenched bureaucracy.

The paradox remains, nonetheless, that great central control is required to achieve a great decentralization of economic control and power. If Gorbachev succeeds, he will lose his centralized power to forces that could undercut the political authority of the regime to a degree that could cause the breakup of the empire. The risks and uncertainties of such a course make one wonder if that is really what he has in mind. It must be if he intends truly systemic change. If it is not, he cannot effect systemic change. This paradox must be clear to Gorbachev; if it is, either he believes he can ride out the danger, or, in fact, he does not intend systemic change. Either way, with the Party's power retained, he faces the second question: How far can reform go if the allocation system remains centralized, essentially driven by "planners' preferences"?

WHAT IS POSSIBLE SHORT OF SYSTEMIC CHANGE?

Periodically it is suggested that the Soviet Union take a lesson from the experiences of East European economies to remedy the failures of the highly centralized Soviet planning system. The Hungarian model and the East German New Economic Model are often cited in this regard without examining the realities of these models in practice. The good press these Soviet allies have enjoyed in the West is somewhat surprising in light of what they have actually achieved. Furthermore, the makeup of their economies is so different from the Soviet setting that the performance advantages they enjoy are difficult, if not impossible, to transfer to the Soviet Union.

In the East German case, bureaucratic and worker discipline is easier to sustain at fairly high levels for cultural and structural reasons. The German work ethic is quite different from the Soviet work ethic. If all Soviet bureaucrats and workers could be imbued with the German work ethic, indeed a better economic performance might emerge in the Soviet system; however, it would be a one-time gain, not a basis for dynamic economic and technological change. A work ethic cannot substitute for private property and market prices in the authority and information functions if an economy is to be dynamic, adapting to new technology, new demands, and structural change. That reality comes abundantly clear from a comparison of the East German and West German economies. Moreover, interzonal trade in Germany ensures a large subsidy for the East German economy. The New Economic Model owes as much to this source of capital and trade as to any feature of East German planning technique. The Soviet economy simply has no equivalent to this sustained subsidy.

The Hungarian system has released control over small parts of the economy, but in almost every case central authorities have set severe limits, often taking back much of the latitude they appeared to give. Jan Prybyla's review of the Hungarian case makes clear the modest degree of decentralization in Hungary and the measures retained to ensure central control.[17] As declining western loans and unfavorable export markets have come to bear on Hungary, so has the cost of central controls. The outlook for the Hungarian model can hardly be a source of inspiration for Soviet planners.

Perhaps the most significant reasons for doubting that East European experiences can show the way for Soviet reform are to be found in the remark a Soviet official made to the author in a lengthy discussion of the Soviet predicament a number of years ago. Why not borrow from the East European experience? He explained that the East European economies are small; they do not have to carry the Soviet responsibilities for a bail-out in the event of catastrophic failure. They can experiment, get into trouble, and, if necessary, the Soviet army can invade them to restore socialism. Who will rescue socialism in the Soviet Union if an economic experiment gets out of control? The political and security context of reform in the Soviet Union is qualitatively different from that in any Soviet client state.

17. Ibid., pp. 211-245.

What about previous Soviet experience? Does it provide a basis for the present situation? The New Economic Policy of the 1920s, of course, is the single example that might have relevance. Some western scholars may argue that a return to NEP is a viable alternative. Private agriculture could be introduced along with small enterprises in the service and consumer goods sectors. The heavy industrial sectors could be retained under central control, keeping the Party in charge of what Lenin called the "commanding heights" of the economy.

Gorbachev has already had an unfortunate experience with the agrarian sector when, as chief of Soviet agriculture, he let the private sector grow. As he noted in his June Plenum Report, that experiment posed a dilemma. Small plots do not encourage the introduction of new technology on the scale needed for major improvements. Furthermore, the industrial sectors are now in serious trouble. How would NEP Mark II cure Gorbachev's woes? In the 1920s, industrial growth came largely through reconstruction of the war-torn economy; as reconstruction was completed, the prospects for continued growth looked bleak. The problem for Gorbachev today is not reconstruction, but is over-construction and inefficient construction in a very large economy, a many times larger industrial sector than existed in the 1920s. NEP simply does not offer a happy solution to the macroindustrial problem. It might, however, boost the consumer sector for services and small unit production much as it did in the 1920s. It could legitimize and expand the present so-called "second economy." Given the industrial modernization Gorbachev seems to demand, NEP II would ameliorate some problems, but at best it would be a partial or temporary solution.

Anthony Sutton has traced an interesting correlation between influxes of western technology with spurts of growth in the Soviet economy.[18] Trade with the West during the 1920s was followed by growth in the 1930s; help from the West during World War II and the transfer of capital stock from defeated Germany after World War II provided the second influx, which was followed by growth in the 1950s. The slowdown in growth in the 1960s was followed by détente and renewed East-West economic interaction in the early 1970s. The expected growth has been less certain, but performance in the military-industrial sector has been significant, even spectacular. A correlation, admittedly, is not sufficient evidence alone to infer a causal relationship, but the sustained Soviet interest in keeping economic interaction with the West

18. Anthony C. Sutton, *Western Technology and Soviet Economic Development*, vols. I, II, and III (Stanford: Hoover Institution Press, 1971, 1971, 1973).

that brings large technology transfers as high as possible suggests that Soviet planners believe the causal relationship exists.

The new Soviet law on joint economic ventures with the West looks, against this historical background, like one more attempt to salvage central planning with a new influx of western aid. Let us set aside the issue of the probable effectiveness of new joint ventures--although initial examination of the rules for such enterprises suggests pessimism--and consider them a gambit for shoring up the present system. If they lead to large western investments on the scale of the Kama River project in a number of key industrial sectors, they could create pockets of improved manufacturing capabilities; they might give the Soviet computer industry a boost, help in communications technologies, and introduce new production organization and management techniques. They will not, however, ameliorate major problems in energy, transportation, and labor allocations or reduce the information reliability and problems in planning and price setting.

In addition to joint ventures, of course, a political climate adequate to stimulate large western credits would also be required for any significant gain from renewed economic relations with the West. To be sure, such a climate may come about, and much enthusiasm in western economic circles may help generate another influx of western aid. If the flow is large enough, for a time Gorbachev might see moderate improvement in the present system's performance. In a few years, however, the inherent inefficiencies of the system would reappear in their old nagging forms, revealing that no real solution had been found.

That day of reckoning can be postponed, nevertheless, if the bureaucracies in the ministries and firms can be made more responsive. How could that behavior be achieved? In the past it was achieved through personnel purges, through turnovers in cadres that broke up informal groups and cliques, which had grown up to resist and cope with the economic directions from the center. Such rejuvenation, however, has not occurred recently. The nearly two decades of Brezhnev's rule allowed thousands of such cliques and circles to flourish. They produced statistics for the center and allocated an increasing part of the state resources to their own interests. The "second economy" reached a scale probably much larger than western analysts perceived, probably greater than Soviet central planners have been able to measure.

The new factor in the Soviet political and economic equation today is a fairly broad recognition within elite circles--especially the intelligentsia, but also in higher Party cliques, the military, and the KGB--of the general predicament of the system. They want improvement. They know they must have improvements if the economy is to be directed away from its present course. They are a source of support and enthusiasm for change, but how can they be harnessed for this purpose without giving them too much leeway in defining the aims of reform?

As suggested earlier, Gorbachev's answer to the question is apparent in the three slogans, *glasnost, perestroika,* and *novoye myshleniye. Glasnost* is a call for the elites to express the political demand for change. As their expressions of criticism lay greater and greater blame on obstinate bureaucrats and officials at middle and lower levels, even at high levels in some cases, the public also joins the chorus. Public discourse cannot be carried on at the level of comprehension of economics that Aganbegyan and Zaslavskaya carry it. Rather, the discussion is already turning to questions of persons, spotlighting individuals, unresponsive officials and Party leaders, as the cause of problems. In this climate, Gorbachev and his aides offer "restructuring" as the solution, retaining the discretion to define this ambiguous term as they choose and to make the definition include changing cadres throughout the bureaucracy. "Restructuring" can also include reorganization and new processes, but its most conspicuous manifestation to date is turnover in cadres. In other words, it is a purge, a purge of new type, a renewal of cadres, a revitalization of *apparatchiki* and Party officials.

Why, one may ask, should Soviet elites and the public believe new *apparatchiki* will behave any differently than their predecessors? Gorbachev's answer is clear: They will practice new thinking. They will abandon the old ways, that is to say, corruption, second economy activities, and abuse of privileges. Again, one is reminded of Stalin's lectures, "The Fundamentals of Leninism," in which he defined the "style of Party work" as new, a combination of "Russian revolutionary sweep" with "American efficiency."

If this is Gorbachev's scheme, how far will economic and social reform go? How far can it go? Again, we are confronted with questions: Whose reforms? Whose image of the future? Whose economic preferences? It seems more and more clear that Gorbachev does not intend systemic change. He is exercising with remarkable energy and cunning the system bequeathed him by previous general secretaries. He is struggling to regain the vitality the system once had but which Khrushchev and especially Brezhnev let slip into decay. If we mean by reform a significant improvement in the standard of living for Soviet citizens and increased protection of their individual rights under law, that kind of reform cannot go very far without bringing systemic change, the kind of change Gorbachev *cannot* want.

What seems to be shaping up, therefore, is a political contest initially between Gorbachev and his allies on the one hand and the entrenched bureaucracy on the other hand. To the extent Gorbachev wins that contest and installs a new set of bureaucrats with new energy and greater responsiveness to central direction, he will slow the decline of the economy and perhaps even improve some limited sectors. To win, he must also have success in drawing resources from the West on a large scale. At the same time, another contest is shaping up between Gorbachev and his allies, the intelligentsia, and others who are taking advantage of *glasnost* to register their own preferences about change, about what *perestroika* should include.

As observers, we must not forget the first contest, although the second may prove more exciting to watch. Gorbachev has certainly renewed the Politburo and the Central Committee as well as a number of regional Party organizations. He has not, however, had much success against the Ukrainian Party, the one he must crack if he is to succeed in a genuine renewal of cadres. The second contest, however, could turn out to be the most significant, particularly for its unintended consequences.

UNINTENDED CONSEQUENCES OF *GLASNOST*

Glasnost as a policy has generated behavior in the Soviet Union most western analysts would never have believed possible. The kinds of criticism voiced in the press, on the stage, in films, and in public demonstrations are truly remarkable. Proposed "restructuring" by the Party has touched on all three of the criteria cited above as tests for truly systemic change in the Soviet Union. The central planning and pricing problem, a wider role for law, and greater freedom from censors have been key issues in the public debate and in some new policies.[19] Thus far, they have remained largely in the domain of *glasnost*,

19. Three recently promulgated laws are particularly noteworthy. The new USSR Law on the State Enterprise, published in *Izvestiya* on 1 July 1987, sets forth the legal basis for economic accountability of enterprises, giving them remarkably wide latitude in hiring and firing labor, in setting wages based on performance with no maximum limit on earnings, in contracting with suppliers and buyers, in accumulating savings, in setting prices within centrally determined guidelines, and in rejecting goods from suppliers when the quality is below standard. Enterprises that do prove profitable--that is, able to meet their debts--can be declared insolvent by the banking authorities. Enterprises may also establish ties with foreign firms, accumulate foreign currency, and execute contracts with foreigners. Precisely which enterprises will operate under this law is to be determined by the Council of Ministers. Central reporting of performance data and planning within the state annual and five-year plans remains obligatory, however. The second law, USSR Law on the Procedure of Encroaching on Citizens' Rights, gives citizens a means for holding Soviet officialdom to account when their rights are property rights in the western economic sense. Finally, a USSR Law on Nationwide Discussion of Important State Issues makes it imperative that laws in draft at the all-Union, Republic, and local Soviet levels must be aired for public discussion. It is too early to assess the likely impact of these laws, but they are of great potential significance, especially the law on enterprises. While it goes far, it does not dismantle central planning.

only foreshadowing *perestroika*. The mere fact that they have gained attention, however, tells us these are not ordinary times in the Soviet Union. Fundamental tensions are near the surface, tensions that go to the very heart of the system's continuing viability.

Can the leadership put the lid back on the voices of *glasnost* that do not accord with Gorbachev's image of *perestroika*? Probably, but it is difficult to see how the lid can be put back as securely as it was before. Certainly it can and most likely will be put back on the broad masses, but the intelligentsia is another matter. Gorbachev has gone quite far in attracting the intelligentsia as an ally in his campaign for system revitalization. The act of bringing Andrei Sakharov back from exile in Gorki and allowing him to appear on American television is a measure of the distance the General Secretary has proven willing to go. He is telling the Soviet intelligentsia, both in the Soviet Union and the emigres, that they can join his campaign--de facto a purge of the bureaucracy. Many, but not all, particularly some who have emigrated, have accepted the invitation. If the campaign does not yield results congenial to those who have joined, what will they do? How will they react? Can they simply be silenced?

Without returning to another period of Great Terror, Gorbachev will find it virtually impossible to close down the activity of a disenchanted intelligentsia. In light of the limited prospects for systemic change, the intelligentsia will almost inevitably turn sour, become embittered, and give up on *perestroika*, confronting Gorbachev with precisely the dilemma of resorting to comprehensive repression or toleration of unprecedented levels of dissident activity.

Not all the intelligentsia will abandon the regime in the event of disillusionment. Many will remain within; they will understand the risks of political instability that would go with a bold move to systemic change. They will see the dangers of fragmentation along nationality lines. They will share the Party fears of losing control of the empire in East Europe. They will accept order and severe curtailment of individual freedom as preferable to the uncertainties accompanying a genuine political transformation.

The great but unintended consequence of Gorbachev's policies will be both the disillusionment of the intelligentsia and its polarization into two camps. One camp will stay with the regime, making cogent arguments that there is no practical alternative to maintaining the old system. The other camp will give up all hope for evolutionary change within the regime and turn to radical opposition, articulating counter ideologies calling for the dismantling of the regime.

Some observers might argue that this polarization has already occurred. The generation that witnessed the thaw in the 1950s has been through a period of hope that ended with the Daniel-Sinyavski trial and the 1968 invasion of Czechoslovakia. Vasili Aksyonov, the emigre novelist who was a key leader in the publication of *Metropol,* a document intended as one last try at bringing the regime around, propounds this thesis in his occasional lectures. Other recent emigres seem to share such a view; they see *glasnost* merely as a ruse to gain their support, not as a serious new opportunity. As Sakharov and others still in the Soviet Union see themselves used by Gorbachev without significant gains for their own aims, they will likely join the ranks of the wholly alienated.

Polarization of the intelligentsia in Russia is not a new phenomenon. It happened in the nineteenth century during the reign of Nicholas I. When genuine reform was tried by Alexander II, the distrust was too great among the radicals. They used the relaxation of police oppression to widen their activities against the regime, giving the Autocracy many good reasons for resorting periodically to crackdowns, to vicious police oppression. The radicals did not join the *zemstvo* movement for local government. They did not support the incipient industrialization that was showing promise in the last decades before World War I. Their counterparts inside the regime used their intellectual talents in support of repression. At the very time constitutionalism had prospects for success, both wings of the Russian intelligentsia worked against it.

If this prognostication for the future of political and economic reforms in the Soviet Union is correct, one is tempted to say that history is repeating itself. In some regards the analogy holds, but there are significant differences. The ethnic minorities are more articulate today. They, too, have an intelligentsia that will participate in the polarization. The East European states are entangled in Soviet developments in a way for which there is no nineteenth century counterpart. To be sure, there was a Polish problem, but there was no Polish state, and the other East European nationalities were struggling against other imperial regimes. The level of mass literacy and the social structure are also different today--in the size of the industrial working class and the scientific elites, and in the character of rural life.

We should also not forget the potential role of the military today. A large, well-educated officer corps exists, unprecedented in both Russian and Soviet history for its technical-cultural level. Will it be able to remain unaffected by the split in the nonmilitary circles of the intelligentsia? We know less about the military in this regard than any other group, but the implications of a polarization there would be truly profound. Disaffected officers are a qualitatively different kind of problem from disaffected scientists, writers, and students. They have leadership and organizational skills that could give a radical movement explosive potential.

Gorbachev has set in motion many forces in the Soviet Union. A few signs of drawing them back are apparent, but if they are abruptly curtailed, all prospects of success for *perestroika* will be destroyed. Yet giving them vent carries all the dangers we have identified.

CONCLUSION

One can only remain uncertain about the true aims of the present steps toward reform in the Soviet Union. Is Gorbachev bent on a fundamental change in the system? If he is, the chances he can control it are small, virtually nil. A halfway house between a centrally planned economy and a market economy in a fragmented polity does not seem to be a real option, which we saw in Czechoslovakia in 1968. Once the system of central controls began to dissolve, it proved impossible to retain censorship, Party control, and arbitrary use of the law. The case of Poland is the same, although the game is still being played out. The regime has not vanquished the opposition, but neither has the opposition brought about systemic change. Without the shadow of the Soviet military over Poland, it is doubtful the regime could survive. In the Soviet Union, letting the forces for change have full sway would call into serious question the territorial viability of the union. Gorbachev surely does not share Solzhenitsyn's view that the nationalities should be let go.

One is forced, therefore, to infer a more limited aim on Gorbachev's part, a revitalization of the old system. And one can discern in his formula--*glasnost*, *perestroika*, and *novoye myshleniye*--an old political strategy with roots in the Stalin and Khrushchev eras. It does not envision the abandonment of socialism and international class struggle. It looks much more like a new variant of "peaceful coexistence," an effort to continue to build socialism within the Soviet camp through greater economic interaction with the industrial states of the West, meanwhile continuing the international class struggle in the Third World and cultivating "progressive" social forces in the West. Gorbachev can achieve some improvements in the economy, particularly in the service and agricultural sectors. He may even realize some industrial gains through western credits and technology transfers. He cannot, in any way, however, overcome the basic structural problems of the economy.

Even modest gains, however, are not assured. Political resistance to his Party revitalization could confront him with the alternatives of returning to policies of the Brezhnev era or losing his post. The Yeltsin affair in the Moscow Party organization and Gorbachev's moderate address on November 2, before the seventieth anniversary of the October Revolution, indicate that he is willing to compromise on the speed of his restructuring. A gradual petering out of *perestroika*, therefore, is not to be discounted. In either case--success in Gorbachev's endeavor or a return to Brezhnevism--Gorbachev's allies in the intelligentsia, domestic and foreign, are bound to face eventual disillusionment.

The most interesting, and perhaps most significant, outcome of Gorbachev's new variant of an old policy is likely to be the further polarization of the intelligentsia when disillusionment sets in. Soviet history can be instructive in helping us anticipate this development, but it will have new dimensions, new consequences, and new dangers. As we watch it, we can only be saddened by the tragedies and hardships it may bring great peoples on whom history has already heaped many painful burdens, not least the Soviet.

5 WEST EUROPEAN PERSPECTIVES ON GREATER EAST-WEST ECONOMIC INTERACTION

Gary G. Meyers

We repeat to your majesty that the Tsar in Moscow, an enemy of any liberty, increases day after day his forces by the profit made by commerce and relations with the civilized nations of Europe. No doubt your majesty does not ignore how powerful, cruel, and tyrannical a ruler he is. Our only hope rests on our superiority in arts and science. But soon he shall know as much as we do. . . and in his insane pride, he will rush against Christianity.

    --King Sigismond of Poland, letter to Queen Elizabeth I of England, 1565

Some day, it appeared to me, this divided Europe, dominated by the military presences of ourselves and the Russians, would have to yield to something more natural--something that did more justice to the true strength and interests of the intermediate European peoples themselves.

    --George F. Kennan, *Memoirs, 1925-1950*, p. 464

On August 24, 1987, a "Special Advertising Section" appeared in the U.S., Asian, and European editions of the *Wall Street Journal*, a supplement entitled "USSR: New Opportunities for Cooperation." In it, the Soviet Foreign-Trade Advertising Agency touted the prospects for western trade with and direct investment in a country whose economic structure was soon to be revamped through *perestroika* (restructuring). Prominently displayed under the masthead,

97

even the most harried commuting capitalist could not help but notice the citation from Mikhail S. Gorbachev's speech to the June 25-26 Plenary Meeting of the Communist Party of the Soviet Union (CPSU) Central Committee: ". . . all wanting to work with us in new, more favorable conditions will gain from the successful realization of the plans of restructuring in our country and the modernization of our economy."[1]

While it is still too early to predict with any precision the ultimate economic impact of Gorbachev's new thinking on the countries of West Europe, it is possible to consider here at least some of its potential consequences by placing current Soviet attempts at reform within the broader historical context of West European economic relations with the Soviet Union. As this examination of previous efforts to achieve a significant measure of economic détente between East and West will demonstrate, while the appeal in the *Wall Street Journal* was aimed principally at American business representatives, it has traditionally been their European counterparts who have proven most willing to engage in extensive trade and investments in East Europe. Their ability to do so in the postwar period, however, was blocked as much by Cold War American strategic goals as by the socialist structure of the Soviet economy. This paper will therefore focus on political and economic changes underway since World War II that ultimately led to a divergence of West European and American interests in economic détente of the type currently envisaged by a Soviet leadership committed to *perestroika*. What emerges from this brief account of East-West economic relations is the conclusion that the future of foreign investment in the Soviet Union may well depend less on *perestroika* than on domestic politics in the United States.

Given this fact, it is somewhat paradoxical that most American planners preoccupied with the construction of a new international economic order between 1943 and 1947 fully anticipated that the East would be part of this nascent postwar system.[2] Although the Soviet Union had been separated between the wars from the international economy by the West's diplomatic reserve and by Stalin's autarkic development policy, the Soviet Union was never completely isolated. Soviet imports of western raw materials and of western technology in this period made an important contribution to that country's growth, and U.S.-Soviet economic interaction revived during the war years through American lend-lease assistance. Furthermore, many of the future Soviet bloc states of East Europe had been closely integrated with the West,

---

1. *Wall Street Journal*, 24 August 1987, p. 9.
2. Marshall I. Goldman, *Détente and Dollars: Doing Business with the Soviets* (New York: Basic Books, 1975), pp. 4-20.

especially West Europe, in the interwar period. After the cessation of hostilities, therefore, the participation of East Europe in the postwar economic order was not initially blocked by western planners. At least some U.S. officials actively sought the participation of the Soviet Union and its satellites in the liberal multilateral system they envisioned as the cornerstone of international economic harmony and prosperity.

According to Stalin, however, only the formation of a separate eastern economic bloc would deepen the crisis of world capitalism and speed its inevitable demise. Economic isolation also was seen as a tool for reinforcing Soviet political and military control and for checking capitalist influence in East Europe.[3] The result was the dramatic postwar reorientation of East European trade later to be institutionalized through the formation in 1949 of the Soviet response to the Marshall Plan: the Council for Mutual Economic Assistance (CMEA).

With the onset of the Cold War, the United States retaliated in kind. Thus, under U.S. pressure, a Coordinating Committee for Multilateral Security Export Controls (CoCOM) was created in 1949 to coordinate the western strategic embargo of the Soviet bloc. There was, however, significant conflict between the United States and its European allies over the list of embargoed items, largely because the United States adopted a broad definition of "strategic goods" that threatened traditional West European trade with the East. To overcome European resistance to American embargo policy, the U.S. Congress passed a "Mutual Defense Assistance Control Act" in 1951 that effectively denied Marshall Plan aid to any country that knowingly permitted the shipment of strategic goods to communist countries.

Yet, while the United States and West Europe had conflicts over trade policies early in the Cold War, the 1960s saw both the first glimmerings of détente and an easing of Alliance restrictions on trade with the East bloc. President Kennedy thought trade might liberalize the East European regimes and wean them from their Soviet dependence. Despite the war in Vietnam, the Johnson administration had similar views and downplayed the traditional notion that trade would strategically benefit the Soviets.

Various West European countries took advantage of this momentary shift in American policy to reestablish economic ties with the East bloc. The West Germans, for example, developed their policy of *Ostpolitik* while France, too, stepped out in front of the United States to expand commercial ties with the Soviet Union and its East European allies under President de Gaulle's vision of

---

3. Joseph Stalin, *Economic Problems of Socialism in the USSR* (New York: International Publishers, 1952), p. 26.

a reconstructed greater Europe from the Atlantic to the Urals. To be sure, European diplomacy toward the USSR occurred within the context of the fundamental "western" orientation of the Atlantic Alliance. Not even de Gaulle ever envisioned some dramatic reversal of alliances. Until the late 1960s, therefore, economic conflict remained at a relatively low level among states that were basically capitalist in structure and therefore benefitted from an international monetary regime that ensured stable exchange rates, cheap energy, and a trading system that moved toward liberalization despite lingering protectionist exceptions. The increasing prosperity of the West Europeans was related to security through the issue of burden sharing, but an expanding economic base made budgetary compromises relatively easy to negotiate. Besides, Europe accepted a degree of American hegemony because it provided security not only for its own territory but for Europe's access to raw materials and markets in the Third World. Thus, even when serious economic conflict erupted in the early 1970s, there was at first little direct linkage to security questions.

At the same time, however, as America's combination of inflation, dollar depreciation, and failure to adjust to high energy prices increasingly offended the interests of both the Europeans and the oil producers, the former grew increasingly skeptical of America's ability to defend their economic interests at home and abroad. Instead, American policy seemed bent on limiting détente in Europe to compensate for U.S. weakness in the world at large. European efforts to build economic bridges across the "Iron Curtain" were subsumed within the Nixon-Kissinger strategy of "leveraged" détente developed in the early 1970s. Kissinger wanted to use the prospect of enlarged East-West commerce as a carrot to supplement the stick of military containment and to combine this with the U.S.-Chinese *rapprochement* to obtain maximum leverage over the Soviet Union.[4] Unilateral forays in East-West relations by our allies, however, were regarded as potentially counterproductive because they failed to take into consideration the overall global perspective of Kissinger's foreign policy.

Thus, as the United States sought to expand its influence over the Soviet Union, its postwar ties with West Europe began to unravel. The capitalist representative democracies of that continent remained American protectorates, but they were nevertheless determined to keep the price for that protection within reasonable bounds. A certain degree of heightened Soviet-American tension outside Europe was not altogether unwelcome to the Europeans because

4. Seyom Brown, *The Crises of Power: An Interpretation of United States Foreign Policy During the Kissinger Years* (New York: Columbia University Press, 1979), pp. 19-48.

it gave *them* leverage for a more independent foreign policy stance. Keeping down the price for their American protection required maintaining "normal," if wary, relations with the Soviets within Europe.

The late 1970s and early 1980s, however, witnessed increasing friction linked to economic competition within the Alliance as the countries of West Europe completed their American-sponsored return to prosperity and competitiveness in the midst of a burgeoning energy crisis. Underlying these conflicts was the growing European influence in a postwar world economy characterized by increased economic interdependence. During this period, also marked by a resurgence of concern on both sides of the Atlantic over the Soviet build-up of its nuclear forces in Europe, politicization of economic issues in the guise of sanctions against the Soviet Union became the common currency of transatlantic controversies. These developments, in turn, inevitably had an impact on western perceptions of the Soviets. Above all, following the nascent expansion of their trade with the East, the European members of NATO felt they had more to lose economically than to gain strategically from an end to détente in their own region. Thus, while the United States continued to regard Europe as a place to put pressure on the Soviets as part of global superpower competition, most Europeans increasingly maintained that their continent should remain a zone insulated from the spreading bipolar confrontations elsewhere in the world. In effect, the Europeans had by the third postwar decade developed their own distinct interests in the maintenance of détente. Following either consciously or inadvertently in the footsteps of Charles de Gaulle, they have done their best in recent years to prevent Washington from exclusively managing West-Soviet relations. In short, a détente policy of their own gave Europeans room to maneuver against American as well as Soviet domination.

In the final years of the Carter administration, however, this relative gain in autonomy was called into question as American attitudes toward the Soviet Union hardened dramatically. The election of a "trilateralist" as president might have augured well for American policies toward West Europe, but the growing self-confidence of the Europeans in economic policy and their continued dependence on what appeared to be an increasingly erratic American security guarantee brought sharp criticism of U.S. leadership. The shifts of Carter foreign policy on the neutron bomb demonstrated the difficulties that could arise when an American president, intending to share decisionmaking in defense, encountered the realities of European domestic politics. The bungling of the neutron bomb decision led to both renewed American resolve not to waver in the future and the determination to assure the Europeans that the United States was committed to their defense.

Yet, as the balance within both the Carter administration and American public opinion shifted toward a harder posture in relations with the Soviet Union following the invasion of Afghanistan, European complaints reversed. After 1979, the Europeans found themselves in a sort of time warp, confronting a United States whose perceptions had shifted dramatically away from the presuppositions of détente and toward those of confrontation with the Soviet Union. Questions of tactics, such as the use of economic sanctions to influence Soviet behavior, lay at the core of the disagreement. The Carter administration introduced a new source of conflict that would only become apparent under the following administration--a mixing of the two tracks of economics and security in the form of the sanctions question.

When domestic politics in the United States took a further sharp turn to the right in the presidential election of 1980, the disarray in the Alliance increased dramatically. The Reagan administration's efforts to restore American military power and to impose its concept of the Soviet threat on West Europe further exacerbated conflict between the United States and its allies. A series of overlapping European-American disagreements arose that concerned not only the older questions of nuclear strategy and burden sharing, but increasingly a growing gray area of economic issues with security implications. To many Europeans, these conflicts seemed to have as their root the attempt of the Reagan administration, which was the least "Atlanticist" of any recent administration, to manipulate such economic issues for domestic political gain.

As it had in its policy toward the Soviet Union, the Reagan administration brought with it a very simple and apparently coherent strategy for mending ties to West Europe. With the reassertion of a clear American line toward the Soviet Union, it was assumed in Washington that the West European allies would respond as they had in the past. In the first Reagan administration, an "essentialist" view of the Soviet Union seemed to hold the dominant position.[5] The rhetorical picture painted of the "Evil Empire" by the president was reminiscent of the 1950s. Soviet expansionist ambitions were perceived to be as ceaseless as they were global. Yet, the Soviet Union was also seen as a giant with feet of clay. Because of the weakness of its economy, in particular, the Soviet Union was presumed to be especially vulnerable to western economic pressure.

Like the Reagan administration, Europeans often accepted a "giant with feet of clay" image of the Soviet Union, but they drew from it very different policy

5. On the "essentialist," "mechanist," and "interactionist" American views of the Soviet Union, see Alexander Dallin and Gail W. Lapidus, "Reagan and the Russians: American Policy Toward the Soviet Union," *Eagle Resurgent?*, eds. Kenneth A. Oye, Robert J. Lieber, and Donald Rothchild (Boston: Little, Brown and Company, 1983), pp. 199-202.

conclusions. First and foremost, the weaknesses they perceived suggested a more manageable threat. Nor did they share with Washington the belief that western economic pressures could change the Soviet system or Soviet foreign policy in any predictable way. In short, the United States, like the Soviet Union, could no longer count on docile proxies to spring loyally to its bidding. Just as the Soviet Union had lost its hold over most of the West European left, the United States could no longer play the European center and right as it had in the 1950s. However much European vulnerabilities might have increased with the simultaneous growth of Soviet military power and international economic interdependence in the preceding decade, the capabilities of the superpowers to influence events in West Europe *had* declined.

In short, West Europe was more insulated from direct manipulation yet remained highly sensitive to changes affecting its security. Still, however negative a view it had of the Soviet Union, elite and public opinion in Europe persisted in seeing the Soviet Union as a state that could and *must* be bargained with because its regime was one that Europeans had lived with for many years as well as having done business with as a trading partner. Unlike questions of military policy, when the British and French often partially endorsed the more pessimistic American view, on the issue of economic sanctions the Europeans stood united against the American effort to burden them and their underemployed economies with a dubious foreign policy strategy. The United States, therefore, found it impossible to reconstruct the elite solidarity that helped it overcome earlier Cold War crises.

This divergence of views stemmed from the structural place of the two economies--European and North American--in the pattern of East-West trade, from different conceptions of how to influence Soviet behavior, and from different readings of the history of détente. The contrasting stakes of American and European economies in East-West trade were clear. Even though Europeans were more deeply involved in East-West trade, more important than volume in determining their position on sanctions was the composition of their trade with the Soviet Union and East Europe. Unlike the United States, whose commerce is concentrated in agricultural exports, European trade is weighted heavily toward manufactures, particularly capital goods. In 1984, for example, European exports to East bloc countries amounted to $28 billion (mostly manufactured products), against $5 billion for the United States (mostly grains).[6] The Europeans argued that trade in such products, unlike trade in grain, could not be turned on and off like a tap without risking disruption to

---

6. As noted in Thierry de Montbrial, "The European Dimension," *Foreign Affairs*, 64, 1986, p. 503.

their domestic economies and to the larger pattern of East-West economic transactions.

If the material burden of sanctions seemed heavy for West European economies, the Europeans also disputed the notion that economic sanctions were an effective means of influencing Soviet behavior. The Reagan administration, however, took office with at least part of the administration arguing that the Soviet economy was in dire straits and that economic warfare on the part of the West would weaken Soviet ability to pursue expansionist policies abroad and to continue its military buildup at home. The effort was not designed to change specific Soviet policies--the "essentialist" view of Soviet behavior could hardly admit that--but rather to weaken the Soviet capability to pursue policies that were unlikely to change.

As noted above, Europeans took a wholly different view. Although reluctantly agreeing with restrictions of strategic technologies toward the East under the continuing aegis of CoCOM, they argued that western credits, trade, and technology transfers were not easily absorbed without changing the Soviet and East European economies. The West European view of economic transactions with the East dovetailed with their reading of détente. In sharp contrast to a Reagan administration that came into office regarding the years of détente as ones in which the Soviet Union increased its military edge over the West and skillfully exploited western divisions to win economic concessions and Third World influence, the Europeans did not view détente as such a one-way street. While the new administration in Washington portrayed economic transactions with the East as a means of relieving the Soviet bloc's economic difficulties, the Europeans saw not only economic benefits from their trade with the the East, but also political bonuses in furthering the stabilization of political relations in Europe. Because the broadening of economic ties produced rising and unrealistic expectations within the "Evil Empire," such links therefore wove the "web of détente" more tightly between East and West.

Poland provided the occasion for demonstrating the fundamental differences between Americans and Europeans on these issues when martial law was declared in that country on December 17, 1981. The United States announced economic sanctions against the government of General Jaruzelski, a move quickly followed by a charge of Soviet responsibility and declaration of sanctions against the Soviet Union. However, even though the American measures were not particularly harsh, the initial European response was less than enthusiastic: no government endorsed the American sanctions or hastened to impose its own. To most Europeans, the growing crisis in Poland seemed to demonstrate that détente policies had worked and that growing interdependence with the West had forced hard choices on the communist regimes. In short, the Polish economy's dependence on a continued flow of western credits made it unlikely that the Soviets would intervene directly to quell the rise of Solidarity, because, whatever the risk of western reaction, the Red Army could not deliver what the Polish economy needed.

The Europeans did agree not to undercut sanctions imposed by the United States, but their interpretation of that assurance remained different from that of the Americans, particularly when the United States focused on two issues that had caused friction since the Carter administration: the natural gas pipeline deal that was being negotiated between the Soviet Union and West European consumers and subsidized export credits in European trade with the East.

The pipeline would prove the most contentious, and no single issue better symbolized West Europe's attachment to East-West economic policies that ran counter to the views of the United States. In scale alone, the proposed pipeline symbolized European reliance on a minimal level of stability in East-West relations. Once completed, this massive 3,500-mile long pipeline project would initially furnish West Europeans with 10 percent of their natural gas, a percentage that was expected to rise to 19 percent by 1995.[7] Plans for the Siberian pipeline had been underway for several years, and the Carter administration expressed concern, which intensified after the Soviet invasion of Afghanistan. The worries of that administration focused on the fear that increased European dependence on Soviet natural gas would lead to increased leverage by the Soviet Union and thus allow the Soviets to exert pressure on their European customers. To the Europeans, on the other hand, Soviet natural gas was a means of necessary diversification of their energy imports away from the insecure Middle East.[8]

Thus, although the Carter administration expressed concern, the dispute inevitably broadened under the Reagan administration. Even before the imposition of martial law in Poland, the pipeline came to symbolize the "web of détente" arguments the new administration totally rejected. It felt the pipeline was doubly dangerous, for not only did it make West European economies increasingly dependent on the Soviet Union, but also contributed directly to Soviet economic well-being and ultimately to Soviet military strength by alleviating the chronic Soviet shortage of hard currencies.

For Europeans, this latter argument was seen as calling into question virtually all East-West economic ties constructed in the 1970s. According to this view, any gain for the Soviet Union economically was automatically a

---

7. Data from *Le Monde* (Paris), 29 January 1985.
8. For the most complete account of this controversy, see Antony J. Blinken, *Ally vs. Ally: America, Europe, and the Siberian Pipeline Crisis* (New York: Praeger, 1987).

loss for the West, a zero-sum view the Europeans were loath to accept. Politically, Europeans saw important gains for their recession-plagued economies in the pipeline deal, particularly for such hard-pressed industries as steel.

The suppression of Solidarity in Poland gave the Reagan administration a final opportunity to convince Europeans to call off the deal. As part of its economic sanctions against the Soviet Union, the American government stopped General Electric from selling $175 million worth of components for gas turbine compressors that were to be built under license for the pipeline by three European firms. Despite this clear signal of American opposition, however, the Europeans refused to budge.

Faced with European recalcitrance, the Reagan administration developed a compromise position on East-West economic relations that it hoped to sell to its erstwhile allies. An implicit bargain was offered to Europeans prior to the Versailles economic and Bonn NATO summits of 1982: no further American resistance to the gas pipeline (and more generally, a turn away from trade sanctions) in exchange for European concessions in tightening the terms and amounts of credits offered to the East European countries. According to administration proponents of this "grand leverage" strategy, less hard currency would deprive not only the Poles but also other East bloc regimes of resources that heretofore had been devoted to military expenditures. In line with this shift in American policy, the summits appeared to produce a consensus among western allies on some of the points at issue between Europe and the United States. For example, an implicit bargain on East-West economic relations seemed to be sealed at Versailles: European willingness to tighten up on economic transactions with the East in exchange for American willingness to stop its efforts to thwart the pipeline.

This new-found transatlantic consensus, however, proved to be short-lived, for on June 18 President Reagan extended the existing American embargo on components for the pipeline to those component manufacturers that were either subsidiaries or licensees of American firms. Such attempts at extraterritorial application of American export controls were authorized under the Export Administration Act of 1969, which gave the executive branch authority to "prohibit or curtail" all commercial exports, including technical know-how, to communist countries from U.S. companies or their foreign subsidiaries. Because American courts can hold the parent firm criminally liable for the acts of its foreign affiliates, there has been great incentive for multinational corporations to cooperate with this U.S. regulation even in cases when the transactions in question were legal under the laws of the host country. Under the Reagan administration, there were even threats to toughen the act by adding provisions that would punish companies that violated its export controls by closing the lucrative American market to them.[9]

The West European response was swift and uniform, because the administration's action had not only reopened the question of economic relations with the Soviet bloc but added to it the equally sensitive issue of extraterritoriality. With the foreign ministers of the European Community displaying a united front in opposition to the ban, the European governments set out to compel their firms to disobey this new *diktat* from Washington. The United Kingdom, for example, enacted counter-legislation prohibiting firms based in Britain from complying with the extraterritorial provisions of the Export Administration Act. The Federal Republic of Germany threatened to follow suit. The United States, however, proceeded to raise the ante, first by threatening and then by imposing its own sanctions on those European firms that continued to participate in pipeline construction.

It was not until late 1982 that concessions from the American side under newly appointed Secretary of State George Shultz led to a truce in this new round of conflict with America's recalcitrant "allies." Within the Reagan administration, the Commerce and State departments had favored less stringent restrictions on economic détente than the Pentagon. Under their influence, the United States shifted from unilateral (and often extraterritorial) efforts toward a greater use of CoCOM. Successive high-level CoCOM meetings were held, the first since the 1950s. During these sessions a series of compromises were reached. The fifteen members of CoCOM agreed unanimously (albeit reluctantly) to prohibit the export to the East bloc of items like computers and telephone systems containing the latest western technology. In exchange, the United States supported European demands that the export of less sophisticated goods no longer be banned. To assist in making such delicate decisions, the United States finally succeeded in winning agreement in October 1985 to establish the Security and Technology Exports' Meetings (STEM), a body designed to offer military and technological advice to CoCOM. In this instance (symbolic of the changed atmosphere on the use of sanctions), the Reagan administration seemed resigned to the European position and unwilling to make it a point of deeper transatlantic conflict. In the end, therefore, pressures within West Europe and in American domestic politics forced at least a partial revision of the administration's distaste for economic détente. The rift with West Europe had been resolved in large measure because the Reagan administration had gradually drifted toward policies it had previously denounced. East-West economic relations were now considered principally in the multilateral forums

9. *Washington Post*, 12 August 1984, p. 15.

like CoCOM favored by the Europeans. The gap between the United States and the European elites--whose positions had shifted much less due to ever increasing levels of domestic unemployment--had narrowed.

Whatever the fashion in Washington, Europeans have had a much higher economic and political investment in détente. Throughout the Reagan administration, for example, ties between the two Germanys have continued to develop and deepen regardless of the political coloration of the government in Bonn. Similarly, other European countries have resisted American attempts to reduce their economic dealings with East Europe and the Soviet Union. Across the political spectrum, including the new forces of the peace movement, the initial "essentialist" and unilateral policies of the Reagan administration have called forth nationalist--even "Gaullist"--responses in unlikely quarters. These responses have taken collective European form in some instances, such as resistance to American extraterritorial demands. And that revived nationalism appears likely to remain a force in future Alliance relations due to the increasing influence of West Europe's less pro-American "successor generation."[10] This development has been especially true of the Federal Republic of Germany in recent years. In February 1987, for example, West German Foreign Minister Hans-Dietrich Genscher urged fellow Europeans to respond positively in both the military and commercial domains to the new thinking of Mikhail Gorbachev. In particular, Genscher supported "large-scale economic cooperation that will help the Soviet Union modernize its economy."[11] As a leader of the Free Democratic Party within the coalition government of Chancellor Helmut Kohl, the German foreign minister has been a forceful advocate for economic détente, echoing the views of leading German industrialists and bankers impressed by Gorbachev's proposals and concerned about both increasing protectionism and a declining commitment to European defense in the United States.

What this West German policy shift also reflects, however, are recent dramatic changes in that country's state of public opinion. A poll conducted by *Der Spiegel* in May 1987 asked a sample of West Germans to place Reagan and Gorbachev on a "sympathy scale" ranging from minus 5 to plus 5. With a rating of +1.2, the Soviet Union's new leader outpolled the American president, who only scored a modest +0.1. In another survey, commissioned by the West German government, 58 percent wanted Bonn in the future to cooperate equally with the United States and the Soviet Union while only 31 percent preferred to

10. Stephen F. Szabo, "The Successor Generation," *The Atlantic Alliance: Perspectives from the Successor Generation*, ed. Alan Platt (Santa Monica: The Rand Corporation, 1983), pp. 45-57.

11. *New York Times*, 18 February 1987, p. 11.

continue working closely only with the United States.[12] Bonn's position of establishing greater economic and more cordial political ties with the Soviet Union has been cautiously endorsed by other members of the Atlantic Alliance. Margaret Thatcher, for one, was favorably impressed with Gorbachev during his 1985 visit to London. Even before her preelection trip to Moscow in the spring of 1987, Thatcher responded positively to the Soviet leader's plans for reform, stating, "We can do business together."[13]

During Gorbachev's visit to France in October 1985, it appeared as if Soviet efforts to take advantage of the divergent western views of economic détente might have some effect in Paris as well. The French, however, have been much more skeptical about the new thinking emanating from Moscow despite their increased cooperation with the Soviets in various high-tech areas, including the commercial aspects of space exploration. In contrast to President Mitterrand, the new French Foreign Minister, Jean-Bernard Raimond (who was ambassador to Moscow before taking up his current post), is known to be concerned about the ultimate aims of the new Soviet overtures to West Europe.[14] His views, influential in shaping the cautious response of the Chirac government to Moscow since the March 1986 legislative elections, also reflect an anti-Soviet trend in French public opinion that has developed over the past decade. Consequently, it is not too surprising that the French premier's reception in Moscow during his May 1987 visit was less cordial than that extended to his British counterpart a short time earlier.

For the time being, at least, Gorbachev's appeal to West Europe appears to be focused on winning support in the two traditional pillars of the Atlantic Alliance--the United Kingdom and the Federal Republic of Germany. In so doing, the new generation of Soviet leaders, intent on pursuing a program of economic modernization that would require western technology, appears to have broken with the past Soviet fixation on superpower relations to focus on fostering more cordial relations with West Europe. Whether Gorbachev's new thinking will succeed in producing significant economic gains for the Soviet economy, however, is contingent on a series of imponderables. It is therefore more appropriate to conclude this effort to gauge the prospects for economic détente in Europe with questions rather than affirmations or predictions.

First of all, will the Soviet Union be looked upon as a good credit risk by those West Europeans being asked to make a sizable investment in joint economic ventures? While the burden of Soviet debt service is considerably

12. *New York Times*, 17 May 1987, p. 18.
13. *New York Times*, 18 February 1987, p. 11.
14. Ibid.

lower than that of Poland and most other East European states, the opportunities for profitable long-term joint ventures are obviously linked to Gorbachev's political longevity. At least in some French financial circles, the memory of the sizable investments lost in the wake of the 1917 Revolution still provides food for thought.

Ultimately of greater importance, however, are the questions raised by the link between the military and economic aspects of Gorbachev's new thinking. As the checkered history of economic détente in the postwar period demonstrates, commercial links between West Europe and the East European states frequently have been determined by relations between the two superpowers. Should the Intermediate-Range Nuclear Force agreement be ratified by the U.S. Senate and the Supreme Soviet, eliminating most medium-range nuclear weapons from Europe, members of the Atlantic Alliance would face the prospect of dealing with the current sizable imbalance in conventional forces between NATO and the Warsaw Pact. As a result, funds that are now available for investment in high technology joint ventures with the Soviets might thus have to be rechanneled into the building of equally sophisticated conventional weapons. In short, should Soviet new thinking coincide with an equally dramatic decline in the credibility of the American nuclear "umbrella" now protecting West Europe, the years to come might well be marked by a stunning reversal in postwar attitudes toward the Soviet Union on the two shores of the Atlantic. While less committed to the United States than earlier NATO leaders, West Europe's "successor generation" could find itself para-doxically obliged to adopt a more suspicious stance in its dealings with the Soviet Union, thereby insuring themselves against the possibility that *perestroika* and *glasnost* will ultimately lead to some form of "Finlandization."

6 FOUNDATIONS AND PROSPECTS FOR SOVIET ECONOMIC REFORMS: 1949 TO 1987

Wladyslaw W. Jermakowicz

Post-World War II Soviet history provides many examples of attempts by the state to reform its economy. Most of these attempts began as a new Party and state leader emerged. Each reform left behind a sense of frustration and disillusionment within three or four years. Currently, the election of the young and vigorous Mikhail Gorbachev as the new General Secretary of the Communist Party of the Soviet Union (CPSU) has created a new wave of hope, optimism, and high expectations. It has also renewed speculation on how serious his *perestroika* is and how long it will last. This paper questions whether the "election" of the most recent General Secretary will move the country on a road toward *real* economic reform. It will examine the historical record of reforms in the Soviet Union, revealing their characteristics, causes, and consequences, compare those reforms with the changes announced by Gorbachev, and provide guarded forecasts on the potential impact of the latest changes.

The author would like to personally thank the following people, whose suggestions have been incorporated into this paper: Dr. Larry Arp from the University of Southern Indiana, Evansville, IN; Dr. Paul Marer from Indiana University, Bloomington, IN; Dr. Reinhard Peterhoff from Forschungsstelle zum Vergleich Wirtschaftlicher Lenkungssystem, University of Marburg, West Germany; and Dr. Wolfgang Quaisser from Ost-Europa Institut, Munich, West Germany.

THE WAVES OF SOVIET REFORMS

"Reform" in this paper is defined as change made in the macro management system (MMS) of the economy, not change made in economic policy or in personnel. The MMS consists of two parts: the subsystem of the organizational structure that includes institutions associated with the production and distribution of goods and services and their interrelationships, and the subsystem of the instruments of regulation, which usually includes direct administrative regulators and indirect financial regulators used to accomplish predetermined goals.

Reforms, then, are the changes made in the organizational structure of MMS and/or within the instruments of regulation. Organizational changes reflect changes in the role and authority of planning bodies, the number and responsibilities of industrial and functional ministries, and the role of Party organs. Instrumental changes, in turn, reflect changes in financial indicators, planned targets, financial incentive funds, methods of their calculation, and the number of indicators.

There are two extreme models of MMS: a fully centralist model of hierarchical organization and management, characterized by exclusive, central, direct, and command regulation, and a fully functional model with an organizational structure of management with *indirect* financial regulation. Between these polar models are an unlimited number of MMS variants. To simplify the discussion, I identify five MMS models that exist (or have existed) in centrally planned economies (Appendix A).

MMS 1 - The War Communism model. This model is an extreme command economy and parallels a military management system. Commands defining the exact volume and structure of production in each enterprise are directed to all economic subjects. Total rationing exists. The economic management and administrative structure is totally dominated by a political structure represented by commissars. The entire economy runs much like an enormous national enterprise. A system of War Communism existed during the 1918-1920 period in Soviet Russia and, through necessity, it also existed in the Soviet Union during World War II.

MMS 2 - The Soviet-type economic model. In this model, a multilevel organizational system prevails and the command system dominates. The financial regulation monitors only plan implementation, and the Ministry of Finance plays the role of an accountant for the entire economy. There is a balance between Party and state structures. This system was dominant in East Europe during the 1950s and still prevails in the Soviet Union.

MMS 3 - The Decentralized model. In MMS 3, plan targets are set by the center. A bi-level organizational structure prevails; at the top, the government is politically controlled by a central Party apparatus, and at the bottom there are strong *obyedineniya* that are formally independent of the political structure. This model appeared after the reforms in East Europe during the 1960s. It existed during the 1970s in Poland and still exists to a certain extent in the German Democratic Republic.

MMS 4 - The Hungarian model. In this model, the central ministries regulate the economy by setting prices and by other financial mechanisms such as taxes, exchange rates, tariffs, and wages. A bi-level organizational structure dominates the economy and has political independence from the Party apparatus at all levels. The center has a right, through the Ministry of Industry, to set compulsory plan targets and state contracts directly, and it may exercise the ownership function over enterprises. This system has prevailed in Hungary since the 1980 reforms.

MMS 5 - The Yugoslav model. In this variant, a central authority simulates market behavior. The center adjusts prices to equate supply and demand, but it does not have any right to regulate directly. Enterprises are independent and ruled by workers' councils. This model is sometimes called a "socialist market model" or a "regulated market model."

An indicator measures the direction and intensity of system changes. The indicator, called the Degree of Parameterization (DoP), shows the relative importance of indirect regulation in the MMS. This indicator is based on twelve parallel descriptors within each of the five MMS models. These descriptors are identified briefly in Appendix A.[1] Because no pure macro management system exists, each MMS is a hybrid; each can be identified by a combination of descriptors from various models. The evolution of the MMS in the Soviet Union from 1944 to 1986 as measured by the DoP indicator is shown in Figure 6-1. Despite fluctuations, the Soviet MMS from the beginning of the 1950s gradually evolved in a dialectic manner from a War Communism form into a decentralized variant.

In the Soviet Union, the first type of reform, which led to the revival of the War Communism method of management and a strengthening of the political rather than state structure, was conducted during the Stalinist period. Such revivals occurred twice, once from 1941 to 1948 and again in 1952-1953.

---

1. See also Wladyslaw Jermakowicz, *Das Wirtschaftliche Lenkungssystem Polens: Indikatoren und Determinanten seiner Entwicklung 1944-1984* (Poland's Economic System: Indicators and Determinants of its Development), Johann-Gottfried-Herder-Institut, Marburg an der Lahn, 1985; and *The Reform Cycles in Poland, Czechoslovakia, GDR, and USSR*, ed. Paul Marer (Bloomington, IN, 1987).

Figure 6-1. The Evolution of the Soviet Macro Management System (MMS):
1944-1986

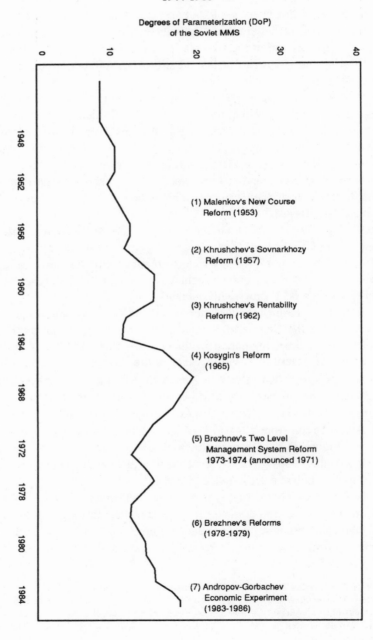

These reforms were made under conditions of resistance to the growing importance of the state apparatus (especially GOSPLAN) and the declining importance of the Party apparatus. The arrest and execution in 1949 of Vosnesensky, the powerful Politburo member and chairman of GOSPLAN, exemplifies the sentiments of that time.[2]

MMS 2, the Soviet-type model of reform, was introduced three times, first by Malenkov in 1953, twice by Khrushchev in 1957 and 1962, and most recently by Brezhnev in 1979. All of these actions were a result of conflicts between the state and Party apparatus.

The decentralized model of reform, MMS 3, was introduced twice in Soviet history. In 1965, reforms that increased the roles of GOSPLAN and lowered organizational units in the economy were implemented. The same type of reform was announced in 1973, but the results were not what was expected, leading the system to revert to MMS 2 a year later. It is my opinion that MMS 3 will be reintroduced in the latter part of the 1980s.

THREE PERIODS OF REFORM

Since World War II, one can distinguish seven attempts at reform, which can then be grouped into three periods. The first period contained the first and second *waves* of reforms. The first wave included changes made during the Malenkov period. There was a reduction in and then a revival of industrial ministries in 1953 and 1954, the splitting of GOSPLAN, and the establishment of *Gosekonomkommissiya* in 1955. The second wave included the Khrushchev reforms, which resulted in the establishment of the *sovnarkhozy* (regional economic councils) in 1957. All changes during the first reform period were in the organizational sphere of the management system--none addressed the instrumental system. During these reforms, the economy was characterized by a highly centralized command system with a large number of detailed planning targets. The first period of reforms is considered to have ended at the Twenty-First Party Congress in 1959. All of Khrushchev's organizational reforms were completed and his personal power seemed unquestionable.

---

2. The political character of arrest and execution can be explained by the accusation Joseph Stalin leveled against Vosnesensky. Stalin accused him of excessively emphasizing "the law of value" (Marxist notion for market mechanism), that is, an attempt on one hand to balance supply and demand and, on the other hand, voluntarism in economic decisionmaking, in other words, lack of respect for "the law of value."

The second reform period began after the Twenty-Second Party Congress in October 1961. The reforms of this period had a mixed character that was both organizational and instrumental. The second period included three reform attempts: the Khrushchev third wave of reforms (1962), the Kosygin fourth wave of reforms (1965), and the Brezhnev fifth wave of reforms (1973-1974). Organizational changes included the establishment of the Committees in 1962, the revival of industrial ministries in 1965, and the introduction of a bi-level economic system in 1973. Changes in the instrumental sphere included the reduction of planned targets in 1962, the development of nine success indicators in 1965, and the introduction of the delivery contract base wage funds in 1974. The second reform period ended in the second half of the 1970s with the stabilization of the political elite.

The third reform period began in July 1979, a year and a half before the start of the Eleventh Five-Year Plan, and resulted from a worsening economic situation and growing discrepancies between plan targets and economic achievements.[3] Changes made during this period were predominantly in the instrumental sphere of the management system. This reform period includes what I call the sixth wave, the Brezhnev reform (1979), and the seventh wave, reforms introduced by Andropov in 1983 and continued by Gorbachev in 1985. These changes were reflected in the introduction of obligatory five-year contracts, which specified the assortment and quantity of products transferred among enterprises. Twelve basic success indicators for enterprises and the *obyedineniya* were introduced. Additional modifications were made in the computation of enterprise incentive funds, bonus funds, and social funds. From 1984 to 1986, a greater degree of experimentation in some industries was permitted.

A conclusion to be drawn from Appendix A is the gradual decomposition of the Soviet MMS over time. The system has moved gradually away from a "pure" or internally consistent system that would embody a complete set of variables belonging to one of the theoretical models. The Soviet MMS was pure only once, between 1951 and 1953. As the MMS evolved, significant blurring of variables occurred, which was especially evident at the beginning of the second period of reforms when various modifications taken from different models were increasingly combined into a hybrid system. In 1965, for example, liberal profitability indices coexisted with strictly specified plan targets for enterprises set by the Planning Commission. Individual enterprises

---

3. See H.H. Hoehmann, Sowjetunion, *Die Wirtschaft Osteuropas und der VR China zu Beginn der achtziger Jahre* (The Economy of East Europe and the People's Republic of China at the Start of the 1980s), ed. H.H. Hoehmann (Kohlhammer: Stuttgart, 1983), pp. 31-32.

were caught between relatively liberal financial regulations and very strict planning regulations.

Central control through financial regulators is more flexible than through rigid directive planning; however, these two methods of control and their respective instruments generally conflict with one another. One inconsistency is the introduction of indirect regulation without significant change in the organizational structure. Such a situation is not unique to the Soviet reforms of 1983; a similar instance arose during the 1973 and 1979 reforms. In general, Soviet reforms seem to begin with the growing independence of the state and end with the growing power of the Party apparatus. By the end of the 1970s, a complete subordination of the economy to the Politburo agenda had occurred.

In 1982, Andropov inherited the Brezhnev system, which resembled the Soviet-type model, MMS 2, characterized by a multilevel organizational structure, centralized decisionmaking, priority of the political structure over the economic system, domination of the Party organs, lack of authority at the lower level of organization, and impressive organizational stability. Personnel reluctant to make organizational changes in the system hindered prospects for reform; reforming such an MMS 2 system requires not only an alteration of instruments of regulation, but also a loosening of the existing organizational structure, which in turn requires strong political power.[4]

POLITICAL PERIODS AND SUBPERIODS: THEIR CHARACTERISTICS AND TIMING

It is possible to distinguish four political periods in the Soviet Union over the last thirty-five years: (1) the *Stalinist period*--pre-1957, (2) the *Khrushchev period*--1957-1964, (3) the *Brezhnev period*--1964-1982 or 1985, and (4) the *Andropov-Gorbachev period*--post-1982.

---

4. Attempts to change the structure by Andropov in 1983 did not succeed at first. After his speech on 15 August 1983, in which he warned a meeting of party veterans of the need for more profound "changes in planning, management, and economic mechanism" (*Pravda*, 16 August 1983), a counteraction occurred. Two days later, Nikolai Baibakov, the 73-year-old veteran chairman of GOSPLAN, declared in a press conference that the Soviet economy was basically healthy and required no major organizational changes. He spoke of the need for increased centralization rather than expanded managerial prerogatives and explicitly said that managers would not be allowed to fire workers, a statement that contradicted the spirit of the much expected economic reform and Andropov's measures directed at improving work discipline. The swift response marked an unprecedented rebuttal of a party chief for expressing his intentions to introduce economic reform. These attempts to change the structure seem to be continued by Gorbachev.

Within each of these periods we can discern two types of political *subperiods*: (1) an offensive subperiod of gaining support and increasing the power of a new group and a new General Secretary, and (2) a defensive subperiod during which the group in power loses support and influence (Table 6-1). The first political period--the Stalinist era--lasted until the spring of 1957, although the offensive subperiod ended with Stalin's death in March 1953. The defensive subperiod of losing power began with the announcement of a "New Course" in March 1953 and ended with the exclusion of the "anti-party group."[5]

The second political period--the Khrushchev era--started in the spring of 1957. The highlight of its offensive subperiod was the Twenty-Second Congress of the CPSU, where Khrushchev announced the second anti-Stalinist campaign. The defensive subperiod began when further reforms were introduced during the November 1962 Party Plenum. The Party apparatus was altered to be organized in strict accordance with the "production principle," and Committees on Party State Control were announced. Although the official purpose of these changes was to achieve a better division of managerial and ideological labor, apparently the objective was actually to replace Party leaders of the Stalinist faction with Khrushchev supporters, and to subordinate control over the Party and the economy to the First Secretary. As a result of this reform, Khrushchev's power was reduced rather than strengthened. Modifications caused increasing resentment among the old secretaries toward the newcomers, as well as toward the organizations that brought them to power. These changes thwarted further movement and led to Khrushchev's eventual overthrow.

The third political period--the Brezhnev era--began with Brezhnev's ascension in September 1964. It is difficult to identify when his power weakened and the defensive subperiod began, but it occurred sometime between 1975 and 1979. Andropov's rise to the Party leadership ushered in the fourth political period during the fall of 1982. Political and economic changes began soon after Andropov's promotion, but a turning point occurred immediately after his death. Chernenko, a representative of the Brezhnev group, returned to the Brezhnev policy of stability in Party cadres; this "retreat" ended, however, when Gorbachev revived the Andropov reforms in the political elite and the economy. The political rule of Gorbachev can be categorized to fall within the framework of the fourth period.

Despite new developments in the Soviet economic and political systems over the past thirty-five years, changes have failed to reform the foundation of

5. *Pravda*, 9 August 1953.

Table 6-1. Waves and Stages of Economic Reforms in the USSR: 1953-1986

| Reform Periods and Events | C h r o n o l o g y | | |
	1953-61	1961-79	1979-86
Defensive Reforms a) Announcement of political program	August 1953	22nd Congress of CPSU	July 1979
b) Announcement of the reform's program	March 1953	November 1962	July 1979
c) Establishment of central management body over Planning Council	May 1955 Establishment of Gosekonommissiya	1963 Establishment at Supreme Council of National Economy	
d) Growth of the number of central administrational institutions	Increase in the number of industrial ministries (18%)	Increase in number of State Committees (100%, from 16 to 32)	Increase in number of State Committees (50%, from 12 to 18)
Offensive Reforms e) Assumption of power. Change of General Secretary and critique of the past	(Formally) September 1953 (Practically) May 1955	September 1964	November 22, 1982
f) Change of Prime Minister (President of Council of Ministers)	May 27, 1958 Bulganin vs. Khrushchev	September 1964 Khrushchev vs. Kosygin	1985 Tikhanov vs Ryzhkov
g) Change of President of Planning Council	1958	1965 Lomako vs. Baibakov	1985 Baibakov vs. Talyzin
h) Abolishing of previous management body in economy	May 1957 Gosekonommissiya was abolished	1965 Supreme Council of National Economy abolished	
i) Announcement of organizational changes	Establishing of Sovnarkhozy	September 1965 Revival of industrial ministries	Establishment of Gosagroprom January 1, 1986.
j) Announcement of the second mutation of the reforms.		1971 The reform of the organization of the economy announced.	
k) Period of stability	1959 - 1961	1975 - 1979	1979-1986

the existing system and have simply represented a continuation or replication of reforms begun in earlier periods. For example, Khrushchev proceeded with reforms initiated by Malenkov in 1953-1955, Brezhnev pushed the reforms planned by Khrushchev in 1962, Andropov advanced the reform program originated by Brezhnev in 1979, and even Chernenko extended some of the improvements introduced by Andropov in 1983. A degree of continuity in these reforms exists, making it difficult to determine which Party secretary in fact started the reforms.[6]

The distinction between offensive and defensive political subperiods allows for making distinctions between offensive and defensive reforms.

CHARACTERISTICS AND STEPS OF OFFENSIVE REFORMS

Offensive reforms begin during a new political period and are most frequently accompanied by the replacement of a General Secretary. The new secretary usually criticizes the previous Party leader, his supporters, and his policies shortly after attaining power, establishing the basis for personnel changes within the ruling center. During the Twentieth Party Congress, for example, Khrushchev politically attacked Stalin and the "cult of personality." During the Kosygin reform in 1965, the critique was both political and economic. During the 1964 October Plenum, Suslov criticized Khrushchev for the disruption in "the efficiency of the Party organization in vain attempts to improve the economy" and for "local tendencies," which disrupted central planning.[7] A year later, Kosygin criticized the economic results of the last years of the Khrushchev administration.[8]

During the fourth political period--Andropov's economic experiment of 1983, which Gorbachev continued in 1985--criticism was largely economic. In his first major speech as General Secretary at the November 1982 Central Committee Plenum, Andropov highlighted the mounting problems of the Soviet economy, pointing out imbalances in the development of primary and advanced industry, the declining growth of labor productivity, wasteful use of resources, problems in feeding the population, and difficulties with transport.[9]

---

6. W. Brus writes about the continuity of Soviet reforms in "Wirtschaftsreformen in der Sowjetunion" (Economic Reforms in the Soviet Union), *Europaeische Rundschau*, 1, 1985.

7. See M. Page, *The Day Khrushchev Fell* (New York: Hawthorn, 1965), p. 55.

8. A. Kosygin, speech to the Plenum of the CC CPSU in September 1965, *Pravda*, 28 September 1965.

9. *Pravda*, 23 November 1982.

A common thread in all three periods was the use of criticism aimed at the preceding political period as a prelude to a major personnel change.

A critique of future plans, in turn, provided good reasons to replace the chairman of GOSPLAN. A similar procedure was followed in all cases. At the beginning of the period, a new secretary would criticize the foundations of the new Five-Year Plan. The draft was deemed unacceptable and sent back for fine-tuning. After a few months, the old chairman was dismissed and a new one installed. During the first political period, the previously approved Five-Year Plan was found to be "ambitious and unworkable" and was revised nine months later during the Plenum of December 1956, precipitating preparations for the irregular Seventh "Five-Year" Plan (1959-1965). Subsequently, GOSPLAN Chairman Kuzmin was dismissed and Kosygin took over his post. Brezhnev used the same strategy. The main foundations of the Five-Year Plan for 1966-1970 were revised, and a new chairman, Baibakov, replaced Lomako in 1965. During the fourth political period (1985), Gorbachev, in his speech of June 11, referred to the draft guidelines for the Twelfth Five-Year Plan as having been considered by the Politburo but accepted "in main" (meaning only in part) with some revisions demanded.[10] As a result, Baibakov, the twenty-year chairman of GOSPLAN, was dismissed and a new chairman, Talyzin, was elevated to the post. Personnel and organizational changes did not stop at the upper echelons of administration, but were followed also by changes at the lower levels of industrial ministries and included many changes of regional authorities. Once the foundations of reforms were announced, it was convenient to dissolve the former leader's base of power.

Institutional changes usually accompanied the personnel and organizational reforms. For example, Khrushchev introduced over 100 *sovnarkhozy* in 1957 and replaced industrial ministries, whose bureaucrats were loyal to the prior political group (Stalin loyalists). Of the twenty-seven industrial and eighteen sectoral central ministries and committees that existed in 1956, only eight industrial ministries and half the sectoral institutions remained after a year. Authority over the economy was transferred to the regional level in the form of 105 *sovnarkhozy*.

In 1965, during the Kosygin reforms, the revival of industrial ministries caused the dissolution of forty-five *sovnarkhozy*, which were the support base for Khrushchev. This time the new elite installed thirty-one new industrial and eleven sectoral ministries and removed twenty-nine of the thirty-five existing economic committees. Of the surviving institutions, six continued their activities as committees and fifteen were transformed into ministries.

10. *Pravda*, 25 May 1985.

Ironically, six of the dismantled committees were re-established with the same chairpersons during the following nine years.

Reforms made during the fourth political period in 1983-1986 concentrated first on personnel changes. In the first seven months of his reign, Gorbachev replaced twenty-one members of the Soviet government. Changes in the organizational structure were more rhetorical than real, and those made primarily affected the agricultural sector and resulted in the creation of GOSAGROPROM.[11] Strengthening the political power of the new elite usually delayed introduction of economic reforms, thus preventing real economic reform. The new system was inevitably similar to the old one.

CHARACTERISTICS AND STEPS OF DEFENSIVE REFORMS

Defensive reforms usually began after a period of relative political stability. GOSPLAN usually assumed the role as the economy's leading management organization, and the *obyedineniya* and the enterprises received some power and authority; however, the Party apparatus was restrained. As opposition to the state apparatus grew, the need for changes became apparent. The acting General Secretary subsequently announced a new Party program.

In August 1953, Malenkov announced programs to increase the standard of living and to develop the consumer goods industries, goals which were to be accomplished at the expense of heavy industry. Nine years later, at the Twenty-Second Party Congress of the CPSU, Khrushchev announced the program of building communism in the Soviet Union to the year 1980, and in 1979, Brezhnev teased Soviet society with the promise of increasing technological progress through the year 2000. These programs sought to motivate Soviet society by proposing an attractive vision of the future as well as providing initiative for the economy. The Party faction that announced the program took responsibility for its fulfillment; it was a good excuse to commence a wave of criticism about state apparatus policies. As a rule, the joint forces of industrial departments and ministries criticized GOSPLAN's role

11. The moderate organizational changes in the structure of the Soviet management system were introduced at the end of 1985. First, the hitherto existing Ministry for Medicine Industry merged with the Chief Administration for Microbiology Industry, and a new Ministry for Medicine and Microbiology Industry was established. Also, beginning 1 January 1986, five ministries in the agriculture and food sector were included in the State Agro-industry Committee. The new Committee contained all-union ministries like Agriculture, Food, Fruit and Vegetable, Meat, Milk Products, and Country Building, as well as the State Committee for Technological Supply in the Farm Industry.

and the over-centralization of the existing system. The Party apparatus stressed that the Central Planning Commission did not leave it any space to maneuver, that planned targets were to be specified, and that planning covered all kinds of economic activity. Primary preparations for new reforms under Party auspices were usually initiated and stressed the further strengthening of democratic centralism, which was accomplished by broadening enterprise rights while simultaneously reinforcing central planning. In effect, the latter was completed at the cost of the former.

The theoretical basis of the 1953 defensive reform drew heavily from Stalin's 1952 book, *Economic Problems of Socialism in the USSR*,[12] in which he recommended permanent changes to the system. By the second Khrushchev period, when defensive reform occurred in 1962, there was a flood of proposals pointing out the many microeconomic irrationalities of the system and the need for greater decentralization. In 1959 and 1960, for instance, the Novozhilov and Nemchinov papers were published. Novozhilov argued that it would be wrong to regard the cost incurred in producing a commodity in isolation as the basis for its value.[13] Nemchinov wrote that "the socially necessary expenditure of labor must be determined by reference not only to the expenditure of labor but also to its results."[14] In 1962, a prominent and critical paper by Liberman, "Plan, Profit and Premium," was published in *Pravda*.[15] The 1979 reform was also preceded by criticisms of the existing system.[16] Each Party leader who started defensive reforms usually had ample time to implement his new reform program, which was in most cases more innovative than previous ones.

Despite the proposed changes, the new elites had no power to put these reforms into practice. Their influence declined rapidly and they were replaced. Their proposals were introduced in the so-called "framework of offensive reforms" by the next elite. For example, the Stalinist idea of weakening the central state apparatus and implementing permanent changes was finally fulfilled by Khrushchev in 1957. Khrushchev's idea in 1962 of establishing economic success indicators was at last accomplished during Kosygin's reforms. Brezhnev's reforms of 1979 were fulfilled during the economic experiments by Andropov, Chernenko, and most recently by Gorbachev. The

---

12. Joseph Stalin, *Economic Problems of Socialism in the USSR* (n.p., Moscow, 1952).

13. V. Novozhilov, *The Use of Mathematics in Economics*, ed. V. Nemchinov (Cambridge, MA: MIT Press, 1965), pp. 210-212. The Soviet version was published in Moscow in 1959.

14. See V. Nemchinov, *Voprosy Ekonomiki*, 12, 1960, p. 87; and *Pravda*, 21 September 1962.

15. E. Liberman, "Plan, Profit, Premium," *Pravda*, 7 September 1962.

16. Compare the examples given by I. Adrim in "Stand und Zunkunfts-ausichten der Wirtschaftsreform in der USSR" (The State and the Future Perspectives of Soviet Economic Reform), *Osteuropa*, December 1985.

lagged implementation of reforms, as mentioned before, seems to be one of the most important characteristics of the Soviet system.

It is noteworthy to stress that defensive reforms, which were better in theory than those described as offensive reforms, resulted in a marked centralization in the economy's management. The planning council in this process was shifted to long-range planning, and a new central management body above the planning commission for operational management was established. In addition, the role and number of industrial ministries were increased. These reforms were officially announced in order to give more power and responsibility to the lower levels of organization. Unofficially, however, they allowed for control over the economy by a new body, and industrial ministries were subordinated to the Politburo and the central Party apparatus.

In summary, defensive reforms are theoretically better based and more progressive than their offensive counterparts, and lead to the strengthening of the central Party apparatus and industrial ministries. Offensive reforms, however, are oriented toward the decentralization of authority. Such decentralization is expected to gain the support of lower ranking personnel for the new leadership and is considered a reward for their support in the battle for succession. The fluctuation and cyclical evolution in the Soviet management system has been a result of continuous competition for control over the economy between the Party and state apparatus. The more pragmatic the state structure, the more it desired strengthening GOSPLAN and increasing the role of the *obyedineniya* and enterprises. These two bodies were not duplicated by the Party structures, and were only indirectly controlled, either through the government in the case of GOSPLAN, or by the *oblast* (region) and republic committees of the Party. Both the *obyedineniya* and the enterprise had some margin of freedom and independence.

The more ideologically oriented Party people were dedicated to establishing a central body controlled by the Politburo and Secretariat, and to strengthening the industrial ministries closely connected and controlled by the Central Committee industrial departments. Most popular during offensive reforms was the Soviet-type vision of the economy (MMS 2). During defensive reforms, attempts were made to implement the War Communism variant (MMS 1), which required a dominant role of the Party.

GORBACHEV'S OPTIONS FOR REFORM

Gorbachev still has many options to reform the Soviet system, the most likely of which include the following:

1. A reversion to the War Communism method of economic control (Reform I).
2. A continuation, without significant change, of the Soviet-type model inherited from Andropov (Reform II).
3. An introduction of a decentralized variant of the current system, such as the Polish WOG reform of the 1970s (Reform III).
4. A replication of the Hungarian economic model (Reform IV).
5. The implementation of the Yugoslav economic model (Reform V).

The most viable options for Gorbachev are Reforms II, III, and IV; Reforms I and V can be excluded from consideration. Advocates of the Soviet-type model include conservative Soviet economists and policy advisors who promote a cautious strategy for revitalizing the centrally planned economy. Economists who support Reform III include two of Gorbachev's most visible new advisors, Abel Aganbegyan, former director of the Novosibirsk Institute of Economics of the Soviet Academy of Sciences, and Tatyana Zaslavskaya, author of the widely popular "Novosibirsk Paper." Those in this group think production decisions need to be made by large, amalgamated industrial enterprises (*Kombinaten*) equipped with resources to conduct research and development and opportunities to coordinate all phases of the industrial process. They also support granting greater flexibility to industrial managers to run their plants as they see fit.[17]

The Hungarian model, Reform IV, is largely supported by theoretical economists, low-level managers, and the staffs of functional ministries. In this model, economic decisionmaking is shifted from industrial ministries to functional ministries, from GOSPLAN to the Council of Ministers. Advocates of the Hungarian model believe in a system in which the choices of suppliers and customers are guided by indirect financial regulators created by functional ministries. For example, Kurashvili, of the Soviet Academy of Sciences, writes, "In this system, enterprises are not subject to any direct instruction from above. Their behavior is influenced by pricing, tax, and credit policies." Kurashvili notes that in such a system, enterprises are motivated to economize on labor and thus, to shed, rather than retain, surplus workers. He proposes the elimination of practically all ministries, leaving only a Ministry

17. The managers support Zaslavskaya's argument in her "Novosibirsk Paper," in which she contends, "If more power over production were shifted to qualified workers they would work more intensively, they would get better results, they would get a better income, and they would lead a more interesting life." Zaslavskaya identifies conservative interests, chiefly bureaucrats in the middle (ministry) layer of the system of economic administration. T. Zaslavskaya, "Ekonomika skvoz' prizmu sotsiologii" (Economics through the Prism of Sociology), *EKO*, 7, 1985, pp. 3-23.

of the National Economy and select ministries for energy, housing, communication, and functional ministries for pricing, finance, foreign trade, and employment.[18]

Professor G. Popov of Moscow State University also supports this type of reform. In the May 1985 issue of *Voprosy Ekonomiki*, Popov called for reordering the functions of central planners, including the elimination of setting specific plan targets. His proposal is consistent with the general line advocated by Kurashvili, which he indirectly supported through kind words about the New Economic Policy of the early 1920s, when a mixed economy coexisted with a regulated market system.[19]

An examination of the theoretical discussions and proposals made by leading Soviet economists seems to suggest that the main battle is between supporters of the Hungarian model and proponents of the decentralized model. Advocates of the Hungarian model propose to introduce self-financing and use profits as a main success indicator. They suggest increasing the role of functional ministers, separating enterprise plans from the central plan set up by GOSPLAN, and grouping the more than sixty industrial ministries into a small number of high-level bodies managing whole sectors. They also propose to give the *obyedineniya* negotiating rights for international trade and contracts. Additionally, as in the Hungarian model, all management positions in enterprises would be chosen by the workers. Advocates of the decentralized model propose control over profits by setting up norms for taxes, wage funds, and social funds. They believe central rationing of some strategic goods should be maintained and that subsidies should still be given to unprofitable enterprises. They propose that candidates for managerial positions be approved by industrial ministries after their election.

In reality, the main debate over reform exists between supporters of the decentralized model and the status quo Soviet-type model. Two documents illustrate this point: the Basic Provisions for Fundamentally Reorganizing Economic Management[20] and the Law on the State Enterprise.[21] The Basic Provisions were approved "in the main" at the June 26 Plenum of the Central Committee, and the New Soviet Law on the State Enterprise was approved by

18. B.P. Kurashvili, "Kontury vozmozhnoi perestroiki" (The Outlines of Possible Restructuring), *EKO*, 5, 1985, pp. 59-80.

19. G. Popov, "O Sovershenstvovanii tsentralizovannogo khozyastvennogo rukovodstva" (About Improvement of Centralized Economic Management), *Voprosy Ekonomiki*, 5, 1985, pp. 82-93.

20. See speech by Gorbachev at the Plenum of the CC CPSU, June 1987, *Pravda*, 26 June 1987, pp. 1-5.

21. See "Zakon SSSR o gosudarstvennom predpriyatii (obyedineniye)" (The Enterprise Association Law), *Pravda*, 1 July 1987.

the Supreme Soviet on June 30, 1987. The latter document, consisting of twelve economic laws, is a central element in the Gorbachev economic reorganization package. One of the proposals, calling for a reorganization of 37,000 industrial enterprises, reflects the spirit of decentralization, and resembles the concept of Poland's WOGs and parts of the Soviet New Economic Policy of the 1920s. The new enterprise law clearly advocates the decentralized model, Reform III, in some areas. The law states that each enterprise is to have an "economically accountable income," referred to here as net income, which can be used to pay wage and bonus funds, production development funds, research funds, and social-development funds. Stable long-term percentage norms, or coefficients, would be set for each of these funds. There are other provisions of the law, however, that are clearly related to the Hungarian model, Reform IV. Enterprises, for example, are empowered to create their own research divisions and to form joint ventures with one another on their own initiative. They can, if necessary, arrange family contracts with their own employees. Enterprises can also go to state arbitration to have ministry instructions that exceed ministerial powers rescinded.

Within the current Soviet-type economic model, Reform II, there are great limitations to reform. The idea of enterprises buying and selling at their own discretion is only partially endorsed. Control parameters and norms "from above" are to influence the enterprise's choice of output, even though enterprises are supposed to control their own annual plans. Also, the central plan targets will be replaced with obligatory "state contracts," "special tasks" and allocations of centrally distributed resources.[22] The law sets no upper limit to the share of output that can be taken by state orders. It says, moreover, that orders will be made by the ministry and will be compulsory. And, the coefficients determining the payment to the state budget will be fixed by ministries, which gives them additional power over enterprises. The ministries are still responsible for the performance of their enterprises and have every reason to intervene in each enterprise's operations by adjusting targets and redistributing tasks among enterprises.

Both the Basic Provisions and the new Law on the State Enterprise contain provisions that can, in reality, be compatible with *any* of three models of

---

22. The supply and use of a number of "most important" products are still centrally planned. The research of two members of GOSPLAN shows that 250-300 product groups are still centrally planned. See F. Klotsvog, D. Matveev, "Chtoby uzhitsa planu s dogovorom," (How to Use the Plan with Agreement), *Pravda*, 3 June 1987. Other authors write that of 12 million goods only the most important 40,000 will be directly and centrally planned, but this represents about 70 percent of all the production. See R. Peterhoff and A. Schueller, "Ursachen fuer die Reformbestrebungen in der USSR" (The Reasons for Reform Attempts in the USSR), manuscript, University of Marburg, 1987.

reform--the Hungarian model, the decentralized model, or the traditional Soviet-type model. It seems, however, that the enterprise law is more conservative in its general implications than Gorbachev's Basic Provisions; it is a compromise document that favors, accordingly, the decentralized model of reform.

If "liberalism" is necessary for the emergence of a "new-approach" Soviet leader, and "conservatism" is needed to defend the status quo, one can argue that the longer Gorbachev delays the start of radical reform, the weaker the support he can expect from his allies and the greater the need for conservatism to defend whatever changes he is able to implement. The introduction of the Hungarian model, for example, would require the full independence of the state economic apparatus. Gorbachev alone will not have the courage to start a battle with the entire Party apparatus; moreover, he is a product of this apparatus and will not limit the rights, privileges, *nomenklatura,* and other benefits that go with it. The Hungarian model will not be considered seriously because it requires the diminution of Party control over the economy. The Soviet establishment seems to be strongly influenced by fear that the Party would lose political power as happened in Czechoslovakia in 1968 and in Poland during 1981, and there is no evidence that Gorbachev is personally inclined toward a Hungarian type of reform.[23] In the majority of his speeches, he seems to support the decentralized option, Reform III, which was especially evident during his speech on June 11, 1985, in which he cited the GDR as a model and implied that industrial associations should be strengthened through what resembles the East German *Kombinaten.* Gorbachev's intent appears to limit the ministries' power and provide a broader scope for initiative at the enterprise level.[24]

Further evidence supporting the likelihood for the decentralized approach to reform is the nature of the personnel changes taking place within scientific institutions. It seems that Gorbachev's intention is to clip the extreme wings of scientists supporting either the conservative Soviet-type model, or the progressive Hungarian model. This policy began in 1983 and 1984, when Chernenko, with the probable support of Gorbachev, strongly criticized two scientific institutes representing opposing positions on reform. The Central

23. There are many positive evaluations of the Hungarian economic model by Soviet officials. This may be inferred from an editorial published in *Pravda* less than three weeks after Gorbachev's succession that talks about a "bold, innovative, and at the same time realistic approach to plans for socioeconomic development." (*Pravda,* 30 March 1985, p. 1). Similarly, Y. Ligachev, in an international press conference during his visit to Budapest, warmly endorsed Hungary's economic, political, and foreign policies and pointed out that different aspects of the Hungarian experience had already served as models for the Soviet Union. This seems to be the first time a Soviet leader has explicitly identified the Hungarian experience as a valid model for the Soviet Union (See report published by TASS on 23 and 25 April 1987).

24. Gorbachev's key speech in June on economic policy, Moscow Television, 11 June 1985; *RFE-RL Research Bulletin,* 26, 1985.

Economics and Mathematics Institute in Moscow, which favored the Hungarian model of reform, and the Institute of Economics at Moscow State University, in concert with the conservative approach to reform, faced organizational changes in 1984. The Central Economics and Mathematics Institute was split into two institutes and its long-term director, Fedorenko, retired,[25] and the progressive Institute of Economics in Novosibirsk faced a similar fate.[26]

Many Soviet academics suggest that the Gorbachev reform program was proposed as a reaction to unfavorable trends in the national economy.[27] I test this assertion using annual growth rates and industrial production indicators for the period 1952-1986 (Table 6-2, Figures 6-2a and 6-2b). Fluctuations in the Soviet economy make it difficult to pinpoint precisely favorable or unfavorable economic conditions for any given period. The data in Table 6-2 illustrate that from one five-year period to the next, industrial production declined. The data suggest that during each period of Soviet development it was "justifiable" to embark on economic reforms. From 1956 to 1960, the five-year average growth in gross industrial production was 2.5 percentage points (a decline of 18 percent) lower than for the 1951 to 1955 period, and national income declined 1.4 percentage points (14.5 percent). This trend continued over most of the next twenty years, with the only exception to this pattern occurring between 1966 to 1970. The same trend is evident in the analysis of yearly annual growth rates of national income and industrial gross production.

A comparison of annual economic indicators and the *timing* of proposals for reforms reveals the following: In the majority of cases, the economic performance the *year before* reforms were proposed was comparatively better than the preceding two years. In 1952, one year before the "New Course" reform, industrial gross production increased by 11.8 percent. In 1956, one year before the *sovnarkhozy* reform, national income increased 12.5 percent (national income in 1957 grew by a less impressive 6.9 percent). In 1970, the year before the announcement of the eventual 1973 reform, income grew 8.7 percent, a 52.6 percent increase over the 1968 growth rate. In virtually all cases, the growth rates for national income were impressive, not in decline, when reforms were introduced. The only exceptions to this pattern were the Khrushchev reform of 1962 and the Andropov program of 1982. In these

25. Philip Hanson, "Economic Advisors and Gorbachev's Leadership," *RFE-RL Bulletin*, 308, September 1985, p. 2.

26. "Otchet o rabote zhurnala" (Review of Journal's Output), *EKO*, 6, 1985, pp. 78-83.

27. Compare, for example, H. Hoehmann, "Sowjetunion," *Die Wirtschaft Osteuropas und der VR China zu Beginn der achtziger Jahre*, p. 11; J. Kosta and F. Levcik, *Wirtschaftskrise in den Osteuropaeischen RGW-Laendern* (The Crisis of East European Economies), Studie 8, ed. Z. Mylnar, Index e.V, (Koeln, 1985); and R. Peterhoff and A. Schueller, *The Reasons for Reform Attempts*.

Table 6-2. Basic Economic Indices in the USSR: 1952-1986

	Annual Growth Rates of National Income Produced	Annual Growth Rates of Gross Industrial Production	Aver. Annual Growth Rates of National Income Produced for Five Years	Aver. Annual Growth Rates of Gross Industrial Production for Five Years
1952		11.8		
1953		10.5	9.6	13.3
1954		14.3		
1955		12.5		
1956	12.5	11.1		
1957	5.6	10.0		
1958	13.2	9.1	8.2	10.8
1959	7.0	11.1		
1960	8.7	10.0		
1961	6.0	9.1		
1962	5.7	10.4		
1963	5.4	7.5	6.7	8.6
1964	8.5	7.0		
1965	7.8	8.2		
1966	7.2	10.6		
1967	9.5	8.2		
1968	7.4	8.9	7.7	8.4
1969	5.7	8.1		
1970	8.7	7.5		
1971	6.0	8.0		
1972	3.8	6.5		
1973	9.1	7.0	5.7	7.4
1974	5.0	8.1		
1975	4.8	7.5		
1976	5.3	4.9		
1977	4.5	6.0		
1978	5.1	4.4	4.2	4.4
1979	2.2	3.4		
1980	3.5	3.6		
1981	3.3	3.4		
1982	3.4	2.9		
1983	4.2	4.2	3.7	4.7
1984	3.4	4.2		
1985	3.5	3.9		
1986	4.1	4.9		

Sources: *Statistical Yearbook of the USSR* and *Reports About Fulfillment of Plan Targets*

Figure 6-2a. National Income Produced Between 1952-1985

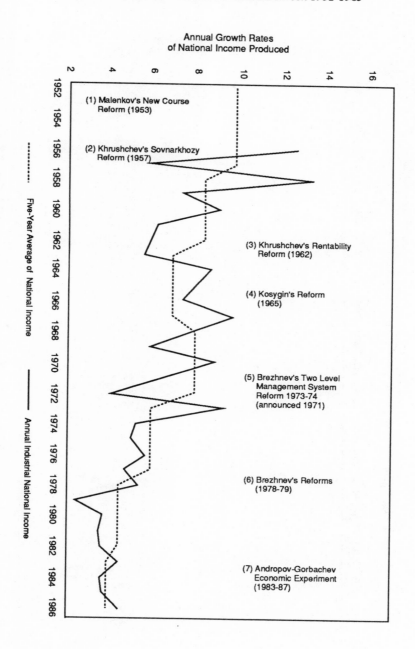

Figure 6-2b. Industrial Gross Production Between 1952-1985

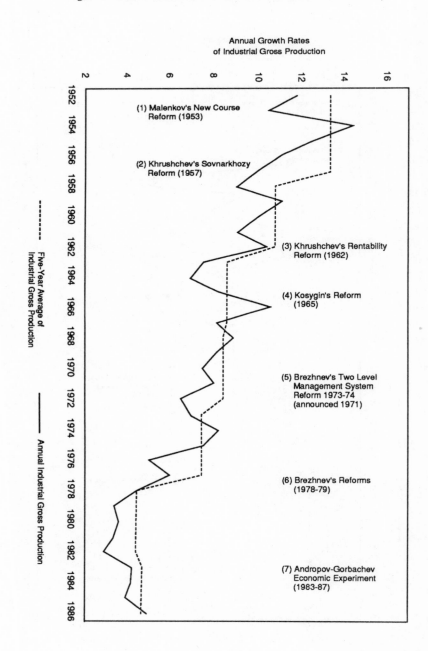

cases, the years preceding the announcements of reform were worse than the years in which the reforms began. In the Khrushchev case, the growth in national income declined 31 percent (2.7 percentage points) in 1961, and in the case of Andropov, the growth in national income in 1981 was 5.7 percent lower (.2 percentage points) than in 1980.

I next analyzed plan fulfillment indicators for national income and industrial production, for reforms generally began following years of improving economic conditions when the fulfillment of national plans was routinely met. It was only during 1982 that one could agree with the assertion that the introduction of reforms was linked to poor economic performance--national income and industrial production were below plan. Yet, even in 1982, reform may have well started simply as the result of a change in Party leadership and was not due to economic conditions. Analyses of such short-term, year-to-year indicators may not fully reflect, however, the steady decline of the Soviet economy since the 1960s. Growth in industrial production and national income fell from 7.7 percent and 8.4 percent annually in the second half of the 1960s to 5.7 percent and 7.4 percent during the first half of the 1970s, and continued to decline into the 1980s. It can be argued that reforms of the 1960s, 1970s, and 1980s were, in part, caused by slowly deteriorating economic conditions. I am of the opinion, however, that, in addition to the earlier argument that reforms were actually introduced in relatively good years (in the short term), other factors, particularly political instability, played at least an equal, if not more important, role in the announcement of reforms.

THE POLITICAL CLIMATE AND REFORM

The notion of "stability" or "instability" is perhaps more difficult to define than economic stagnation. I have attempted to measure the degree of political stability by examining the turnover rate of leading personnel in both the Party (full and alternate members of the Politburo and secretaries of the Central Committee) and the state apparatus (members of the Council of Ministers).[28] The turnover rates provided in Table 6-3 and Figure 6-3 suggest that the early reforms were undertaken primarily in periods of instability in the Party apparatus. Proclamation of the "New Course" by Malenkov was the result of political instability, which led to a vying for power between Party (Khrushchev) and government (Malenkov) groups. Announcement of the 1957

---

28. The turnover rate is computed as a percentage of officials who, at the end of the year, changed positions, left, or joined the elite compared to the number of all officials in the elite at the beginning of the year.

Table 6-3. Turnover Rate of Personnel Among Soviet Elites

Turnover Rate of Personnel

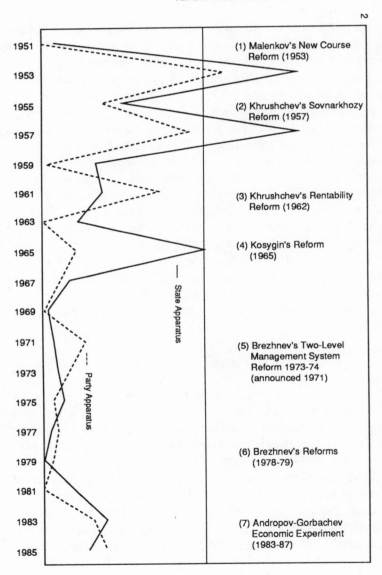

Figure 6-3. Turnover Rate of Personnel Among Soviet Elites

Year	Number of Members of Council of Ministers	Numbers of Personnel Changes in Council of Ministers	Turnover Rate of Members of Council of Ministers	Number of Party Elite Members (Politburo Secretaries)	Number of Changes in Party Elite Members	Turnover Rate of All Party Elite Members	Number of Members in Both Elites	Number of Changes in Both Elites	General Turnover Rate in Both Elites	General Turnover Rate (Moving Average)
1951	67	5	0.07	16	0	0.00	83	5	0.06	0.06
1952	66	13	0.20	16	2	0.13	82	15	0.18	0.56
1953	35	55	1.57	17	19	1.12	52	74	1.42	0.67
1954	60	31	0.52	16	0	0.00	76	31	0.41	0.77
1955	69	34	0.49	19	7	0.37	88	41	0.47	0.39
1956	69	19	0.28	19	8	0.32	94	27	0.29	0.68
1957	40	63	1.58	32	29	0.91	72	92	1.28	0.65
1958	45	21	0.47	32	8	0.25	77	29	0.38	0.62
1959	46	15	0.33	34	1	0.03	80	16	0.20	0.38
1960	41	22	0.54	34	19	0.70	68	41	0.60	0.39
1961	46	17	0.37	25	18	0.72	71	35	0.49	0.43
1962	53	24	0.45	34	0	0.00	87	24	0.28	0.46
1963	55	12	0.22	34	0	0.00	89	12	0.13	0.30
1964	57	5	0.09	26	9	0.35	83	14	0.17	0.19
1965	66	66	1.00	28	6	0.21	94	72	0.77	0.36
1966	65	1	0.02	30	12	0.40	95	13	0.14	0.36
1967	73	12	0.16	30	4	0.13	108	16	0.15	0.35
1968	78	4	0.05	30	2	0.07	109	6	0.06	0.12
1969	79	1	0.01	30	0	0.00	111	1	0.01	0.07
1970	81	8	0.10	30	0	0.00	113	8	0.07	0.05
1971	83	6	0.07	30	8	0.27	114	14	0.13	0.06
1972	82	4	0.05	30	2	0.07	113	6	0.05	0.07
1973	83	7	0.09	32	5	0.16	114	12	0.11	0.09
1974	86	15	0.18	32	0	0.00	118	15	0.13	0.10
1975	86	11	0.13	30	2	0.07	118	13	0.11	0.11
1976	86	12	0.14	32	10	0.31	117	13	0.11	0.14
1977	85	4	0.05	32	3	0.09	117	22	0.19	0.12
1978	85	1	0.01	32	0	0.00	126	7	0.06	0.08
1979	94	0	0.00	32	2	0.06	129	1	0.01	0.03
1980	97	49	0.52	32	2	0.06	127	65	0.52	0.02
1981	98	18	0.19	32	16	0.50	132	18	0.14	0.22
1982	103	14	0.14	29	0	0.00	127	22	0.17	0.28
1983	101	40	0.39	29	8	0.28	128	49	0.37	0.23
1984	103	19	0.19	27	9	0.31	127	21	0.16	0.24
1985	99	28	0.28	28	11	0.39	127	39	0.31	0.31

sovnarkhozy reform by Khrushchev was a result of his victory over the "anti-party group." In this case, 45 percent of the personnel in the Party apparatus and 79 percent in the government apparatus were changed. Between 1956 and 1961, 70 percent of the Politburo's full members were changed, and 75 percent of the secretaries of the Central Committee, 67 percent of the members of the Council of Ministers, and 79 percent of the Republic First Secretaries were removed.

In 1962, a second Khrushchev reform began after a large pre-Congress purge in which about 70 percent of the Party leadership changed. Kosygin's reform in 1965 followed a Party purge in 1964, which was a result of Khrushchev's ouster. One year earlier, however, the turnover in the state apparatus recorded its lowest rate since 1951. A similar situation occurred before the reforms in 1973. In March and April of 1971, during the Twenty-Fourth Congress of the CPSU, when the ideas of the new reforms were announced, four new Politburo members, three new alternate members, and one secretary were removed. The situations before the reforms of 1979 and the 1980s were much like the proverbial calm before the storm and differed from earlier reform periods. In 1978, turnover in both the Party and state apparatus was negligible, and in 1982 and 1984, there were even fewer changes. Political instability was one of the most important factors precipitating the announcement of reforms in the 1950s, 1960s, and the first half of the 1970s, but there is no evidence that this variable was a factor in the reforms introduced in the late 1970s and the 1980s.

From the discussion above, one can distinguish between two periods and two causes of reform (Table 6-4). The reforms of the 1950s were caused initially by political factors and were made exclusively within the organizational sphere of the economy. The reforms of the 1960s (1962 and 1965) and 1973 were introduced in response to both political and economic factors and resulted in both organizational and instrumental changes. The most recent reforms (1979, 1982, and 1984) were initiated primarily for economic reasons and focused on instrumental changes in the financial system. It appears that reforms instigated by political causes led to a restructuring of the organizational system and to changes in the political elite, while economic factors led to changes in the types of financial regulators, yet left the ruling elite intact.

SUMMARY AND CONCLUSIONS

The real reason for change in the Soviet Union is seen in the results of reforms, not in their announced causes. If the causes for reform are accepted as having been both economic and political, the results have been largely

Table 6-4. Combination of Factors Initiating the Announcement of Economic Reforms in the Soviet Union

	Favorable economic situation (1950-1960)	Unfavorable economic situation (1960-1985)
Unstable political situation	Changes occur only in the organizational sphere of the management system • decreasing or increasing the number of industrial ministries • removal or revival of industrial ministries • establishment of the new center over the planning councils Reforms of 1953 and 1957	The changes both in organizational and instrumental spheres of management system • remodeling of organizational structure • reduction of plan targets • reduction of number of success indicators • introduction of new principles of calculation of bonus fund, etc. Reforms of 1962, 1965, and 1973
Stable political situation	No reforms	The changes only in instrumental sphere of management system: • reduction of number of plan targets • reduction of number of success indicators • introduction of new principles of calculation of bonus funds, etc. • introduction of novelty prices Reforms of 1979, 1982, 1984

political. In my opinion, *all* economic reforms undertaken in the Soviet Union during the last thirty-five years were motivated by political rather than economic reasons. The primary aim of the reforms was to replace members of the old elite; if economic efficiency was achieved, it was a secondary concern and a positive byproduct.

In the post-war history of the Soviet Union, the strongest political battle occurred in the 1950s between Stalin and Khrushchev factions and resulted in the most radical of Soviet organizational changes, including the abolition of the branch structure of the economy in favor of a regional structure. A second significant political battle occurred in the 1960s between the Khrushchev and Brezhnev factions. This power struggle generated the Kosygin reform and the revival of industrial ministries. Generally speaking, the stronger the opposition group, the greater the effort required of the new elite to change the system, which results in more radical reforms and a longer time period to introduce them.

A quite different principle can be observed at the end of the 1970s and the beginning of the 1980s. The turnover rates within the Party and government showed a remarkable symmetry and the same rate of change. This relationship suggests that, since the end of the 1970s, the Soviet leadership (Party and government) has become highly unified. Changes in one apparatus result in parallel changes in the other, reflecting the close cooperation among members of the collective leadership and the shift of economic decisionmaking from the state apparatus to the Party.[29] Also, competition within the Party has shifted; in place of factional Party in-fighting, competition has shifted to the individuals--between leading personalities like Andropov and Chernenko or Gorbachev and Romanov. These Party leaders demonstrate a high degree of loyalty to the collective body and a readiness to cooperate; there is little room for the type of struggle known in Khrushchev's era. If changes need to be made, they are made only among personnel and not to political or economic programs. The Soviet leadership in this respect has become anti-ideological, evidenced by the continuity of changes undertaken in the economy by Brezhnev, prolonged by Andropov, supported by Chernenko, and implemented by Gorbachev.

The most recent era of economic experiments concluded and an era of "radical reforms" began on June 26, 1987, when the long awaited Plenum of the Central Committee of the CPSU took place. The draft law on the

---

29. See the study on relationships among the Politburo, Soviet government, army, soviets, and other sectors conducted by M. Kostecki, *Corporate Construction and Corporate Action: Policy, Society, and the Economy in the USSR*, manuscript at the Hoover Institution, Stanford University, 1986.

enterprise was endorsed and a set of guidelines (Basic Provisions) for complementary changes in prices, central planning and the management of industrial branches was "in the main" approved. Although these documents were approved, it is too early to predict which reform option will be adopted in the Soviet Union. Resistance to reform is very strong. During the June Plenum, Gorbachev apparently had been unable to secure an agreement on a detailed set of reforms; no organizational and instrumental barriers to faster growth had been removed. Experiences of other East European states show that the real battle over reform begins when the documents outlining proposed changes become laws and decrees. The path of reform can follow either the Hungarian or the less radical decentralized model, though past experience indicates the Soviet leadership will probably follow the more conservative blueprint.

The reorganization scheme that has emerged so far is close to the more moderate decentralized model. Rather than make a complete break with the hierarchical system as the Hungarians did in 1980, the reformers seem to be aiming at a blend of indirect market regulation and central administration, combining a top-down approach to management *and* a market-resource allocation system. Such a combination, as East European and especially Poland's experience shows, does not work very well or for very long. There is no doubt that the enterprise's increased powers will mean little unless there are changes at the levels of branch ministries and central planning. The fate of the ministries remains a key issue in the politics of the reform processes. As long as branch ministries exist, are responsible for the output of subordinated enterprises, and have enough staff to check up on what is happening in those enterprises, senior officials will have good reason to interfere in enterprise decisions. As long as enterprise directors owe their positions to particular ministries, they will accept the "interference." Gorbachev was apparently unable to be specific about modifying the status of branch ministries. During the last Plenum he reiterated his belief in the idea of a small number of high-level bodies managing whole sectors instead of a large number of separate branch ministries. He did not explain how this regrouping of authorities and functions would proceed, yet he acknowledged the changeover would be very difficult. It appears rumors concerning the dismissal of these central agencies were much exaggerated.

The new enterprise law gives the work force the right to elect a workers' council, as well as to elect the enterprise director and other senior management. In reality, the powers of the work force and its council remain very limited. The choice of top management has to be approved by the superior organ of the enterprises (the ministry), and the law also declares the enterprise's Party organization is to direct or guide the work of the collective.[30] After some time, this collective has a chance either to become the arm of the Party organization and a subject of Party control from above or a body without authority. The self-government in socialism, according to Ligachev, the Politburo member responsible for Party work, "should be conducted by the state."[31]

The role and tone of the Soviet economic press seems to have changed in an ironic way and perhaps reflects much of the pessimism for real reform under Gorbachev. The greatest number of publications devoted to economic experiments was published in 1984, during the tenure of a conservative, Chernenko, and in the spring of 1986, after the Congress of the CPSU. In 1987, during introduction of radical reforms, journals such as *Ekonomicheskaya gazeta* and *EKO* treated the experiences of the new mechanism quite marginally. Instead of proposing positive changes, the press has concentrated on negative aspects of the reform experiments.[32] The picture being portrayed of the current situation in the economy is largely pessimistic.

I am rather pessimistic about the future of Soviet reforms. Past Soviet and East European experiences show that each new leader allows reforms to proceed until they have helped him consolidate political power. If he consolidates power successfully, he will not continue the reform program--at least not in its original and most comprehensive form. The key to understanding the Gorbachev era and the future of Soviet reforms lies in Gorbachev's attempt to secure power; his struggle for power is now the essential element for the Soviet future. The longer Gorbachev remains Party leader and has opposition in the Party and among government elites, the further the reform process will be advanced. Complete victory over the opposition *or* complete defeat will result in the end of radical Soviet reforms. Mikhail Gorbachev's reformist undertakings, judging from lessons of past reforms, will only last as long as necessary to make the most important personnel changes in the political system. Unfortunately, after some changes occur the exuberant expectations will most likely die.

30. Philip Hanson, "Central Committee Plenum on the Economy," Radio Liberty Research RL 234, June 1987, and "The Enterprise Law and the Reform Process," Radio Liberty Research RL 269, July 1987.

31. Y. Ligachev, "Sovetujas's s partiey, s narodom" (Consulting the Party and the Nation), *Kommunist,* 16, 1985, p. 81.

32. See Abel Aganbegyan, "Perelom i uskoreniye (Breakthrough and Acceleration), *EKO,* May 1986, p. 3; P. Bunich, *Trud,* 6 and 7 May 1987; *Izvestiya,* 7 June 1987; and "Kranke Betriebe muessen geschlossen werden" (Sick Firms Must Be Closed), *Der Spiegel,* 26, 1987.

APPENDIX A: FIVE MODELS OF MMS SYSTEMS

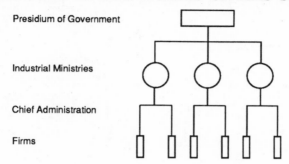

Presidium of Government

Industrial Ministries

Chief Administration

Firms

DESCRIPTOR	WAR COMMUNISM MODEL (MMS 1)
I. ORGANIZATIONAL STRUCTURE	
Organizational structure, measured structure, measured by ratio of branch ministries to functional ministries	Linear: Large number of industrial branch ministries. No functional ministries. At each level, departmentalization by product
Basic legal entity	Entire economy is one large enterprise
Intermediate supervisory unit over enterprises	Military administration with commissars as part of political structure. Main function is transmission of commands from top down and monitoring their implementation
Relative significance of system's levels: 1) center of management system 2) State Planning Council 3) industrial ministries 4) functional ministries 5) *obyedineniya* 6) firms	1) Council of Commissars 2) None 3) As divisions of the Council 4) None 5) As departments of industrial divisions 6) As subdepartments of departments
II. DIRECT REGULATION	
Structure of central economic plan	No structured national plan: Production oriented toward fulfilling national campaign
Degree of enterprise autonomy in designing own plan	No operational plan by enterprises. Activity of economic units oriented toward execution of directives from above
Types of instruments and their range	Differentiated commands directed to all economic units that define exact volume and structure of production
Scope of administrative rationing over supplies	Comprehensive
III. INDIRECT REGULATION	
Types of instruments	No functional instruments. Qualitative output targets
Success indicators	No financial success indicators or direct influence by state
Sources of bonus funds	No bonus funds. Salaries paid in physical goods. No relationship between amount of goods given as wage to worker and quality of work
Degree and scope of control over wholesale prices	No money and no prices. Physical rationing

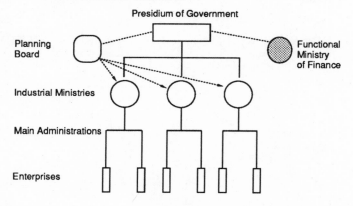

DESCRIPTOR	SOVIET-TYPE MODEL (MMS 2)
I. ORGANIZATIONAL STRUCTURE	
Organizational structure, measured structure, measured by ratio of branch ministries to functional ministries	Quasi-Linear: Dominated by branch ministries, departmentalized by product. Only functional ministry is Ministry of Finance
Basic legal entity	Industrial branch ministry
Intermediate supervisory unit over enterprises	Main administration: Intermediate, administrative organ between ministries and firms. Main function is transmission of command from above and of reports from below
Relative significance of system's levels: 1) center of management system 2) State Planning Council 3) industrial ministries 4) functional ministries 5) *obyedineniya* 6) firms	1) Government or new center of economy 2) Part of new center or executive body for government 3) Basic level and unit of management system 4) As advisory body (Ministry of Finance) 5) As administrative units grouping enterprises 6) Without importance
II. DIRECT REGULATION	
Structure of central economic plan	Divided into sectors, branches, classifications, groups, and individual products. Ministry of Finance prepares own financial plan
Degree of enterprise autonomy in designing own plan	Enterprise totally dependent on hierarchical national plan
Types of instruments and their range	Differentiated commands directed to all economic units that define minimum volume and structure of production
Scope of administrative rationing over supplies	Comprehensive, with exception of certain consumer goods
III. INDIRECT REGULATION	
Types of instruments	Relies mostly on variable turnover tax and subsidy system to level enterprise performance
Success indicators	Leading criterion: Gross enterprise production measured by large number of other financial indicators
Sources of bonus funds	Plan targets. The bonus fund stresses the fulfillment and surpassing quantitative production targets established by plan. Base salary is predetermined
Degree and scope of control over wholesale prices	Marginal. Industrial wholesale prices are fixed on basis of "cost-plus-formula"

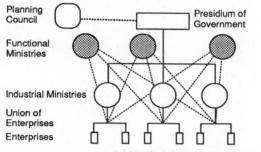

Planning Council

Presidium of Government

Functional Ministries

Industrial Ministries

Union of Enterprises

Enterprises

DESCRIPTOR	DECENTRALIZED MODEL (MMS 3)

I. ORGANIZATIONAL STRUCTURE

Organizational structure, measured structure, measured by ratio of branch ministries to functional ministries	Functional-Linear: Equal number of functional and branch ministries
Basic legal entity	Trust; hierarchically organized on branch principle; union of enterprises
Intermediate supervisory unit over enterprises	Union of enterprises a formally independent economic unit, operating on profitability principle
Relative significance of system's levels: 1) center of management system 2) State Planning Council 3) industrial ministries 4) functional ministries 5) *obyedineniya* 6) firms	1) Council of Ministers 2) As part of center responsible for national plans 3) Limited role as representative of different branches and management units in strategic areas 4) Limited role with functional authority 5) As basic economic unit 6) As department of *obyedineniya*

II. DIRECT REGULATION

Structure of central economic plan	Hierarchical and functional plans: Former prepared by branch ministries and coordinated by Planning Board, the latter by functional ministries, in cooperation with Planning Board
Degree of enterprise autonomy in designing own plan	Plan is in part dependent on national plan, with limited margin of freedom. Enterprises can start new production if it does not impede execution of plan. Can reduce plan targets if no demand for production established in plan
Types of instruments and their range	Differentiated commands define minimum production volume only of enterprises producing investment and raw materials
Scope of administrative rationing over supplies	Partial rationing over basic materials only

III. INDIRECT REGULATION

Types of instruments	Relies on price, tax, subsidy, wage differentiation as incentive or disincentive to output
Success indicators	Rentability: The ratio of outputs to inputs, supplemented by a significant number of financial indicators
Sources of bonus funds	Two simultaneous sources: Plan and Rentability. Two types of bonus funds: one depends on degree of fulfillment of plan targets, another determined as percentage of "profit"
Degree and scope of control over wholesale prices	Partial. State fixes prices on basic raw materials and certain protected industrial goods and services

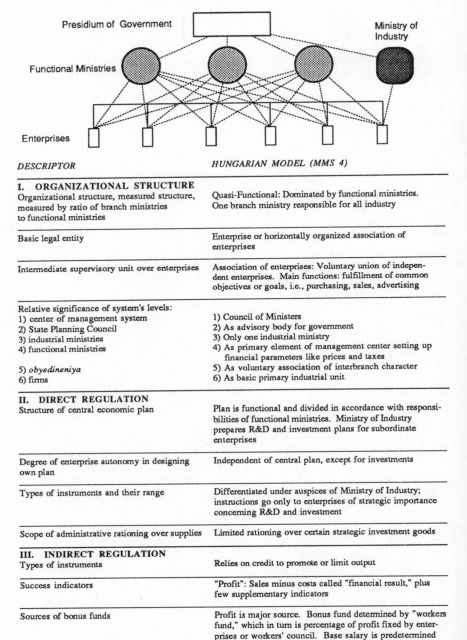

DESCRIPTOR	HUNGARIAN MODEL (MMS 4)
I. ORGANIZATIONAL STRUCTURE Organizational structure, measured structure, measured by ratio of branch ministries to functional ministries	Quasi-Functional: Dominated by functional ministries. One branch ministry responsible for all industry
Basic legal entity	Enterprise or horizontally organized association of enterprises
Intermediate supervisory unit over enterprises	Association of enterprises: Voluntary union of independent enterprises. Main functions: fulfillment of common objectives or goals, i.e., purchasing, sales, advertising
Relative significance of system's levels: 1) center of management system 2) State Planning Council 3) industrial ministries 4) functional ministries 5) obyedineniya 6) firms	1) Council of Ministers 2) As advisory body for government 3) Only one industrial ministry 4) As primary element of management center setting up financial parameters like prices and taxes 5) As voluntary association of interbranch character 6) As basic primary industrial unit
II. DIRECT REGULATION Structure of central economic plan	Plan is functional and divided in accordance with responsibilities of functional ministries. Ministry of Industry prepares R&D and investment plans for subordinate enterprises
Degree of enterprise autonomy in designing own plan	Independent of central plan, except for investments
Types of instruments and their range	Differentiated under auspices of Ministry of Industry; instructions go only to enterprises of strategic importance concerning R&D and investment
Scope of administrative rationing over supplies	Limited rationing over certain strategic investment goods
III. INDIRECT REGULATION Types of instruments	Relies on credit to promote or limit output
Success indicators	"Profit": Sales minus costs called "financial result," plus few supplementary indicators
Sources of bonus funds	Profit is major source. Bonus fund determined by "workers fund," which in turn is percentage of profit fixed by enterprises or workers' council. Base salary is predetermined
Degree and scope of control over wholesale prices	Dominant. Prices fixed by state on all goods and services in all sectors except some strategic investment where a "cost-plus-formula" is in force

Presidium of Government

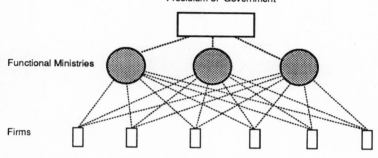

Functional Ministries

Firms

DESCRIPTOR	YUGOSLAV MODEL (MMS 5)
I. ORGANIZATIONAL STRUCTURE	
Organizational structure, measured structure, measured by ratio of branch ministries to functional ministries	Functional: Only functional ministries or decentralized territorial structure of management
Basic legal entity	Firm as part of enterprise represented by self-governing body
Intermediate supervisory unit over enterprises	No intermediate control units over enterprises
Relative significance of system's levels: 1) center of management system 2) State Planning Council 3) industrial ministries 4) functional ministries 5) *obyedineniya* 6) firms	1) Council of Ministers 2) As advisory body for government 3) Without importance 4) As primary element of management center. There exists: Ministry of Economy, Ministry of Market, Ministry of International Trade, etc. 5) None 6) As basic economic unit
II. DIRECT REGULATION	
Structure of central economic plan	Plan is exclusively functional and consists of large number of separate plans devoted to different functions, prepared by functional ministries and coordinated by Council of Ministers
Degree of enterprise autonomy in designing	Fully independent of central plan
Types of instruments and their range	No commands and no directives
Scope of administrative rationing over supplies	None. Auction mechanism
III. INDIRECT REGULATION	
Types of instruments	Relies on tariffs, R&D allowances and investment to promote or limit output
Success indicators	Net added value without supplementary indicators
Sources of bonus funds	Net value added of enterprise. Basic salary as well as bonus funds fully dependent on financial performance of enterprise. Value added divided by workers' or enterprise councils
Degree and scope of control over wholesale prices	Total. Prices fixed by state on all goods and services

7 CONTRACTUAL FORMS FOR INDUSTRIAL COOPERATION: NEW THINKING IN THE EAST... AND IN THE WEST?

John E. Parsons

New times demand new thinking. The Soviet Union and other socialist countries, having analyzed the experiences of the last two decades, are drawing fundamentally new conclusions regarding many issues in the international arena. Among the most provocative are those suggesting a change in business and corporate financial relations among firms in socialist and capitalist countries. Such new thinking has the capacity to alter fundamentally the basis of East-West economic relations. Future capitalist and socialist economic interaction depends in no small part on whether the West is up to the challenges these developments pose.

This paper outlines the logic of the socialist states' new thinking and its influence on their approach to business relations between East and West. My characterization of this logic leads to a fundamental question: How does the West evaluate its previous economic cooperation with the East? If the logic that led the socialist community to new thinking makes sense, then the West

The material in this paper is based in part on a series of research visits to the German Democratic Republic sponsored jointly by the Ministry of Higher Education in the GDR and the International Research and Exchanges Board (IREX) in the U.S. The author gratefully acknowledges the helpful discussions with my colleagues at the GDR Academy of Sciences, the Humboldt University of Berlin, the Institute for Politics and Economics, and the University of Economics.

must also reevaluate its earlier approaches to the issues. I argue that the West has not yet met this challenge, and I explain how it must adapt its thinking if it seeks broader economic cooperation. I illustrate this thesis with examples from the analyses made by academic economists, business representatives, and policymakers based on industrial cooperation agreements of the 1970s.

It is time for some new thinking in the West. A critical examination of western preconceptions and past errors is a prerequisite for developing a successful trade negotiating strategy. A correct and honest assessment of the socialist negotiating strategy and its logic is also essential. The capitalist states must recognize and eventually overcome their deep-rooted prejudices if they are to develop a fair strategy for negotiating acceptable contractual forms of industrial cooperation with the socialist states.

WHAT IS NEW IN THE NEW THINKING?

What is the nature of Mikhail Gorbachev's new thinking? The typical western response is that it recognizes the failure of the socialist model in general, and national economic planning in particular, to provide prosperity and economic growth comparable to the free market.

> If Gorbachev is to solve the Soviet Union's economic shortcomings, he *must* impose on the country a structural economic reform--or, as he calls it, "a profound transformation in the economy"--that will set free the Soviet Union's inventive, productive, and investment spirits. The implications of such a far-reaching reform are potentially very disruptive. For a starter, most proposals involve the abandonment of central planning. As Marx would have said, the central plan has become a fetter.[1]

This view is a fundamentally mistaken assessment of the thinking that motivates the socialist countries' new approach to economic relations. It is self-satisfying and underestimates or ignores the positive features of the plan and socialism. New thinking is a complicated synthesis of positive and negative experiences and lessons from socialism's history. It represents a basic questioning, which grew out of the confrontation between Marxism and the experiences of the last two decades, of particular dogma identified with socialism. Frank recognition of the successes and failures of socialism has resulted in a strategy for greater East-West interaction. The successes have

---

1. Marshall I. Goldman, "Gorbachev and Economic Reform," *Foreign Affairs*, vol. 64, pp. 56-73, Fall 1985, pp. 57-58 and 60.

confirmed in the minds of socialism's leaders certain aspects of their political and economic ideologies. The failures, on the other hand, have called attention to unrealized changes for which previous strategies were inappropriate.

In more concrete terms, history has confirmed two key tenets of socialist political economy with regard to international economic relations: (1) the importance and value of economic planning to general national welfare, and (2) the primacy of national economic independence for political self-determination and the importance of political self-determination for economic success. The socialist community of states has seen its basic commitment to planned economies confirmed. Socialist states have established planning's workability-- its ability to manage social and economic development and yield broad improvements in economic well-being--while avoiding such sources of social crises and conflict as unemployment, uneven development, and social divisions based on race and class. They also have witnessed their commitment to the integrity and sovereignty of their individual national economies and that of the socialist community as a cohesive unit. They long ago rejected the capitalist notion that individual states' prospects are tied to the profitability of individual corporations. Discussions with socialist economists give me the impression that while the particular interpretation or implementation of these two key principles is often hotly debated, the basic tenets are not widely questioned.

If these two principles represent a continuity in socialist political economy, then it is appropriate to question what is "new" in the thinking of the socialist community. First, in Marxist terminology defined by socialists, the objective material conditions under which these two principles must be implemented have changed. Two key changes are present, although only one is readily and publicly admitted by spokespersons in these countries: (1) technological development has made industrial production necessarily international in a qualitatively new sense, and (2) the relatively stable growth in the capitalist world since World War II and the development of an effective international trade and financial structure, combined with the relative failure of the socialist community to develop a competing form for a multilateral international economic system, have guaranteed an international trading and financial system that is similar to the present capitalist system.

Second, and again in Marxist terminology, the subjective conditions have changed. Dogmatic Marxist rejection of various forms of economic relations, and of key concepts developed under the hegemony of the neo-classical paradigm in the West, has given way to a more sophisticated differentiation and analysis of these concepts. Marxists and communist parties have traditionally fought any attempt to identify the social problems of capitalism with personal, technological, and juridical features of capitalism. This approach has been a central distinguishing characteristic of communists vis-à-vis other socialists and reformers of capitalism. However, since the Stalinist era, a dogmatic rejection of key economic forms and intellectual developments in the West has become a hallmark of economic theory in socialist states; this is changing.[2] While the exploitative nature of capital remains central to orthodox Marxist dogma, specific juridical forms of economic relations fall outside these ideological constraints.

Much of the dispute among western analysts regarding the likely direction and extent of the reforms revolves around each analyst's position vis-à-vis the continued commitment of socialist policymakers to the two ideals--planning and national economic sovereignty. Westerners who hope the current reforms and new thinking herald a recognition of socialism's failures and the market's virtues--and that they portend large-scale future movements toward market systems--fancy that policymakers do not maintain the serious commitment to these two principles that I claim does exist. These analysts do not recognize that these principles are not only an element of the political orthodoxy of these states--something to which various political leaders and intellectuals continue to cling for obvious reasons of personal interest--but are honestly maintained propositions. They do not recognize that these principles have been essentially confirmed by socialist economists. When other western analysts pronounce their deep skepticism about the future direction and magnitude of the reforms, it is because they understand these fundamental tenets are not under question, but they themselves cannot conceive of qualitative change *unless* these tenets are challenged. They ignore, however, the significance of the ideological developments borne out of a reassessment of the old dogmas within the framework that maintains a commitment to planning.

COMPENSATION AGREEMENTS: LESSONS FROM THE 1970s

East-West industrial cooperation was an exciting and important subject in the 1970s; any discussion of the current prospects for cooperation and trade is certain to look back to this period for lessons. One of the key new forms of

---

2. The principle behind this abandonment of dogma is stated in Leonid Abalkin, "A Creative Approach to Developing the Political Economy of Socialism," *World Marxist Review,* vol. 29, pp. 80-88, 1986; one example of its consequences appears in Gerhard Grote and Horst Kuhn, "Komparative Vorteile und ihre Ausnutzung im Aussenhandel sozialitischer Länder," *Wirtschaftswissenschaft,* 34:1138-1156, 1986. (Comparative Advantages and Their Application in the Foreign Trade of Socialist Nations.)

economic relations between socialist and capitalist firms developed during détente was the industrial compensation agreement. This form of agreement allowed socialist firms to purchase large-scale capital equipment--whole plants and machinery--from western firms, and the western companies agreed to long-term purchases of the products manufactured or processed by the socialist buyer. An important feature of this form of industrial cooperation was its integrative character--a chain of production from raw materials to finished or intermediary goods. It required planned and tightly coordinated production at each stage, but could not admit to coordination arranged exclusively by market signals.

De facto coordination of economic decisions inevitably arises when large-scale purchases of raw materials, consumer goods, or light manufactures occur repeatedly between socialist and capitalist states. However, the character of cooperation and integration engendered by industrial compensation agreements is qualitatively higher than that engendered by the simple repeated sales of goods characteristic of East-West trade prior to the late 1960s and 1970s. Industrial compensation agreements differ because they require long-term organization of closely related and strategically significant industrial operations across political, ideological, and economic boundaries.[3]

Industrial compensation agreements are important to study for a second reason. During the 1970s, several socialist countries experimented with different forms of economic cooperation with western firms and states. Industrial compensation agreements were, however, perhaps the only new and significant form for financing and organizing large-scale industrial cooperation advocated by every socialist state. For example, an industrial compensation agreement was one component in the long-term cooperative effort of the Council of Mutual Economic Assistance (CMEA) countries to modernize and restructure their chemical industries.[4] Thus, the industrial compensation agreement had a degree of centrality, acceptance or institutionalization, and significance that exceeded other forms with which all parties experimented in those years.

Compensation agreements are a peculiar form of contract. They do not conform to the traditional sale agreement of capital equipment in which the equipment is delivered and payment is made--presumably via traditional loan financing arrangements. In a compensation agreement, the seller of the capital equipment has a long-term stake in the project because the seller is obligated to purchase and somehow market a portion of the products manufactured at the

3. Sergei Ponomarev, "Compensation-Based Cooperation and the Western Countertrade Concept," *Foreign Trade of the USSR*, vol. 11, pp. 28-32, 1983.

4. *East-West Trade in Chemicals*, OECD, Paris, 1980.

new factory. But a compensation agreement is not a direct equity investment, either. In a direct equity investment, the suppliers of the capital equipment would have a stake in ensuring that the plant operated efficiently, and they would earn a corresponding profit or suffer a loss according to how well the plant operated and how well the products sold. On the other hand, in a compensation agreement, the operator of the plant--the socialist firm--bears the full cost of operation and earns the profits. In the field of corporate finance and investment banking, a compensation agreement is one of a wide range of special or peculiar project financing arrangements that are sometimes referred to as "left-handed financing."

"Peculiar" is not meant, however, to be pejorative. In this case, it might be best to reword the description to say that a compensation contract is "custom tailored"; it is the appropriate financing package for particular situations. There are a number of market environments in which certain market imperfections require such custom-tailored packages to provide incentives for efficiency from all parties. One problem, well known to economists as the "the lemons problem," arises when the seller of the plant and equipment has superior information regarding the quality and/or future value of the commodity to be produced in the plant. In this case, sellers of the plant and equipment are willing to purchase a large quantity of the plant's output to demonstrate their confidence that the delivered equipment will produce high quality or highly valued products. The buyer of the plant and equipment can then accede to paying a high price for the plant and equipment. Had the seller demanded the more traditional sale contract, the buyer would have demanded a discount on the basis of the suppliers' lack of willingness to stand behind their product. The compensation agreement, then, offers advantages to both sides: Buyers receive high quality plant and equipment, and sellers receive a higher price for their equipment corresponding to its quality. Several similar situations would warrant the use of a compensation contract over any other form of financing. The importance of these considerations has been documented repeatedly.[5]

THE SOCIALIST PERCEPTION

How did socialist economists view the compensation contracts of the 1970s? Why were compensation contracts considered an acceptable form of cooperation

5. John E. Parsons, "A Theory of Countertrade Financing of International Business," *Sloan School of Management Working Paper, #1632-85*; John E. Parsons, "Forms of GDR Economic Cooperation with the Non-Socialist World," *Comparative Economic Studies*, vol. 29, Summer 1987; Rolf Mirus and Bernard Yeung, "Economic Incentives for Countertrade," *Mimeo*, May 1985.

while other forms of contracts and financing were not widely accepted? What does the socialist conception of compensation contracts tell us about the likely future openness of socialist economists, business representatives, and policymakers to alternative forms of arranging cooperative ventures?

Most western accounts of the socialist countries' use of countertrade policies in general, and compensation agreements in particular, assert that these policies conform to the emphasis in socialist countries on industrial production and long-term planning of supply and demand. They also view these policies as a consequence of the socialist companies' inflexibility and their failure to accept the rigors of "true" supply and demand for the products manufactured with the newly purchased capital goods. These assertions are generally meant to argue that this "deficient" form of contract stems logically from their "deficient" understanding of economics. There is some truth to this idea, but it is wrapped in a bundle of false arguments.

The acceptability of this disposition is challenged by my argument above: The compensation contract, far from being a "deficient" form of industrial cooperation, is the "efficient" form, custom-tailored to provide the best incentives to all parties. Socialist economists have identified compensation contracts as useful for the purpose that I already outlined. They have argued long and hard, and generally correctly, against western assertions that this contract form was inefficient.

There is, however, a kernel of truth to the common western description of the socialist acceptance of compensation contracts as essentially related to the broader ideological character of socialist political economy. The socialist acceptance and promotion of compensation contracts as a form of industrial cooperation did not follow from an analysis of various juridical forms of cooperation and their incentive characteristics. Systematic analytic modeling of incentives is extremely backward and not very widespread in socialist states. A survey of the economic literature in the German Democratic Republic shows, for example, that virtually no other form of contract has been given serious attention, and certainly the incentive properties of alternative forms of contracts have never been the central focus of discussion. One can see the narrowness of thinking regarding alternative forms of juridical contracts for organizing the financing of cooperative capital projects in the regulations governing joint large-scale capital projects of this CMEA country. The only acceptable form is equity ownership by the host country and repayment of capital contributions with interest for all other participants. The restrictions on the forms of CMEA cooperation are not merely a result of the practical problems of organizing an international agreement. In the German Democratic Republic, alternative forms are not even broadly debated or entertained by academic specialists involved in the field.[6] Even today, the joint venture is the only new form of business contract between socialist and capitalist firms the Soviet Union is explicitly considering.[7]

How, then, did socialist states come to endorse compensation contracts and articulate correctly their valuable features? The socialist acceptance and endorsement of industrial cooperation stemmed from three factors that converged during the years of détente and the expansion of East-West trade.

1. The objective basis for industrial cooperation was large and demanding of complex forms of coordinated operations.
2. Compensation contracts are, in fact, an appropriate form of contract, especially for capital projects focused on the processing of natural resources, a sector on which the socialist countries were interested in concentrating and for which the basis for trade was great.
3. As western authors have stressed, compensation contracts "fit with," or at least did not patently contradict, the reigning ideological conception of socialist planning and proper forms of cooperation with the West.

The objective opportunities for trade and the objective need for industrial cooperation forced socialist states to consider new forms of cooperation. The compensation contract accommodated the objective conditions and did not require too serious an adaptation of unacceptable ideological structures.

THE WESTERN PERCEPTION

The western perception of compensation agreements has been the hostage of the ideological misconception and narrowness with which we approach the subject of socialist economies and East-West economic relations. It is ironic that a form of financing large-scale capital projects, which appears perfectly rational when viewed from the framework of abstract western economic theory, is analyzed in a prejudicial and irrational fashion because it is the focus of East-

---

6. Of course, there are differences among the socialist countries in this regard. The Soviet Union is currently actively advocating joint ventures among socialist firms and has succeeded in incorporating the principle of "direct relations" among firms in different socialist countries in the most recent communique concluding the meeting of ministers of CMEA countries. The GDR, on the other hand, while signing the communique, is stonewalling any actual development of "direct relations" involving contractual or formal obligations such as those which are the subject of this paper.

7. Vladimir Kamentsev, "Restructuring the USSR: External Economic Aspect," *World Marxist Review*, vol. 30, pp. 89-96, 1987.

West trade and is therefore summarily denounced and dismissed. The following incorrect accusations have been made in typical western analyses of the subject.

1. A compensation agreement is an inherently cumbersome form of financing trade and industrial cooperation because it conforms to the inflexibility of planning and is imposed on the more innovative and flexible western firm seeking to trade with a socialist country.
2. A compensation agreement is a bureaucratic solution to the deficiencies of planned economies and backward management techniques. It is an attempt to push low-quality goods on western markets, or is a means by which socialist management can bring western management into the process of ensuring the quality of goods produced in socialist countries. Western management has an interest in the operation, and a legal foundation for participating in operating decisions, because it must purchase the products. The compensation contract, then, is a means by which the socialist firm is able to shift or sell the risk of marketing to the better-equipped western firm.
3. Socialist countries demand compensation contracts because they want to force a bilateral balancing of trade on their western partners.
4. Socialist countries prefer compensation contracts because they believe the fallacy that the agreement is a means through which they can save on scarce foreign exchange when purchasing large-scale capital equipment.[8]

While each of these accusations may be valid--in the right context, and with the correct qualifiers--it would be fair to assert that they do not accurately characterize the important role a properly designed compensation agreement can serve, and they reflect instead the prejudicial views of western analysts toward nearly every legal, administrative, or policy device used by a socialist firm or economy. The accusations are wrong. We are not studying the problem with an open mind. Recent studies have established the unique role of compensation contracts, but the common view continues to focus on the presumed irrational motivations for their use by socialist states.

---

8. A good example of the strikingly polemical character of the discussion is given by Philip Beckerman of Philip Brothers, Inc. in a statement issued to the *Journal of Comparative Business and Capital Market Law*, vol. 5, pp. 407-408, 1985: "For the past four years U.S. multinational corporations have been forced to consider a group of trade methods which fall under the rubric of 'countertrade.' Although these practices have been utilized outside the U.S. for many years, many U.S. corporations believe the relationship between buyer and seller should be symbiotic, whereas countertrade assumes a parasitic posture in favor of the buyer."

PROBLEMS WITH COMPENSATION CONTRACTS IN THE 1970s

The problems the West encountered during experiments with compensation contracts in the 1970s stemmed from the great differences in the way capitalist and socialist states managed and regulated their respective economies. These fundamental differences led to conflicts regarding the sets of obligations and commitments acceptable in most forms of long-term industrial cooperation agreements.

The most well known compensation agreement involved the large flow of chemicals from East Europe, chemicals that were produced in western built factories and contracted for delivery to West Europe.[9] The contracts were written with reasonable expectations that the contracted supplies would be needed by the western buyers. As it turned out, over the course of the contract period, West Europe experienced an oversupply of the same chemicals and had to close several plants, which cost many workers their jobs. Many persons, therefore, advocated cancelling the obligations to purchase the products and denounced the initial decision to organize the compensation agreements. Of course, it is possible to play down this debate as just the inevitable wrangling that follows the disappointing performance of a project on which any two parties, be they socialist or capitalist, embark. *Caveat emptor* is certainly an important principle to remember. When the western suppliers of the capital equipment agreed to the buyback of the chemicals, they knew their obligations and the potential for a weakening market for chemicals. However, to dismiss the larger problem in this way would be incorrect. The policies available to the West European governments to influence the future performances of their economies were constrained or modified by the existence of contracts with firms operating in the socialist countries. Government policymakers have the right to exercise various policy controls to affect aggregate demand, employment policies, industrial development, and, in socialist countries, to adjust the planned operation of a given firm and its commitments to other firms. Capitalist and socialist states, however, using different controls and policies, have made different choices regarding acceptable tradeoffs. Any industrial compensation agreement must impose a set of obligations on both parties; how the obligations are to be interpreted and incorporated into different systems will remain a troubling issue, an issue to which little careful attention has been given.

9. "Are East-Bloc Buybacks Worth the Price?" *Chemical Week*, 8 November 1978, pp. 29-34; "Countertrade in Chemicals," *Chemical and Engineering News*, 14 August 1978, pp. 32-44.

This problem is similar to that caused by the international capitalist economy transcending the borders of any single capitalist state. It is difficult and inefficient to adhere to different national monetary and fiscal policies and regulations. The fact that political and economic systems involved in East-West trade are so disparate intensifies the problem. A confrontation among industries that operate within distinct social systems--with different forms of economic regulations and responses to changing economic circumstances--means that policies in one country may conflict with those in the other, or that a contract written between partners cannot define like obligations given conflicting regulatory systems. Firms in socialist countries will seek greater levels of commitment than western firms are used to offering, or can reasonably offer, given a regulatory system that expects the individual firm to weather adverse conditions. Firms in socialist countries will be less willing than their capitalist counterparts to permit the labor market to absorb the costs of adjustments in operating decisions to new conditions .

Although this problem became apparent in the compensation agreements during the 1970s, it is not a problem with compensation contracts per se; it is a problem with any form of cooperation in which large-scale industrial processes are coordinated across ideological boundaries, and will arise with any contract form. Individual states must develop a *modus operandi* for the impact of national prerogatives and systems on projects of intersystem industrial cooperation. The socialist states have recognized that this *modus operandi* cannot be what they sought ten, twenty, or thirty years ago; they have realized that it will incorporate many features basic to the capitalist financial system. They seem prepared to enter into negotiations on a new compromise. But westerners will be fooling themselves if they believe any new agreement will be on their terms alone. They will be fooling themselves if they expect the framework for East-West industrial cooperation agreements to mirror that of economic cooperation agreements among capitalist economies. The West must identify those elements of a planned economy it can accept within the framework of any industrial cooperation agreement.

The capitalist states, then, cannot view this problem from an exclusively western perspective. They will, of course, legitimately attempt to assert their own notion of the proper regulatory environment in economic negotiations. As long as the capitalist states recognize they are negotiating, and do not fool themselves into believing they are championing the only framework for an agreement (as I claim they did in their response to the socialist advocacy of compensation agreements), the negotiations can proceed rationally and fruitfully. But if those negotiating on behalf of the capitalist states limit themselves by imagining theirs is the "correct" form of regulation, whereas the socialist conception is "irrational," they will obstruct the negotiations as they have done with the compensation and countertrade forms of organization.

NEW FORMS OF ECONOMIC COOPERATION

Compensation contracts are a specialized form of economic cooperation or financing arrangement for industrial projects, custom-tailored to resolve a specific market problem. Other forms of contracts are necessary to accommodate other problems and to provide the proper incentives and efficiencies for other situations. Joint ventures are also a limited form of relationship. Westerners tend to view joint ventures as political compromises when direct equity investments would be optimal. While this was certainly true of past East-West joint ventures--and also explains the Soviet Union's restrictions on cooperation with western firms, remember that joint ventures are a common form of corporate structure, even within the boundaries of a single capitalist state. Joint ventures are one example in a long list of juridical patterns of financial liabilities; each form, it should be repeated, is appropriate to a particular circumstance.

How open will all parties be to the development of sophisticated contractual forms for arranging the obligations in an industrial cooperation project? Our earlier discussion of the approach of socialist economists toward compensation contracts and the character of new thinking in socialist countries can help us discern those areas in which the new openness to economic cooperation is likely to be great. It can also clarify whether we should anticipate obstacles to significant progress in expanding economic relations. My conclusions about the impact of new thinking on increased economic cooperation are the following: (1) there will be large obstacles and little imagination or flexibility in the short term, and (2) the intellectual obstacles will, in the medium term, be overcome. The socialist states, as I mentioned above, do not yet show any appreciation of the logic behind various forms of economic cooperation. Analysis of incentives and economic calculus remains very poor, but the socialist states are committed to changing that, and some changes are already visible. Their acceptance of new forms of cooperation results from their acknowledgement that something must be done, that agreements with the West cannot be all bad, and that somehow the struggle between the two social systems must be conducted in a world that allows these forms of cooperation, if only because they have been forced upon the socialist community. They have not yet identified the ideological conception that incorporates an understanding of the rational kernel behind these forms of cooperation into an orthodox Marxist analysis of exploitation. Nevertheless, there is broad consensus that this must change, that these forms cannot be the essential problem, and that they do not conflict with Marxism, even orthodox Marxism.

One must ask the same frank question of westerners as well. To what extent will we approach the new openness as an opportunity to push the narrow view of what economic cooperation means (that is, direct investment by U.S. multinationals on terms they are familiar with in the United States)? To what extent will the capitalist states respond to the problem, abandon their prejudices, and analyze the ingredients for cooperation more objectively? If they did not learn some lessons from the limitations in their own approach, which was clear in the 1970s, then they will contribute to the frustration. I fear that they will be in a poor position to design a set of feasible objectives that serve their own interests, as well as a strategy to implement them. Some new thinking is also needed from the West.

8 GORBACHEV'S REFORMS AND EAST EUROPE

Michael Kraus

In principle, all socialist countries are in one way or another going through the process of searching for renewal and profound transformations. But each country, that is its leadership and its people, decides independently what scope, scale, forms, rates, and methods these transformations should have.
--Mikhail Gorbachev

We may have affairs with the West, but we sleep with the Soviet Union. This is not a matter of ideology, it is a matter of economic necessity.
--A Polish Journalist

In a broad sense, the role of East Europe in Gorbachev's reform program is inseparable from the role the region plays in Soviet policy in general. That is to say, East Europe--comprising Bulgaria, Czechoslovakia, the German Democratic Republic, Hungary, Poland, and Romania--has been the mainstay of the Soviet-led economic and military alliance system for forty years. Along these lines, Soviet reforms and Moscow's new thinking have opened up a whole host of issues that bear on ideological, political, economic, and security

Research for this paper was facilitated by grants from the Joint Committee on Eastern Europe of the American Council of Learned Societies and the Social Science Research Council and from the United States Department of State under Title VIII awarded by the Hoover Institution, Stanford University. The author would like to thank Joe Brada for comments on an earlier version of this chapter.

questions.[1] Because it is beyond the scope of this paper to address the four dimensional subject in full, the comments below concentrate on two dimensions only, the political and the economic, touching on the others only parenthetically. The first part of the paper attempts to reconstruct Soviet economic objectives in East Europe; the second outlines the impact of Gorbachev's policies to date, and the third points to future prospects for *perestroika* in the region.

SOVIET REFORM OBJECTIVES IN EAST EUROPE

In the 1980s, economic issues have come to dominate the Soviet-East European policy agenda. This trend reflects four overlapping concerns on the part of Moscow. Briefly, they are the following: first, the opportunity costs of Soviet subsidies to East Europe; second, the quality of East European machinery and goods imported by the Soviet Union; third the relationship between East European economic performance, political stability, and bloc cohesion; and fourth, the nexus between economic performance and the requirements of Warsaw Pact military planners.

Because these concerns shape the parameters of Moscow's prescriptions for East Europe, each deserves a separate, if brief, discussion. In the 1980s, East Europe, like the Soviet Union, has experienced a long-term decline in economic growth (see Table 8-1). Unfavorable facets of the current situation range from the low productivity of labor in the Council of Mutual Economic Assistance (CMEA), which is about a third less than that of the advanced industrial countries, to East Europe's debt to both the Soviet Union and the West: the latter debt exceeds 70 billion dollars in 1988.[2] There is no need here to recite the familiar litany of the underlying reasons for the patterns of these developments. Suffice it to say that while external factors have influenced the economic slowdown, the fundamental causes are internal to the region, rooted as they are in the systemic defects of command planning. To that extent, of course, East Europe shares the symptoms of the Soviet disease. But the converse also holds true. As far as Moscow is concerned, Soviet reforms,

1. For the best informed studies assessing the state of the Soviet bloc economies, see *East European Economies: Slow Growth in the 1980s*, vols. 1-3, Selected Papers, Joint Economic Committee of the U.S. Congress (Washington, DC: U.S. Government Printing Office, 1985-1986). Also see the chapters by Odom and Jermakowicz in this volume for a discussion of the aims and methods of reforms.

2. Abram Bergson, "Comparative Productivity: The USSR, Eastern Europe, and the West," *American Economic Review*, June 1987.

Table 8-1. Real Gross National Product Growth
(In Constant Prices)

Average Annual Rate of Growth

	1961-65[a]	66-70[a]	71-75[a]	76-80[a]	81-85[b]	81[a]	82[a]	83[a]	84[a]	85[b]	81[b, c]
E. Europe	3.9	3.8	4.9	1.9	1.2	-1.0	0.9	1.8	3.3	0.6	2.7
Bulgaria	6.4	5.1	4.7	1.0	0.9	2.7	3.2	-1.8	2.9	-3.3	2.2
Czech.	2.4	3.4	3.4	2.2	1.4	-0.5	2.0	1.5	2.7	0.4	1.5
GDR	2.9	3.1	3.5	2.3	1.7	2.0	-0.4	1.8	3.2	2.3	2.0
Hungary	3.9	3.0	3.3	2.0	0.9	0.7	3.7	-1.0	2.7	-2.5	1.4
Poland	4.5	4.0	6.5	0.7	1.2	-5.3	-1.0	4.9	3.4	1.1	2.9
Romania	5.4	4.9	6.7	3.9	2.0	0.2	2.6	0.0	4.6	0.9	5.7

a. CIA Directorate of Intelligence, *Handbook of Statistics* (Washington, DC: U.S. Government, 1986).
b. L.W. International Financial Research, Research Project on National Income in East Central Europe, Occasional Paper no. 95, tables 1-61, 16-71 (New York, 1987).
c. Preliminary figures.

insofar as they address the common ailments of "developed socialism"--and with some particular variations on the general theme--point to the future direction for East Europe as well.[3]

In this connection, one motivating factor for change in East Europe is Moscow's effort to reduce implicit subsidies to East Europe, which are imbedded in the structure of Soviet-East European trade. East Europeans import primary materials, especially energy, and export to the Soviet Union their machinery and other manufactured goods. The subsidy is largely a function of the underpricing of Soviet energy and raw material exports--via a CMEA formula--to East Europe relative to the world market prices of these goods, on the one hand, and of the overpricing of the East European manufactures. The oft-cited study by Marrese and Vanous estimated that between 1970 and 1984, the Soviet subsidy reached about $110 billion in 1984 dollars.[4] Though other research indicate that this estimate is on the high side, most western specialists agree that in the last fifteen years Soviet economic

3. See O. Bogomolov, "Sotsialisticheskii mir na perelomnom etape, "*Mezhdunarodnaya zhizn*, 1987, no, 11, pp. 3-14.
4. Michael Marrese and Jan Vanous, *Soviet Subsidization of Trade with Eastern Europe* (Institute of International Studies, University of California, Berkeley, 1983).

ties with East Europe have become costly.[5] The strange thing is that Soviet economic ties have become--some would argue that they have been all along-- costly to East Europe as well. Among other things, this has to do with the adverse trends in East European terms of trade with the Soviet Union, namely the rising price of Soviet fuels. One graphic way of putting it is to say that for the same quantity of goods imported from the USSR in 1985, East Europe had to deliver to Moscow twice the amount of goods compared to 1970.[6] More recently, however, as the world price of oil declined in 1986-1987, so did the Soviet subsidy, while East European terms of trade improved somewhat.

Moscow's second concern has to do with the quality of the East European imports, more specifically the low quality of East European machinery and manufactured goods. It is worth noting in this context that East Europe accounts for more than half the value of Soviet trade--62 percent in 1987--(see Table 8-2 for a country by country breakdown), and that the share of foreign trade in Soviet national income is roughly 10 percent. Unlike oil, which is the major earner of Soviet hard currency, East European machinery imported by the Soviet Union is generally unmarketable in the West. While the CMEA countries prefer to sell their best machinery to the West for hard currency, in the 1980s Moscow has stated its unwillingness to serve as a dumping ground for substandard products. Given that East European machinery plays an important role in Soviet modernization strategy, Moscow's hard-nosed attitude about the quality of CMEA imports is here to stay.

Third, there appears to be growing Soviet recognition that economic performance is closely tied to political stability within the alliance and to bloc cohesion. Beginning in the early 1980s, several Soviet analysts have argued that the economic slowdown must be reversed, lest it cause "crises situations."[7] In this connection, one must single out the impact of the 1980-1981 Polish crisis on Soviet new thinking. There is little doubt that Solidarity's sixteen months, or what Soviet commentators called "the dual power" in Poland, influenced Soviet thinking about "crises situations" in socialist systems, inclu- ding their own. To put it in other words, when the history of the intellectual

5. For a discussion of the various estimates and issues involved, see Keith Crane, *The Soviet Economic Dilemma of Eastern Europe*, Rand Report, R-3368-AF, May 1986. For a dissenting view see Paul Marer and Kazimierz Z. Poznanski, "Costs of Domination, Benefits of Subordination," *The Dominant Powers and Subordinate States: The United States in Latin America and the Soviet Union in Eastern Europe*, ed. Jan F. Triska (Durham: Duke University Press, 1986), pp. 383-399.

6. See Jan Vanous, "East European Economic Slowdown," *Problems of Communism*, July- August 1982, p. 5. The figure for 1985 is Vanous's estimate.

7. For a thorough discussion of a wider set of issues involved, see Ernst Kux, "Contradictions in Soviet Socialism," *Problems of Communism*, November-December 1984.

Table 8-2. *Soviet Trade with CMEA*
(Billion Rubles)

	1970	1980	1985
Bulgaria	1.8	7.1	12.5
Hungary	1.5	5.7	9.4
Vietnam	0.2	0.6	1.5
GDR	3.3	9.2	15.2
Cuba	1.0	4.3	8.0
Mongolia	0.2	0.9	1.5
Poland	2.4	8.0	12.0
Romania	0.9	2.8	4.2
Czechoslovakia	2.2	7.2	13.4
Total	13.5	45.8	77.7

Source: *Ekonomicheskaya gazeta,* no. 45, 1986.

origins of Gorbachev's reforms is written, Solidarity will have its own chapter.

Finally, the fourth reason for Moscow's quest for change in East Europe relates to declining economic growth rates as an impediment to the modernization of the Warsaw Pact. On this score, clues to Soviet discomfort in the 1980s can be gleaned from a series of commentaries by East European economists and military strategists, whose common themes are the countervailing requirements of domestic prosperity and alliance burden-sharing.[8] Given the likelihood of low East European growth in the next few years, Moscow will find it difficult to extract higher rates of defense spending from its allies.[9]

RESTRUCTURING THE CMEA

While the foregoing considerations had shaped Soviet-East European economic ties even before Gorbachev's ascendancy, they have received renewed attention since 1985. Moscow has advocated a closer coordination of five-year plans of the CMEA members, the development of long-term bilateral specialization

8. See Michael Kraus, "Czechoslovakia and the Soviet Bloc: From Stalin to Gorbachev," *The Political Economy of Bloc Cohesion,* eds. Cyril Black and Kenneth Oye, forthcoming.

9. Keith Crane, *Military Spending in Eastern Europe,* Rand Report, R-3444-USDP, May 1987.

agreements between the Soviet Union and the East European countries, and joint efforts in research and development. These objectives are being facilitated by changes concerning Soviet foreign economic relations. The decentralization of the export-import decisions of more than twenty ministries and seventy major associations is being supervised by the new State Commission on Foreign Economic Relations. "Measures to Perfect the Direction of Economic and Scientific-Technical Cooperation in Socialist Countries" were enacted in 1986, giving Soviet enterprises the right to choose their socialist trading partners, set prices, and conclude contracts and production cooperation agreements. Though by the end of 1987, over 700 intergovernmental agreements were signed between Moscow and European CMEA partners to encourage the establishment of "direct ties," only 500 of nearly 40,000 Soviet enterprises established direct links with East European firms.[10]

Seeking to broaden cooperation in production, science and technology, the Soviets (and their CMEA counterparts) have also enacted new legislation on joint ventures with (capitalist and) socialist partners. Although interest in joint East-West and East-East ventures in the CMEA is considerable, so are the obstacles. While twenty-eight joint ventures with socialist partners were under consideration by November 1987, only 4 had been created, and letters of intent had been signed to establish 8 others.[11] As a result, Soviet officials were quick to express their disappointment with the slow pace of developments for "direct ties" in intra-CMEA relations.[12] Because the non-convertibility of local currencies had long been regarded as one of the key barriers to integration in CMEA, Soviet recognition in 1987 that direct ties between the enterprises can be effective only if the bloc creates a convertible currency represented a conceptual breakthrough of sorts.[13]

On the face of it, the performance of the CMEA can be no better than that of its individual members. But in fact, it is worse because the CMEA system actually hinders economic advancement. That the CMEA governments have come to share this conclusion is a measure of a substantial change in official attitudes since 1985. While common reform goals for the coming years include reducing the bureaucratic impediments to socialist integration, such as

10. Ivan Ivanov, "Restructuring the Mechanism of Foreign Economic Relations in the USSR," *Soviet Economy*, 1987, vol. 3, no. 3, p. 207; Jackson Diehl, "Kremlin Decides It Can Learn From Its Allies," *Washington Post*, 13 October 1987.

11. Ivanov, p. 209.

12. For example, see *Foreign Broadcast Information Service*, USSR, no. 67, 18 April 1987; see also "Convertible Rouble: What Will the Economy Gain?" *Moscow News*, no. 37, 20-27 September 1987.

13. See the article by Oleg Bogomolov, influential director of the Institute on the Economics of the World Socialist Systems, in *Izvestiya*, 13 June 1987.

the size of the CMEA secretariat, enlarging the direct ties, and restructuring the financial system, there are disagreements about the more specific reform strategies.   In 1987, the new convertibility plan (proposed by Hungary) encountered opposition from Romania, which has consistently opposed many Moscow-initiated specialization programs, and the GDR, normally a loyal Soviet ally.   In this instance, the Romanian-East German coalition of foes of change was predicated on their common resistance to market-oriented solutions.[14]

There is little doubt that the restructuring of the CMEA exerts a powerful pull toward the realignment of all East European economies.   In the words of one Soviet Foreign Ministry official charged with CMEA affairs, "Now, with the reforms of the system, it will be very important to have coinciding economies in details: systems of prices, systems of wages, currency values."[15]

SOVIET POLICY AND EAST EUROPEAN RESPONSES

In the three years under Gorbachev, Soviet policy toward East Europe has been calibrated on a country by country basis, taking into account the widely different local political and economic circumstances.   And while a full discussion of the East European response to Soviet reforms--analyzing the mix of elements that favor or hinder the reform process on a country by country basis-- is beyond the scope of this study, an overview of the emergent trends is not.[16]

Poland and Hungary have been at the forefront of economic reform, though it remains to be seen whether or not the local leaderships have the political will and muscle to implement the reformist blueprints.   And while Warsaw has kept ahead of Moscow in both openness and restructuring, Budapest, which in the past probed the limits of Soviet tolerance, has, more recently, experienced a loss of reformist vigor and stagnating living standards.   Paradoxically, at a time when the Soviets openly acknowledge their learning from the Hungarian reforms, some western specialists warn that "the economic and social situation

14. See Vladimir Sobell, "Convertibility in the CMEA: The Long Road Ahead," Radio Free Europe, Background Report/208, 5 November 1987.

15. Jackson Diehl, "Soviet Leadership Decides to Imitate East Europeans' Economic Recipe," *Washington Post*, 13 October 1987.

16. See also Charles Gati, "Gorbachev and Eastern Europe," *Foreign Affairs*, Summer 1987; Michael Kraus, "Soviet Policy Toward East Europe," *Current History*, vol. 86, no. 523, November 1987; see also the country analyses in the same issue.

in Hungary has been bleak for the past decade and in quantitative terms the situation is approaching that which precipitated the Polish crisis."[17]

By 1987, Bulgaria and Czechoslovakia, the more reluctant reformers, had also embraced the principle of changing their economic mechanisms. The former, in fact, carried out a series of dizzying economic and administrative maneuvers that prompted Moscow before the year was over to advise Sofia to scale down the projected changes and slow down the implementation.[18] For the Gustav Husak regime in Czechoslovakia, which had taken shape under the anti-reformist ethos of "normalization," Gorbachev's adoption of reforms bearing many similarities to the Prague Spring proved to be an acute political embarrassment. But the opposite was also true. Prodded by Moscow, Husak promised to carry out the "most radical intervention in the economic mechanism" in forty years. By December 1987, that promise also happened to be the swan song for the first bloc leader replaced during the Gorbachev period. Ironically, Husak ended his nineteen years in power by reintroducing the previously taboo word *reform* into the Czech political vocabulary. His successor, Milos Jakes, despite his orthodox credentials, is likely to press harder for a much overdue economic restructuring.

For different reasons, the German Democratic Republic and Romania belong to the rejectionist front vis-à-vis *perestroika* and *glasnost*. East Berlin has argued--not without some foundation--that it has already "perfected the planning mechanism" and that, in any event, the GDR's sound economic performance preempts any need for changes in economic policy. That Moscow is receptive to this line of argument--as much as it recognizes the GDR's exposed security position--is evident in the absence of any Soviet criticism of East Berlin's censorship of Gorbachev's calls for "democratization." In the eyes of some western observers, initial Soviet steps toward a new economic strategy have had more in common with the GDR's "model"--which successfully adapted to technological change without any concessions in the political sphere--than they had with, for example, Hungary.[19] By contrast, the Romanian "model" appeals perhaps least of all to Romanians who experience first-hand harsh austerity measures, designed in part to repay the hard currency debt. Bucharest's

17. Josef Brada, "Soviet Reforms and East European Responses," paper prepared for the Eleventh U.S.-Hungarian Economic Roundtable, Indiana University, October 28-November 2, 1987.

18. Henry Kamm, "Bulgaria Parley Is Foretaste of a Scaling Down of Change," *New York Times*, 29 January 1988.

19. Philip Hanson, "The Shape of Gorbachev's Economic Reform," *Soviet Economy*, vol. 2, October-December 1986, 318, 322. For a balanced examination of the GDR's *Kombinate* system, see Thomas A. Baylis, "East Germany's Economic Model," *Current History*, vol. 86, no. 523, November 1987.

economic policy in the 1980s has been comprised of "a series of *ad hoc* emergency measures to deal with the short-term effects of essentially long-term problems" centering around energy and food supplies.[20] Recentralization and cuts in domestic consumption have gone hand in hand with workers' unrest--despite the increasing reliance on the use of the military to enforce Draconian rationing measures. Small wonder, then, that at the end of 1987, Romania's human rights record left Ceausescu's regime very much isolated within the Soviet bloc.

FUTURE PROSPECTS

Clearly, the program of Soviet domestic reform has legitimized and widened the scope of reforms in East Europe, strengthening the ranks of reform-oriented elements in the region in the process. But while there has been a notable change in attitudes toward the concept of a market-oriented reform, the implementation of such measures is likely to encounter a two-tiered barrier, upstairs and downstairs. Let us take the upstairs first. Historically, Soviet leadership successions have involved contending factions in the struggle over power and policy. Because the accompanying personnel turnover affects the existing Soviet-East European elite coalitions and because they entail both policy changes and a policy vacuum, leadership changes in Moscow have contributed to instability in East Europe. In that sense, the transition to Gorbachev has been managed effectively in terms of East Europe. Moreover, Moscow's domestic priorities have required quiet on the East European front, favoring leadership continuity. But there is little doubt that the Brezhnev holdovers in the East European capitals are ill-equipped to rally the masses under the banner of Gorbachev's *glasnost* and *perestroika*.

At the same time, the East European power cliques, much like the Brezhnev-entrenched Soviet elites, will resist adopting measures that would weaken their own hold on power, including openness and restructuring. But given that East European prospects are fraught with the twin hydras of poor economic performance and political instability, then Gorbachev--assuming he can maintain the reformist course--will have ample opportunities to replace the aging oligarchs within the bloc. Divisions in the local leadership over future

20. Alan H. Smith, "Romania: Internal Economic Development and Foreign Economic Relations," *The Economies of Eastern Europe and their Foreign Economic Relations*, ed. Philip Joseph (NATO Economics Directorate: Brussels, 1986), pp. 263-266; Ronald H. Linden, "Socialist Patrimonialism and the Global Economy: The Case of Romania," *International Organization*, vol. 40, no. 2, Spring 1986.

policy course at a time of political and economic change will give rise to contending factions, from which Moscow can help to choose the successor generation.[21]

In several respects, the downstairs in East Europe represents a far more uncertain prospect for Gorbachev. According to western specialists, beginning in the late 1960s, something of a tacit social compact came into being in East Europe. It entailed the trading of political rights and liberties in exchange for a range of socioeconomic benefits that include full employment, a relatively lax work ethic, and steadily rising living standards.[22] But in the course of Brezhnev's last decade, East Europe had learned to live with what local wits describe as the seven miracles of socialism:

1. Everybody has a job.
2. Though everybody has a job, nobody works.
3. Though nobody works, the plan is always fulfilled.
4. Though the plan is always fulfilled, there is nothing to buy.
5. Though there is nothing to buy, you can get what you need.
6. Though you can get what you need, everybody steals.
7. Though everybody steals, nothing is missing.

As in so many other areas, Gorbachev wants to eliminate the Brezhnev legacy that has engendered such attitudes, though the prescription for curing the malaise is potentially destabilizing. In Hungary, for example, the course of action now openly advocated and partly adopted calls for the rollback of food subsidies, the creation of income and value added taxes, and invoking the specter of bankruptcies and unemployment. In a sense, Gorbachev's new deal is the opposite of Brezhnev's old deal: more trade union participation, more self-management, elections to lower posts within the Party and without, cultural thaw, a freer press, greater tolerance for dissent in exchange for labor discipline, wages tied to performance, tough quality control, increasing wage differentials, and, at least in the short run, a declining standard of living for many. Thus, for large segments of the East European societies, Gorbachev's new deal is not an attractive prospect.

Clearly, the Brezhnev era had created its own social base in the Soviet Union and East Europe. And in many respects, the drive for reforms runs counter to the existing elite-mass linkages and power coalitions. In Poland, for

21. For a well-informed assessment of this issue in the context of United States policy, see William H. Luers, "The U.S. and Eastern Europe," *Foreign Affairs,* Summer 1987.

22. See, for example, Stephen White, "Economic Performance and Communist Legitimacy," *World Politics,* vol. XXXVIII, no. 3, April 1986, pp. 468-469.

example, those groupings that generally tend to favor reforms, like the non-Party intelligentsia and skilled workers, do not trust the government. By contrast, those groups that have tended to line up behind the government, including the non-skilled workers and the Party apparatus, oppose the reforms. The November 1987 defeat of the government-sponsored policy package in Poland--in an unprecedented public referendum--illustrates the political quandary of economic reform in today's East Europe. On the one had, the principle of a sound economy involves the introduction of a market-oriented reform and requires tough-fisted measures that would overcome the resistance of those groups whose interests are adversely affected. On the other hand, the principle of "democratization" requires that any fundamental or "radical" changes that redefine the social compact be subjected to consultation with the society. The recent Polish experience suggests that there is a good deal of tension between economic and political change currently contemplated.[23]

CONCLUSIONS

The underlying facts of East Europe's economic slowdown speak for themselves. To quote the conclusions of a recent study, ". . . because the East European countries have by and large exhausted the resources that could be mobilized from domestic, Soviet, or western sources under their Soviet-imposed economic and political system, they face not temporary but fundamental economic difficulties."[24] Because there is no obvious solution to this basic problem, the East European malaise is here to stay for the foreseeable future. But in the near term, even the reform-oriented East European allies face major dilemmas. Thus, if the current trends continue, it will make very little difference whether Hungary is the future of Poland or the other way around. For all the attention lavished on the Hungarian economic model, most Hungarians have experienced a steady erosion of living standards in the 1980s, with a proportion of those below the official poverty level approaching 40 percent.[25]

As we have seen, Soviet motivations for change in East Europe range from those having to do with narrow economic objectives, such as the reduction of the purported subsidy, to wider concerns about the very viability of the client regimes. Whether as a market for otherwise unmarketable goods, or as a

23. For additional evidence, see Michael Kraus, "L'Europe de L'Est a L'Heure de Gorbachev," *Politique Internationale*, no. 38, Winter 1987-1988.

24. Marer and Poznanski, "Costs of Domination, Benefits of Subordination."

25. Ivan Volgyes, "Hungary: Before the Storm Breaks," *Current History*, November 1987, p. 376.

supplier for otherwise unobtainable raw materials and energy, the Soviet Union's bargaining position vis-à-vis East Europe is formidable. At the same time, there are real limits to Soviet leverage, stemming from the overriding concern with stability within the alliance.

One of the ties that binds the Soviet-led alliance today links the fortunes of Soviet and East European reformists and conservatives. Already, Gorbachev's three years have legitimized and widened the scope of policy debate and reform in East Europe. If and when Soviet reforms gain momentum, their impact within the bloc is likely to grow. But, as Reszo Nyers, one of the architects of the Hungarian reform of 1968, has put it, "East European reform will be influenced by progress or setbacks of Soviet reform . . . . A setback will have a limiting impact. It will warn everybody to be more cautious."[26] Such caution was very much in evidence in the aftermath of the Yeltsin affair. Following his criticism of the slow pace of Soviet reforms, Boris Yeltsin, the leader of the Moscow Party organization and a candidate member of the Politburo, was dismissed in November 1987. Both the reform-minded and conservative elements within the bloc could view his ouster as a signal that even ardent supporters of Gorbachev's program in high places can be defeated and their policies emasculated.

But while change in East Europe will be influenced by the ebb and flow of Soviet domestic reforms, the converse also holds true. Undoubtedly, a failed economic reform in Hungary or Bulgaria would weaken the pro-reformist elements in the Soviet Union. That is why, for example, Soviet advocates of change have repeatedly praised the Hungarian model--despite the mounting evidence of problems. Along the same lines, in October 1987 Gorbachev reportedly cautioned Bulgaria's Todor Zhivkov against precipitous and radical reforms that would fundamentally change the relationship between the Party and society.[27] Though Gorbachev, too, seeks to redefine this relationship, he views the renewed Party as the agent of change "from above." In his conception, "socialist pluralism" recognizes the multiplicity of--often contradictory--interests in modern socialist society. "Democratization" entails making the Party more accountable and responsive to the diversity of such interests "from below." "We need *glasnost* as we need the air," Gorbachev points out.[28] Yet in "socialist pluralism" the accent remains decidedly on the "socialist": the Party must remain at the forefront of change. How Gorbachev expects to contain the contradictory and diverse impulses of Soviet society

26. *New York Times*, 5 January 1988.
27. Kamm, *New York Times*.
28. Mikhail Gorbachev, *Perestroika: New Thinking for Our Country and the World* (New York: Harper & Row, 1987), p. 78.

within the framework of one-party rule is unclear. But in the process of trying, he has taken the Soviet Union into uncharted territory.

Looking ahead, Gorbachev must be mindful of East European responses to earlier attempts at Soviet reforms. In each instance, internal Soviet reforms had unintended consequences within the bloc: Khrushchev's de-Stalinization campaign stimulated developments in Budapest that eventuated in the Soviet invasion of Hungary in 1956; and when the logic of the Kosygin-Liberman economic reforms was extended to the political sphere in 1968 Czechoslovakia--much along the same lines now advocated by Gorbachev--another Soviet intervention followed. Next to defining the limits of Soviet tolerance for diversity within the bloc, the events of 1956 and 1968 set back the clock of Soviet internal reform as well. Clearly concerned that *glasnost* and *perestroika* in the Soviet Union would generate demands for more radical change in East Europe, Gorbachev has hedged his advocacy of Party-sponsored change in the bloc with elements of continuity. His policy must weigh carefully the costs of the Brezhnev-like immobilism against the risks that precipitous change "from above" might stir uncontrollable forces demanding change "from below." In this sense, Gorbachev's dilemma is how to mobilize the East European populations to avert the systemic decline of the socialist camp without, simultaneously, raising the expectations of East Europeans beyond the capacity of the local power elites to satisfy or contain them.

Three years into the Gorbachev era, Moscow's policies toward East Europe have shown more flexibility and innovation than expected. Let us recall that as late as 1986, leading western specialists deemed the question "whether Gorbachev and his colleagues will tolerate, or even encourage, reforms within the East European systems" as "unanswerable."[29] In light of the foregoing evidence, it would appear that by 1987 Moscow had answered the question in the affirmative on both counts. And while Soviet policies have created a more conducive bloc environment for fundamental reforms in East Europe, the mix of factors that promote and constrain the reform process varies from country to country. The new questions center around three related issues: (1) the ability of the East European regimes to implement the emerging reformist blueprints, (2) the internal ramifications of such changes, and (3) the extent to which internal economic and political reforms in East European states will spill over into demands for a redefinition of their relationships with Moscow. On answers to these questions ride Gorbachev's prospects in East Europe.

---

29. Timothy Colton, *The Dilemma of Reform in the Soviet Union* (New York, 1986, revised and expanded edition), p. 213.

9 THE BAM AND PACIFIC DEVELOPMENT

Victor L. Mote

The convenors of this conference have charged that our focus is Mikhail Gorbachev's economic and social reforms and their potential impact on Soviet trade with the West. After three short years in office, Gorbachev's influence on the image of the Soviet Union has been nothing short of dramatic. This has included impact in the arena of regional development, where Soviet planners have always faced the dichotomous dilemma of whether to invest in the developed western or underdeveloped eastern and southern parts of their country. The aim of this paper is to examine the economic feasibility of the eastern alternative in terms of labor costs, infrastructural development, and environmental problems.

GORBACHEV, THE BAM, AND THE PACIFIC

Two of the hallmarks of communist ideology are civil and spatial equality. Without one there cannot be the other. In the utopian sense of true communism, human beings share equally in all resources, and all regions of the country advance equably with all others. As a condition that is one of "transition" to communism, socialism theoretically can, and does, have a certain measure of inequality, but its practitioners should never lose sight of the aspiration for equality. In this respect, the ideal plan for spatial

175

organization is "planned proportional development," whereby no area of the country lags economically behind any other.

Although obviously a pipe dream, planned proportional development subtly lurks in the shadows of Soviet regional planning and, on occasion, becomes more or less important depending on the administration in power. In light of his approach to the development of new frontiers in Siberia, Leonid Brezhnev evidently considered the ideal policy as costly but necessary. He invested heavily in assets that would have little immediate return in anticipation of long-term future benefits. One such asset was the Baikal-Amur Mainline railway (BAM) in the southern tier of East Siberia and the Soviet Far East.

A problem with the BAM and other geographically large projects is that they incorporate so many diverse resources and landscapes that they require a planning approach that is at odds with traditional Soviet methods. Such an approach should not only incorporate developmental factors (labor, infrastructure, and industry), but also environmental considerations. Soviet scientists and planners call this a program-oriented approach. It is a true regional or territorial planning method that simultaneously integrates the expertise and technologies of dozens of sciences and ministries in a thoroughly comprehensive, interministerial way. The program-oriented approach is, as western geographers are wont to say, an example of "holistic" planning.

The program-oriented approach to regional planning collides head-on with sectoral planning by ministries that pettily vie with one another for scarce revenues and projects. For years these ministries have indurated into pyramids of power that deal only vertically, rarely communicating with other pyramids on the horizon. This planning option has been called departmentalism. Even Brezhnev, and Khrushchev before him, recognized the hazards of this kind of mentality, but they failed to alter the course significantly. The fleeting administrations of Andropov and Chernenko had little chance to make significant changes.

Now Gorbachev has arrived on the scene with what can only be described as an intensive approach to the Soviet economy. Some claim that, in so doing, he has repudiated many of Brezhnev's Siberian development projects, including many major schemes within the BAM service area. This study indicates that, although Gorbachev's policies may be considered at least a temporary retreat to renovate industry in the western parts of the country, the long-term plans for the BAM and other projects may very well be right on target. Moreover, with long-time Siberianist Abel Aganbegyan as his chief economic advisor, Gorbachev has begun to lower the boom on departmentalism in regional planning.

In view of his putative anti-BAM stance, it may seem paradoxical that Gorbachev asserted in a key address in Vladivostok in the summer of 1986 that the Soviet Union is "also an Asian and Pacific country," to wit:

> It is aware of the complex problems of this vast region. It is directly contiguous to them. This is what determines the balanced and overall view of this giant part of the world with its mass of diverse nations and peoples. Our approach is based on the recognition and understanding of existing realities.[1]

Among those "existing realities" is the fact that the Soviet Union thus far has played only a very minor role in the Pacific Basin. True, the country's largest naval fleet is based in the Far East, which represents the country's most open and reasonably navigable coastline. True, there are more than fifty armed land divisions confronting the China border (but in the absence of "voluntary settlers," this is one way to fill a significant, potentially hostile gap in the country's defenses). Indeed, even with the developments associated with the BAM construction project, Pacific trade as a share of total Soviet foreign commerce declined slightly from 7.7 percent in 1970 to 7.4 percent in 1985. "This reflects the fact that trade with East Europe and the industrialized West has grown at a faster rate."[2] Gorbachev obviously would like to reverse this trend, but the only practical way to do this is to increase trade with Japan, and "if one disaggregates the Pacific Basin trade data and examines the growth of trade with socialist countries and Japan, it is clear that trade with the socialist states is continuing to grow, while trade with Japan is in decline."[3]

Geopolitically, Gorbachev and his comrades find themselves in Asia between the proverbial rock and a hard place. They know that if they are to experience any economic progress in the Pacific Basin they must "pacify" the region. Gorbachev has paid lip service to a possible compromise on the divisive Amur River boundary with China, a potential withdrawal of "substantial" numbers of troops from Mongolia (where there are five Soviet divisions), and an overall reduction of land forces on the China border to go along with the recent agreement signed in Geneva that will have Soviet troops out of Afghanistan by next year. A number of economic ties related primarily to fishing rights have been made with microstates in the South Pacific. The Politburo logically supports New Zealand's anti-nuclear stand, and it has

1. Mikhail S. Gorbachev, "For Peace, Security, and Cooperation in Asia and the Pacific," *Soviet Life Supplement*, October 1986, pp. i-v.
2. Michael Bradshaw, "Soviet Trade with the Pacific Basin: Toward the Year 2000," paper presented at the Annual Meeting of the Association of American Geographers, Portland, Oregon, 23 April 1987.
3. Ibid.

cajoled the new Aquino administration in the Philippines in hopes that the island state would put an end to U.S. military bases there. Simultaneously, in 1986 Soviet Foreign Minister Eduard Shevardnadze toured six states in Asia and the Pacific.

Clearly, Gorbachev's approach to the Pacific is more aggressive than that of many of his predecessors, and it has not gone unrewarded. In the fall of 1986, Soviet and Chinese foreign ministers met in New York, and border talks between the two countries resumed in February 1987. Even the Japanese were willing to resume negotiations over joint exploration of Sakhalin's oil and gas reserves, despite continuing difficulties over the status of the southern Kurile Islands. However, in light of geographic realities, all of these are minor successes.

In the Pacific, the Soviet Union is flanked by strategic "choke points." From the Bering Strait to the often ice-bound Sea of Okhotsk to the Soya, Tsuguru, and Korea straits, the massive Far Eastern fleet traditionally has been monitored with little difficulty by the defense networks of Japan and North America. Ironically, because of its geographic proximity, it was a Japanese conglomerate (Toshiba), not a North American one, that facilitated Soviet aspirations for quieter submarines. Yet, acknowledging Soviet difficulties of turning ideas and foreign imports of high technology into universal practical realities, even this major blunder should not seriously affect the balance of power in the Pacific.

THE QUESTION OF ECONOMIC FEASIBILITY

In July 1986, during his visit to the Soviet Far East, Gorbachev posited the question of a plan for the long-range comprehensive development of the eastern regions of the Soviet Union and later appended the subject to the agenda of the Politburo.[4] As summarized in a later report, "The goal of this program is the establishment of a highly efficient economic region complete with its own large-scale resource and industrial base, an optimized economic structure, and a developed social sphere that is organically tied to the domestic and international division of labor.[5] Nothing more was mentioned of this plan for over one year. In fact, skeptics felt that the BAM and Pacific development projects might be dead in the water under Gorbachev--at least temporarily.

After all, by middle 1985, after a decade of arduous labor under some of the worst imaginable working conditions, the cost of the BAM was estimated to

4. *Gudok*, 17 August 1986.
5. *Pravda*, 26 August 1987.

have surpassed 20 billion rubles,[6] which represented only two-thirds of the "short-range (to 1995)" investment in the service area. The remaining 10 billion-ruble short-range expenditures were to be absorbed in the following way: half would go to residential needs, 38 percent to the construction of new industries, and 12 percent for other purposes. These investments, allocated with few prospects for immediate return, must have been viewed by the pragmatic General Secretary with a bit of the jaundiced eye, especially in view of potential costs and benefits. Such would surely add insult to injury in a muddling economy, such as Gorbachev had inherited from his predecessors. Moreover, his known personal antipathy for Brezhnev must have prejudiced the new leader against many of the "Brezhnev projects," among which the BAM was the vanguard. In fact, not once during his five-day tour of the Soviet Far East in 1986 did Gorbachev publicly mention the BAM or its service area. This starkly contrasted to the uproar surrounding the project when Brezhnev visited the same areas in the late 1970s. Was Gorbachev discreetly shelving the project by sapping it of its financial resources?

Numerous scholars in the West seemed to think so, including the late Theodore Shabad, who keenly surmised from the early "catchwords" of Gorbachev's restructuring policy that the leader might be turning away from Siberian development except in Western Siberia. After all, didn't "intensification" signify more effective use of existing plans and equipment? Wouldn't emphasis on "scientific and technological progress" bring investment to Moscow, Leningrad, and other big cities of the Western Soviet Union? Modernization, by definition, implies a preexisting factory or plant, thus eliminating the possibility of building one from scratch. And, finally, the criterion of "savings of energy and resources" clearly emphasizes the need for conservation of old, already discovered raw materials, not the exploitation of new ones.

But the worst was yet to come for the BAM and its development. Somewhere lurking in one of the State Planning Committee's (GOSPLAN) inscrutable filing cabinets (inscrutable at least to western scholars like us), there must have been a cost-benefit analysis of the project, to which Gorbachev would have been privy, specifying the amount of traffic needed to be generated by the BAM so that it might someday become a viable enterprise. Not to be denied, resourceful western scholars exercised a little exchange theory of their own and concluded that "from an accounting point of view, the BAM seems a marginal investment." In current (1983) prices ". . . traffic needs to be 50

6. *Pravda*, 7 September 1985.

million ton-km per kilometer *merely to break even"* (my italics).[7] In the early 1970s, GOSPLAN projected traffic flows for the BAM to average 35 million ton-km per kilometer per year between 1983 and 1985, and 70 to 75 million ton-km per kilometer per year between 1985 and 1990, with even heavier cargoes thereafter. Up to three-fourths of the initial freight was to be West Siberian oil bound for Pacific markets.[8] By 1983, BAM's chief economist and academic director, Abel Aganbegyan, concluded that the new line would not be able to haul more than 30 million ton-km per kilometer before 1990.[9] Surely, Gorbachev had the statistical firepower to shoot down the BAM before it became a major boondoggle . . . *if he would only choose to do it.*

Shabad certainly thought he had done it. Some of the proof in the pudding was the fact that appropriate investments for the BAM sister-project, the Amur-Yakutsk Mainline (AYAM), were not forthcoming during the new five-year plan. Designed to reach Yakutsk by 1995, the AYAM was barely out of the starting block before suffering radical cuts in financing. Estimated to need at least 2 billion rubles, half of which should have been earmarked for the period between 1986 and 1990, the AYAM reportedly was given a piddling 150 million rubles for that period.[10] With unpromising data like these and an overall slow down in news coverage of BAM-related developments, by mid 1987 even diehard BAM enthusiasts had to agree that the crafty Shabad was onto something. Or was he?

Indications were that things were better on the BAM than met the eye, even a jaundiced one. With only half of BAM's 3,115 km in full service, it still had exceeded plan in 1986 and 1987.[11] Transport costs had dropped sharply, labor productivity was up 5 percent, and workers had saved the government 2 million rubles in subsidies. Between 1981 and 1987, 150 million tons of freight were shipped over the BAM, meaning 110 million tons had been carried over the railroad during the last three years. (In August 1984, a BAM spokesperson noted the BAM had carried some 40 million tons to date.[12]) Thus, BAM, at 36 million ton-km per kilometer, had already exceeded Aganbegyan's projection and apparently was well on its way to the western-calculated "break-even point."

7. J. Ambler, H. Hunter, and J.N. Westwood, "Soviet Railways: Lethargy or Crisis?" *Soviet and East European Transport Problems, European Transport Problems,* eds. J. Ambler, D.J.B. Shaw, and L. Symons (New York: St. Martin's Press, 1985).

8. *Ekonomicheskaya gazeta,* no. 5, January 1975, p. 13; N.P. Belenki and V.S. Maslennikov, "BAM: Rayon tyagoteniya i gruzovyye perevozki," *Zheleznodorozhnyy transport,* no. 10, October 1974, pp. 39-46.

9. *Gudok,* 22 April 1983; originally he had said, "before the end of the century."

10. *Pravda,* 6 March 1986.

11. *Gudok,* 7 and 14 August 1987.

12. *Izvestiya,* 17 August 1984.

Moreover, Gorbachev never stated publicly that he was repudiating the BAM. In fact, by announcing his commitment to a long-range development program for "the Far East Major Economic Region, Buryat ASSR, and Chita Oblast to the year 2000," he clearly defined the major geographical limits of the BAM service area, even though he did not mention the mainline by name. And how does one repudiate an already 20 billion-ruble investment, anyway?

THE COMPREHENSIVE PLAN FOR THE FAR EAST AND VICINITY

The plan that emerged in August 1987 had the blessing of GOSPLAN, the Soviet and Russian Republic Councils of Ministers, and local soviets and organs of the Party. The plan foresees a 2.5-fold growth of industrial output, a 2.6-fold increase in the generation of electric power, up to a 3.8-fold rise in the production of oil and gas condensate, and a maximum of a 9.3 fold expansion of natural gas output. To ensure that these targets will be reached, 232 billion rubles of State and enterprise investments will be allocated to the Far East region (198 billion rubles) and Transbaikalia (34 billion rubles) through the end of the century.

Certain economic spheres receive priority under the plan guidelines. Investments will be allotted to Far Eastern fisheries, which by century's end will account for 45 percent of the country's total fish catch. Because provisioning of the region has been a serious problem through the years, with almost half of the food needs being drawn from other parts of the country, major investments will be allotted to this. By the year 2000, the demands of Far Eastern consumers and Transbaikal region will be fully satisfied by locally raised potatoes, vegetables, milk, eggs, pork, and poultry. A substantial portion of the beef also will be produced locally. Yet, the plan does recognize that butter, cheese, warm-weather vegetables, and the balance of the beef will have to be imported.

One of the important focuses of the plan deals with the comprehensive utilization of regional resources in closed-cycle integrated plants, whose production will go exclusively to the needs of the region to reduce its dependence on long-haul imported finished goods. Emphasis will be given to the production of machines needed for the extraction of regional raw materials. Even here, Gorbachev's goal of intensification and restructuring is important: Older plants like "Amurstal'" and the steel mill at Petrovsk-Zabaikalski will be upgraded, and the long-promised integrated iron and steel plant based on South Yakutian coking coal and iron ore will be built somewhere in the region. The new plant will produce 3 million tons of rolled metal by the year 2000. The tin processing operations at Solnechny near Komsomolsk will be expanded and improved to fully utilize not only the tin but also valuable trace metals in the ore.

Wood and wood processing will expand several times over. The output of wood pulp will rise by 2.1 times, cardboard by 3.2 times, particle board by a factor of 5, and plywood no less than six-fold. "And all of this will occur as exports of wood grow by only 11 percent," meaning most of the wood products will be going for local and domestic needs.

The electricity and energy demand of the region will be fully satisfied by local sources as early as the Thirteenth Five-Year Plan (1991-1995). Coal output in the region will increase by 85 million tons. From new oil and gas condensate wells in western parts of Yakutia will come 3 million tons of petroleum and 5 billion cubic meters of gas. An additional 5 million tons of oil and 10 billion cubic meters of gas will be extracted from the continental shelf off Sakhalin Island.

A special section of the plan is devoted exclusively to the BAM and its service area. The entire railroad (except for the 15.3-km North Muya Tunnel) is slated to be fully operational by 1990; a tunnel bypass will work temporarily until 1992, when the North Muya is expected to be complete.[13] As the full program has not yet been published, few details have transpired on which parts of the BAM zone will obtain priority investment. We can certainly imagine that one will be South Yakutia, another the Komsomolsk region, and another in the Urgal area, where coal output is slated to more than double by 1990.[14] BAM industrial production as a whole will increase 2.9 times by century's end, while the population of the service area is slated to increase only 1.7 times (1.7 to 2 million persons). Production of electricity, coal, nonferrous metals, wood, wood pulp, and lumber will rise rapidly. The highest rates of growth, however, will occur in the construction materials industry, which is obviously important for the development of the virtually nonexistent infrastructure of the BAM service area. In fact, 30 percent of the total investment for the entire Far Eastern and Transbaikal regions (70 billion rubles) during this period is earmarked for infrastructural development.

Is the Gorbachev plan realistic? Is it economically feasible? It means an allotment of at least 20 billion rubles of investment capital every year for the next decade or so. This is double the annual allocation now going to the development of West Siberian oil and gas. Considering the limited immediate return from this substantial investment and the burdens that the investment

13. *Gudok*, 31 July 1987.
14. *Gudok*, 27 August 1987.

will place on an already overextended economy, it is unlikely that the comprehensive plan for the Far East and Transbaikalia will meet with early approval. Other reasons are linked to labor, infrastructural, and environmental constraints.

Labor and Infrastructure Problems

The ills of Siberia's labor turnover are legendary. In the early 1970s, one out of three oilfield workers departed West Siberia within the first year. More recently, only one out of every four BAM workers, who endure their entire three-year term in the region, reenlists for further tours of duty, [15] and one 1984 study indicated that only 13 percent of the BAM workforce wanted to make the BAM their lifetime home.[16] Even excluding the costs of losing trained or semi-trained labor, when turnover occurs, Siberian salaries must be subsidized by the rest of the country to the tune of 1.25 to 5.0 or more, depending on the skills and/or hazards involved. Beginning BAM workers, including office staff, for example, receive a salary that is consistently 1.7 times greater than the average Soviet wage.[17]

Deborah Kaple's excellent research on Far Eastern and BAM labor problems notes the great transience of the workers. The inducement in part relates to the high wages offered in the region. Once skilled, a worker theoretically can find a better paying job in a more northerly and/or easterly location. Labor management is uncoordinated and encourages workers to move from job site to job site; thus, a sense of community is lacking in most Siberian towns. Transient workers take no pride in the towns in which they live. Without such "civic pride," it is difficult to improve the quality of local life. Add to this the high living costs and generally poor living conditions, irrespective of climate, and labor turnover is an inherent feature of Siberian life.[18] Given the remoteness of the eastern regions and the ubiquity of job availability, the situation induces unemployment from downright shirking, drifting, or seasonal labor. Workers opting for this course often just "bum around" in the major cities. "Why not?" Kaple asks. They have a right to work and are in demand

15. *Gudok*, 22 November 1986.

16. *The Economist*, 12 May 1984.

17. S.N. Zhelezko, *Sotsial'no-demograficheskiye problemy v zone BAMa* (Moscow: Statistika, 1980).

18. Deborah A. Kaple, "The BAM: Labor, Migration, and Prospects for Settlement," *Soviet Geography*, 27, 1986, pp. 719-720.

everywhere. Thus, "the BAM was built by a steady stream of constantly changing cadres."[19]

Poor living conditions, often due to the low quality or virtual nonexistence of infrastructure, is the problem most often cited by departing BAM families and workers. Women living in Novy Uoyan, a new town on the BAM northeast of Lake Baikal, as late as August 1987 complained about a 2,000 seat shortage in preschool accommodations, the fact that their children (some as old as seven years) had never tasted ice cream (!!) in a country awash in ice cream, the lack of maternity wards in a region with the highest birth rate in the Russian Republic, and the ubiquitous shortage of consumer goods and spare parts.[20] Temporary housing, some of which dates back to the original BAM settlement (1974), is a problem throughout the service area. Kaple again notes that as late as 1984, fourteen of seventeen neighborhoods consist of such housing, including such shelters as old railroad cars, quonsets, trailers, ramshackle wooden hovels, and tents.[21] These descriptions can be repeated for Neryungri, Chara, Ulkan, Ust-Kut, Zvezdny, and any number of other settlements.

Because emphasis must be placed on replacing the inferior housing as quickly as possible, other elements of infrastructure must suffer. Social and cultural needs go wanting. Some towns have no libraries. Some have movie theaters--without heat. Some have kindergartens for 200 children, but room is needed for 300 more. Worst of all, many towns have no hospital facilities at all.[22]

Incidentally, these same anecdotes were told five and ten years ago. No wonder there are labor shortages. Some towns, like Ikabya in the eastern BAM zone, are near ghost towns. When work teams leave, the population is slow to replenish. As a result, the "in-filling" and upgrading of infrastructure suffers from want of sufficient laborers. The great irony in all this is that the money needed to create the infrastructure is there--it just does not get spent. Thus, of the 3 million rubles earmarked for infrastructure in Ikabya last year, only 1.1 million rubles were actually expended.[23]

In March 1987, a senior BAM service area engineer wrote that technically "full operations" of the railway include completion of railroad support functions, such as locomotive and car repair depots and facilities.[24] In the decade or more that the BAM has been under construction, only one out of

19. Ibid., p. 732.
20. *Gudok*, 6 August 1987.
21. Kaple, *Soviet Geography*, p. 733.
22. *Gudok*, 16 July 1987.
23. *Gudok*, 5 September 1987.
24. *Gudok*, 31 March 1987.

three projected depots is now being built, and this is at Tynda. Even here, progress is slow. As in Ikabya, only one-fourth of the funds allotted for depot construction has been spent during the entire decade. "At this rate, it will take thirty years for the depot at Tynda to be built." So, technically, the BAM may not be in full operation for a long time.

Environmental Problems

The environment of the BAM service area and the Soviet Far East ranks among the world's harshest and simultaneously most delicate places on earth.[25] At 3.1 million square miles, the area of the region is larger than the continent of Australia and spans fully 30 degrees of latitude. It is thus difficult to speak of a single environment for the region as a whole. One needs to focus on discrete segments. The BAM service area lends itself to such a focus and will serve as the case study here.

To ensure that environmental considerations are taken into account in the course of economic construction, the Soviet Union, like the United States, uses a variant of environmental impact analysis. Potentially harmful environmental changes brought about by development are predicted and evaluated and, wherever possible, measures are taken that might reduce or eliminate the severity of these effects.

Although environmental impact analyses are now commonplace in the Soviet Union, the government has no specific law that states when such analyses should be prepared or what types of issues should be discussed. Instead, officials rely on broad enactments that govern the use of land, water, wildlife, air, and other natural resources.

Within the Soviet Far East, the BAM project has received considerable environmental study. The research is intended to assemble baseline data on features, such as geology and vegetation, that can be used to assess changes created by future economic development. Criticisms of the studies note that they seem to lack appropriate mitigation measures to help overcome the anticipated environmental problems. For instance, a project known as "The Territorial Comprehensive Plan for Environmental Protection Along the BAM" provides a thorough analysis of the territories and resource potential of the service area and forecasts potential pollution and environmental damage, but it includes no specific proposals to protect the primary topographical features and

---

25. Victor L. Mote, "Environmental Constraints to the Economic Development of Siberia," *Soviet Natural Resources in the World Economy*, eds. R.G. Jensen, T. Shabad, and A.W. Wright (Chicago: The University of Chicago Press, 1973), pp. 15-71.

basic ecosystems.[26] Because of these omissions, and because the project was begun *after* the start of work on the rail line, the plan does not meet the requirements of an American environmental impact statement. The baseline data provided in the project are nonetheless valuable and served as the subject of a national conference on the BAM development scheme in 1984.

Although there are a few environmental horror stories connected with the BAM construction project, chiefly concerning shabby regard for timber along the railway easement, poaching of wildlife, erosion and pollution problems associated with quarrying or dredging for subgrade and construction materials, and so forth, the BAM has received considerable environmental review by competent scientists. The recommendations of this stellar group have been responsible for shifting the proposed BAM route away from the northwest shore of Lake Baikal through a series of four cape tunnels. This action increased costs but made good environmental sense. Heavy industry thus far has been banned from most of the BAM service area because of the persistent temperature inversions that occur, especially during the long winter months. All along the BAM, workers and children alike are taught the value of preserving the environment, and the vast majority of residents possess a keen awareness of nature and its value.

Sometimes, however, the best intentions go awry. In the North Baikal region in the Buryat Republic, a Peoples' Control Committee has been assigned the task of overseeing the regulations specified in a State law dealing with the protection and rational utilization of the resources of Lake Baikal. A number of towns and settlements have been built in the vicinity of the lake and each is supposed to take measures to avoid polluting the lake. Given the aforementioned failures in the creation of infrastructure, it is understandable why, since the beginning of 1987, only thirty-one of fifty-seven of the measures required to protect Lake Baikal have been realized. Seven towns near the lake were supposed to have sewage treatment plants by this time; only one exists, in Severobaikalsk. Oil spills regularly stand in the motor pools of places like Angoya, Kichera, Uoyan, and Yanchukan, all of which are located on the Upper Agara River, which drains into Lake Baikal.[27] Apart from these isolated instances, the railway itself serves as a threat. It is estimated that Soviet railway industries produce some 400,000 tons of air pollution per year and only 13 percent are treated in any manner at all.[28] Eventually most BAM trains will be electric, thus avoiding an air pollution problem.

---

26. *Current Digest of the Soviet Press*, 36/40, 1984, p. 23.
27. *Gudok*, 26 March 1987.
28. *Gudok*, 7 July 1987.

CONCLUSION

At the present time, the BAM remains a "frozen asset" with very little economic justification except as a springboard for future settlement. Its abundant resources, except for timber, coal and a few rare and precious metals, have numerous competitors in the Pacific Basin. Development of BAM service area resources depends integrally on the appeal of foreign markets. Moreover, the lead-times inherent in developing these raw materials are extensive, and most of the resource sites are still undeveloped, meaning it will take years, perhaps even decades, for these operations to come on stream.

It is somewhat surprising, then, that a person as economically pragmatic as Mikhail Gorbachev would urge the development of a comprehensive scheme for the development of the Far East, Buryatia, and Chita Oblast at this time. The cost of the resultant program is 232 billion rubles, and the highly speculative benefits remain very long-term. With few prospects of payoffs within the next score of years, the proposed investment does not appear to be economically feasible.

Moreover, the nagging problems of an unreliable labor supply exacerbated by a poor and slowly developing infrastructure further discourage an optimistic outlook. Finally, whether it is a success or failure, environmental protection in the Far East and Transbaikalia costs a great deal of money, just one more hand in the coffers of the aching Soviet treasury.

10 JAPAN AND THE ECONOMIC DEVELOPMENT OF THE SOVIET FAR EAST

Michael J. Bradshaw

During the second half of 1986, events in the Soviet Union suggested the possibility of increased trade between Japan and the Soviet Union. First, Mikhail Gorbachev's speech at Vladivostok in July called for accelerated economic development of the Soviet Far East and improved relations with the states of the Pacific Basin. Second, the reform of the foreign trade system and the allowance of joint ventures paved the way for new forms of economic cooperation. This paper seeks to place these events within the perspective of past developments in Soviet-Japanese trade, and to evaluate the potential for increased Japanese involvement in the development of the Soviet Far East.

PAST: SOVIET-JAPANESE RELATIONS

Factors Affecting Trade

As with most trading relations, there are factors that promote Soviet-Japanese trade and others that hinder it; while economic factors have tended to favor trade, political factors have served to reduce it. The Soviet Union and Japan have yet to sign a peace treaty following World War II. Japan still lays claim

This paper is based on research conducted while the author was a graduate student at the University of British Columbia. He would like to acknowledge the support of the Max Bell Foundation, the Izaak Walton Killam Trust, and the Department of Geography.

to the Northern Territories (Kurile Islands) seized by the Soviet Union at the end of the War. As an industrially developed capitalist nation and a member of the Coordinating Committee for Multilateral Security Export Controls (CoCom) strategic embargo, Japan is in the opposite ideological camp. Finally, Japan does not appreciate the heavy-handed diplomacy of the Soviet Union.[1] On the other hand, Japan relies on the import of natural resources to fuel its industries, and the Soviet Far East has a wealth of natural resources. Thus, there exists a basic complementarity that promotes trade between the two countries. In addition, the resources of the Soviet Far East are relatively close to Japanese markets, although not necessarily accessible until the Baikal-Amur Mainline railway (BAM) is fully operational. At the same time, there are factors external to Soviet-Japanese trade that must also be considered. First, despite the construction of the BAM, the Soviet Far East has received relatively low priority in Soviet economic plans, and a lack of economic infrastructure continues to hinder resource development. Second, whenever possible Japan has tried to diversify its sources of raw materials. This "multiple sourcing" means that the Soviet Union now finds itself in resource markets that are characterized by oversupply and price cutbacks. To appreciate fully the interplay between these many factors, it is necessary to examine the dynamics and structure of trade between Japan and the Soviet Union.

Trade Dynamics

The growth of Soviet-Japanese trade is shown in Table 10-1 and Figure 10-1. In October 1956, Japan and the Soviet Union signed a joint declaration of intent to enter into treaties and agreements on trade.[2] Starting in 1960, a number of "Trade Payment Agreements" have been signed, and since 1965 these have been coordinated with Soviet Five-Year Plan periods. The most recent agreement for the period 1986-1990 was signed in January 1986 during Soviet Foreign Minister Shevardnadze's visit to Tokyo.[3] In 1965, the Japan-Soviet Economic Committee and the Soviet Japan Economic Committee were established, and joint meetings initiated the first cooperative agreement on Siberian development--the First Soviet Far East Forest Development Project, signed July 24, 1967. However, it took the combination of East-West détente

---

1. K. Ogawa, "Japan-Soviet Economic Relations: Present Status and Future Prospect," *Journal of Northeast Asian Studies,* vol. 2, no. 1, 1983, pp. 3-15.

2. Yu. S. Stolyarov and Ya. A. Pevzner, *SSSR-Yaponiya: problem torgovo-ekonomicheskikh otnosheniy.* (Moscow: Mezdunarodnyye otnosheniya, 1984), pp. 201-207.

3. Kel'n, "Novoye soglasheniye s Yaponiyey," *Vneshnyaya torgovlya,* no. 6, 1986, p. 14.

Table 10-1. Soviet-Japanese Trade, 1965-1986
(Million Foreign Trade Rubles)

Year	Exports	Imports	Total	Balance
1965	166.5	159.6	326.1	+6.9
1966	214.8	201.8	416.1	+13.0
1967	317.7	352.1	466.8	-34.4
1968	149.1	166.5	518.6	-17.4
1969	321.3	237.4	558.7	+839.0
1970	341.1	377.4	652.3	-36.0
1971	377.4	356.2	733.6	+21.2
1972	381.7	433.9	815.6	-52.2
1973	622.0	372.4	994.4	+249.6
1974	905.7	777.5	1,683.2	+128.2
1975	668.9	1,253.5	1,922.4	-584.6
1976	784.5	1,372.1	2,120.5	-623.6
1977	853.4	1,444.4	2,297.8	-591.0
1978	736.1	1,583.7	2,319.8	-847.6
1979	944.4	1,653.5	2,597.9	-709.1
1980	950.2	1,772.6	2,722.8	-822.4
1981	816.8	2,212.7	3,029.5	-1,395.9
1982	756.6	2,925.8	3,682.4	-2,169.2
1983	828.5	2,175.5	3,004.0	-1,347.0
1984	840.0	2,054.3	2,894.3	-1,214.3
1985	958.0	2,287.1	3,126.0	-2,286.9
1986	979.9	2,205.4	3,185.3	-1,225.5

Source: Vneshnyaya torgovlya v SSSR (Moscow, various years).

and the energy crisis to initiate large-scale trade agreements. Following a summit meeting in Moscow in 1973, the Japanese government agreed to make credit available from the Export-Import Bank of Japan to finance Siberian development projects. Between 1974 and 1975, a number of large-scale, long-term compensation agreements were signed, including the South Yakutian Coal Development Project, the Second Soviet Far East Development Project, the Yakutia Natural Gas Exploration Project, and the Sakhalin Continental Shelf Project.

In the late 1970s, the availability of credit and windfall profits from Soviet resource exports promoted a steady increase in Soviet-Japanese trade. Following the Soviet invasion of Afghanistan in December 1979, the Japanese

Figure 10-1. Soviet-Japanese Trade, 1965-1986

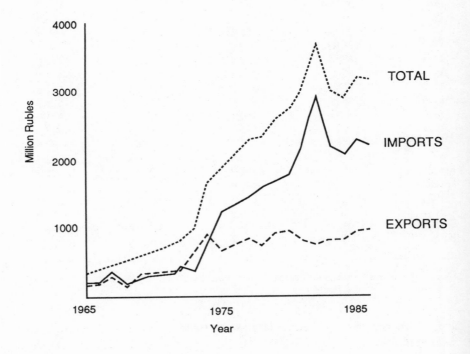

government implemented economic sanctions against the Soviet Union, $1.4 billion worth of credit was cancelled in early 1980, and meetings of the Japan-Soviet Economic Conference were suspended.[4] For a while, imports from Japan continued to expand. A third forestry agreement was signed in 1981, and Japanese companies picked up some additional contracts from the Siberian gas pipeline project when U.S. companies, in particular Caterpillar, were prohibited from participating in the project. However, in the absence of cheap credits and a positive political environment, trade faltered and declined between 1982 and 1984.[5] Despite the impressive growth recorded in the 1970s, Soviet-Japanese trade played a modest role in the foreign economic relations of both states. According to Soviet foreign trade statistics, Japan's share of total Soviet foreign trade turnover peaked at 3.8 percent in 1976. That same year, Japanese trade figures show the Soviet Union accounted for 3.3 percent of total exports and 1.8 percent of total imports.

Trade Structure

The general commodity structure of Soviet-Japanese trade is shown in Table 10-2. Japanese trade statistics have been used because they include information on nonferrous metal exports not reported in the Soviet Foreign Trade Yearbook (*Vneshnyaya torgovlya v SSSR*). From these data it can be seen that Soviet exports to Japan are spread among raw materials, fuels, and manufactured goods. The trade classification system distorts the structure of Soviet exports, because nonferrous metals are included among manufactured goods. In the raw material category, wood is the most important commodity, accounting for 24.5 percent of Soviet exports to Japan in 1985. The majority of wood is exported as uncut logs, providing a basic raw material for the Japanese forest products industry. Coal is the most important fuel export, and in recent years the volume of coal deliveries has increased as compensation deliveries from South Yakutia have begun. Among the nonferrous metals, platinum and platinum group metals, nickel, aluminum, and gold are the most important commodities. Fish and shellfish are also exports worthy of note.

Soviet imports from Japan are predominantly heavy industrial goods, which are used to provide "western technology" to improve the performance of

---

4. Leslie Dienes, *Soviet Asia: Economic Development and National Policy Choices* (Boulder, CO: Westview Press, 1987), p. 512.

5. G.B. Smith, "Recent Trends in Japanese-Soviet Trade," *Problems of Communism*, vol. 36, no. 1, 1987, p. 62.

Table 10-2. Structure of Soviet-Japanese Trade

Soviet Imports from Japan	1970	1975	1981	1985
TOTAL VALUE (Million U.S. $)	340.9	1,626.2	3,259.4	2,750.6
Percent of Total				
Raw Materials & Fuels	1.4	1.0	2.4	3.0
Light Industrial Products	36.2	14.2	7.9	9.2
Heavy Industrial Products	60.0	82.2	83.2	81.6
(Metals & Metal Products)	(16.2)	(36.1)	(43.0)	(34.1)
(Machinery & Instruments)	(31.8)	(35.3)	(32.1)	(38.1)
Other	2.4	2.6	6.5	6.2

Soviet Exports To Japan	1970	1975	1981	1985
TOTAL VALUE (Million U.S. $)	481.0	1,169.6	2,020.7	1,429.2
Percent of Total				
Foodstuffs	2.1	2.8	4.3	7.1
Raw Materials	56.6	57.6	34.7	32.3
Minerals & Fuels	15.8	19.5	15.7	24.6
Manufactured Goods	25.1	19.8	18.5	24.7
(Nonferrous Metals)	(15.9)	(15.0)	(11.7)	(16.1)
Other	0.4	0.3	26.7	11.3
(Gold)	n/a	n/a	(26.5)	(10.8)

Source: *White Paper on International Trade: Japan* (Tokyo, various years).

industry or to accelerate the development of Siberian resources. Much of the equipment used in the Soviet Far East is related to large-scale, long-term compensation agreements. Equipment deliveries under these agreements have not only included "high-tech" items such as pulp mills or coal processing plants, but also large volumes of "low-tech" products such as bulldozers, timber carriers and trucks.[6] These imports compensate for the illogical branch structure of the Siberian machine-building industry, which is ill-equipped to

6. Michael J. Bradshaw, *East-West Trade and the Regional Development of Siberia and the Soviet Far East,* unpublished Ph.D. thesis (1987), Department of Geography, University of British Columbia, Vancouver, pp. 268-293.

supply the region's resource industries with equipment suited to the harsh environment. Among metal and metal product imports, the most important item is large-diameter pipe. The Japanese steel industry was not initially a supplier of large-diameter pipe, but the development of the West Siberian oil and gas fields created an enormous demand for pipe in the late 1970s and early 1980s. In 1975, Japanese pipe exports to the Soviet Union were worth 207.8 million rubles and accounted for 15.7 percent of total Soviet pipe imports. In 1985, the value of exports had risen to 555.9 million rubles and the share of total imports to 29.4 percent. Soviet demand for large-diameter pipe will decline in the second half of the 1980s as the pipeline networks are completed.[7] Clearly, the structure of Soviet-Japanese trade reflects the basic complementarity that exists between the two regions. In the case of the Soviet Union, imports of Japanese technology and products are used to compensate for problems in the domestic economy. For Japan, resource imports from the Soviet Union serve to diversify further raw material sources; in the case of the forest products sector, the willingness of the Soviet Union to supply unprocessed logs provides a basic resource for the forest products industry in Japan.

The Role of the Soviet Far East

Since 1967, Japan has provided over $2.5 billion of credit to aid in the development of the Soviet Far East. The projects have concentrated on the development of the forest, coal, oil and gas resources, and also the improvement of port facilities at Nakhodka/Vostochny. Projects already complete include three forestry development agreements, under which the Japanese provided equipment to enable harvesting and processing. These credits were paid off with deliveries of timber. Japanese involvement in the South Yakutian Territorial Production Complex (TPC) has aided in the development of the coal mining and processing facilities at Neryungri. Off the coast of Sakhalin, the Sakhalin Oil Development Company (SODECO), a Japanese Consortium, has confirmed reserves of 140.5 billion cubic meters of gas, 86.5 million tons of crude oil, and 19.5 million tons of condensate. In short, the contribution of Japanese imports to the development of the Soviet Far East has been to aid in the exploitation of the region's natural resource base.

Data on regional trade participation are not available. However, a recent Soviet study suggested that Siberia and the Soviet Far East account for nearly

7. Smith, "Recent Trends in Japanese-Soviet Trade," p. 60.

80 percent of Soviet exports to Japan.[8] If one examines the structure of the regional economies of Siberia and the Soviet Far East, it is easy to see how this might be the case. Much of the trade between Japan and the Soviet Union has been internalized within compensation agreements. Between 1969 and 1979, 12 percent of Japanese exports to the Soviet Union and 11 percent of Soviet exports were under compensation agreements. By 1981, the share had risen to 32 percent of Japanese exports and 25 percent of Soviet exports.[9] Since then, coal exports from the South Yakutian TPC have come on stream and the proportion of Soviet exports under compensation agreements has increased. The role of compensation in Japanese exports has declined because there have been no agreements since 1981.

Stolyarov and Pevzner estimated that the Soviet Far East accounts for 44 percent of forest product exports to Japan.[10] This figure may seem low, but because the forests of the Soviet Far East are dominated by stands of larch, the East Siberian region has to supply other species, such as pine, fir, and spruce. A large part of these exports has been delivered under compensation agreements, but timber is also sold under short-term contracts and barter agreements.[11] Coal exports have traditionally come from the Kuznetsk basin in West Siberia and the Toro Basin on Sakhalin Island.[12] However, since 1984, coal has been delivered via the Little-BAM railway from the South Yakutia coal basin. Exports of nonferrous metals and minerals are also dominated by production in Siberia and the Soviet Far East. The Soviet Far East is the Soviet Union's only source of natural diamonds. The most important Soviet producer of nickel and platinum-group metals is the Norilsk Metallurgical combine north of the Arctic Circle in the East Siberian Economic Region. Norilsk accounts for 60 percent of Soviet nickel production and 75 percent of platinum production. About 60 percent of Soviet aluminum smelting capacity is located in the upper reaches of the Angara-Yenisey river system in East Siberia, and, no doubt, the region makes a substantial contribution to Soviet aluminum exports to Japan. The Soviet Far East has traditionally been the center of the Soviet gold mining industry, but in recent years mining

8. Stolyarov and Pevzner, *SSSR-Yaponiya*, p. 186.

9. Leslie Dienes, "Soviet-Japanese Economic Relations: Are They Beginning to Fade?" *Soviet Geography: Review and Translation*, vol. 26, no. 7, 1985, p. 512.

10. Stolyarov and Pevzner, *SSSR-Yaponiya*, p. 186.

11. R.T. Fenton, "The Eastern USSR: Forest Resources and Forest Products Exports to Japan," *FRI Bulletin*, no. 123 (Rotorua, New Zealand: Forest Research Institute, 1986), pp. 24-25.

12. R.S. Mathieson, *Japan's Role in Soviet Economic Growth: Transfer of Technology Since 1965* (New York: Praeger, 1979), p. 69.

operations have been developed in Central Asia.[13] Nevertheless, the Far Eastern region still accounts for 50 to 60 percent of Soviet gold production and therefore contributes to sales to Japan. Together, all of these raw material sources could easily account for 80 percent of Soviet exports to Japan.

While it is clear that Siberia and the Soviet Far East account for the bulk of Soviet exports to Japan, the regions' share of imports is far more difficult to determine. Mathieson's study of Japan's role in Soviet economic development suggested that a large part of Soviet imports from Japan was destined for the core regions of the European USSR. This finding is also supported by Sobeslavsky and Beazley's 1980 study of western technology transfer to the Soviet chemical industry. Thus, to a certain degree, exports from the Soviet Far East finance imports for consumption elsewhere. However, as the data in Table 1 show, the Soviet Union has a sizable hard currency deficit in trade with Japan. Therefore, to pay for Japanese imports, a hard currency surplus must be generated elsewhere. The likely source of this additional hard currency will be the export of Siberian oil and gas to West Europe. This means that the level of trade between Japan and the Soviet Union is not only determined by the value of Soviet exports to Japan and the availability of credit, but also by the size of the trade surplus with West Europe.

PRESENT: SOVIET-PACIFIC BASIN TRADE AT THE DAWN OF THE PACIFIC CENTURY

Since coming to power in March 1985, Gorbachev has made a number of diplomatic moves to try to improve relations with Japan.[14] For example, in January 1986, Shevardnadze visited Tokyo. However, Gorbachev's scheduled 1987 visit to Japan was postponed due to an inability to agree on a program and Soviet insistence that Friendship and Economic Cooperation documents be signed during the visit.[15] While the two sides have agreed to renew negotiations on a Peace Treaty, the Northern Territories still remain a major obstacle. In August 1987, the Soviet Union allowed fifty-two former residents of the Islands to visit ancestral graves. The visitors were allowed to enter the Soviet

13. M. Kaser, "The Soviet Gold Mining Industry," *Soviet Natural Resources in the World Economy*, eds. R.G. Jensen, T. Shabad, and A.W. Wright (Chicago: University of Chicago Press, 1983), p. 559.

14. T. Satoshi, "The Soviet Union Smiles at Japan," *Japan Quarterly*, vol. 33, no. 2, 1986, pp. 129-137; and R.U.T. Kim, "Warming Up Soviet-Japanese Relations?" *Washington Quarterly*, vol. 9, no. 2, 1986, pp. 85-96.

15. "Gorbachev's Visit to Japan in January Impossible: Ministry," *Japan Times Weekly*, 20 December 1986, p. 2.

Union without passports and visas to avoid recognition of the Islands as Soviet territory. As part of this general improvement in relations, sanctions imposed to protest the invasion of Afghanistan and martial law in Poland were also lifted, and Japanese government credits are now available. However, political events during 1987 took a turn for the worse. In August 1987, the Soviet Union expelled a Japanese business executive and naval attache. Japan responded with the expulsion of Soviet trade representatives. At the same time, U.S. reaction to Toshiba's illegal export of computerized milling machines has made the Japanese wary of trade with the Soviet Union.

Despite the short-lived thaw during 1986, Soviet-Japanese trade has shown no signs of returning to the levels of the late 1970s. One of the major reasons for this decline in trade is the demise of the compensation agreement as a means of financing trade.[16] There are a number of reasons why the Japanese have lost enthusiasm for compensation agreements. First, the Soviet Far East has remained a low priority region within Soviet economic plans, and the resultant lack of economic infrastructure hinders resource development. Despite Gorbachev's Vladivostok speech and the recent announcement of a comprehensive plan for the economic development of the Soviet Far East, it is difficult to see from where the investment required to accelerate the economic development of the Soviet Far East will come. The present policy of restructuring is likely to focus development on the European regions of the Soviet Union.

The second reason is the poor experiences the Japanese have had with past compensation agreements. For example, Japanese forest products companies have continually complained about the inability of EXPORTLES to provide quality timber of the correct species mix and dimensions when domestic demand is high. The inability of the Soviet economic system to respond to the dynamics of the Japanese economy has often led to an oversupply of timber when demand is slack, leading to severe storage problems. At the same time, the percentage of larch in Soviet deliveries remains a constant source of friction.

A third and related reason is that conditions in world resource markets no longer favor large-scale, long-term compensation agreements. Under the terms of the South Yakutian coal development project, the Japanese are expected to take delivery of 104 million tons of coking coal between 1979 and 1998. At the time the agreement was reached in 1974, the Japanese steel industry predicted an increasing demand for coking coal during the 1980s and 1990s. Since then, global recession, changing technology, and the restructuring of the

16. Dienes, *Soviet Geography*, p. 519.

Japanese economy have reduced demand for steel and coking coal. Under the terms of the compensation agreement, delivery of South Yakutian coal was to start in 1983, and by the late 1980s deliveries would reach 6.5 million tons a year. In actuality, coal deliveries did not start until 1984, when 0.8 million tons of coal were delivered.[17] According to the Japan External Trade Organization (JETRO), Japan imported 1.6 million tons of coal from the Soviet Union in 1984, so the Kuzbas must have supplied the balance. The 1985 plan called for the delivery of 3.2 million tons of coking coal; according to JETRO figures, only 2.9 million tons were actually delivered. Western sources reported that during 1986, the Soviet Union asked the Japanese steel mills to accept 6.5 million tons of coal, while the Japanese wanted 3.7 million tons. An agreement was reached on 4.2 million tons.[18] It seems very unlikely that Soviet coal exports will reach the 6.5 million-ton level in the near future, because Japan has commitments to accept coal from producers in the United States, Western Canada, Australia, South Africa, and China.[19]

A similar situation has plagued the Sakhalin project. The imposition of U.S. sanctions to protest the invasion of Afghanistan and martial law in Poland hampered the project by denying SODECO access to U.S.-designed drilling rigs. However, in 1983, an agreement was finally reached on the development phase. SODECO was to participate in the construction of a liquefied natural gas (LNG) production facility at De Kastri on the Soviet mainland. LNG would be moved to Japan by tanker rather than by pipelines, as originally proposed. During 1986, the rapid fall in oil prices cast the future of the project in doubt. By late 1986, both sides were reconsidering the project. The Soviet Union was concerned with the economic viability of the project, which in itself was something new. Japan felt that energy prices in the 1990s would be high enough to make the project viable, but the Japanese power utility companies, the major consumers of LNG, were no longer agreeing to accept delivery from the Soviet Union. In July 1987, it was announced that the Soviet and Japanese governments had agreed on a joint crude oil development project off Sakhalin Island.[20] The announcement made no mention of LNG deliveries, possibly because the Japanese have promoted a

17. Victor L. Mote, "A Visit to the Baikal-Amur Mainline and the New Amur-Yakutsk Rail Project," *Soviet Geography: Review and Translation*, vol. 26, no. 9, 1985, p. 704.

18. "Japan-Soviet Coal Terms," *Mining Journal*, 27 March 1987, p. 238.

19. Michael J. Bradshaw, "Soviet-Pacific Basin Trade: A Canadian Perspective," *Institute of Asian Research, Working Paper #29* (Vancouver: The University of British Columbia, 1987).

20. "Sakhalin Oil Project Gets Green Light," *Japan Economic Journal*, 11 July 1987, p. 18.

number of LNG projects in the Pacific Basin, and they now face a potential oversupply.[21]

All of the above factors combine to undermine the economic effectiveness, from a Japanese viewpoint, of large-scale, long-term compensation agreements. A second reason for the decline in the level of Soviet-Japanese trade is the rise of the Pacific Basin as an economic system in its own right. Japan is clearly the most important component in this system and has actively promoted the industrialization of the region to meet its own needs. As Gorbachev has recognized, the Soviet Union at present is not considered part of this economic system. In 1986, the Pacific Basin accounted for a mere 9.9 percent of Soviet foreign trade turnover.[22] Gorbachev's Vladivostok speech can be seen as an attempt to ensure that the Soviet Union benefits from the coming Pacific Century; however, current trade patterns suggest that the only countries with which the Soviet Union is likely to increase trade are the socialist states of the Asia-Pacific region: North Korea, China, Vietnam, Kampuchea, and Laos.[23] The Soviet Union's trade with Vietnam, Kampuchea, and Laos is really a form of foreign aid, and the Soviet Union has a large trade surplus with them. As countries such as Japan, the United States, Canada, and Australia promote the idea of a Pacific Basin economic system, the Soviet Union will find it very difficult to compete in the region.

The final reason for the decline in Soviet-Japanese trade relates to the decline in the oil price and its impact on Soviet trade with West Europe. Since 1984, the combination of production problems and a rapid decline in world prices has reduced the Soviet Union's hard currency purchasing power. During 1985, Soviet exports of oil earned $13 billion; in 1986, earnings fell to $7.9 billion.[24] To counter the falling price, the Soviet Union has increased the volume of oil exports, but a 15 percent increase in oil exports can only partially compensate for a 30 percent drop in the price.[25] The nature of natural gas markets means that gas sales cannot suddenly be increased to compensate for lost oil revenues.[26] The strength of the Japanese yen serves to compound this problem because the majority of Soviet hard currency trade is conducted

21. R.A. Morse, "Japan's Liquefied Natural Gas Dilemma: Oversupply and Lower Demand," *U.S.-Japanese Energy Relations, Cooperation and Competition*, eds. C.K. Ebinger and R.A. Morse (Boulder, CO: Westview Press, 1984), pp. 179-195.

22. Bradshaw, *Working Paper #29*, p. 6.

23. Michael J. Bradshaw, "Soviet/Asian-Pacific Trade and the Regional Development of the Soviet Far East," *Soviet Geography: Review and Translation*, April 1988, forthcoming.

24. I. Gorst, "Oil Exports Rise in 1986," *Petroleum Economist*, vol. 54, no. 3, 1987, pp. 93.

25. "Soviet Union Set to Sell More Petroleum to West," *Globe and Mail*, 13 August 1987, p. B18.

26. J.P. Stern, *Soviet Oil and Gas Exports to the West*, Royal Institute of International Affairs, Energy Paper No. 21 (Aldershot, Hants.: Gower, 1987).

with U.S. dollars. The impact of this decline in revenues is dramatically illustrated by the fact that in 1984, total Soviet exports to the European Community were valued at 16.6 billion foreign trade rubles, and the Soviet Union had a 6.7 billion ruble positive balance of trade; by 1986, the total value of exports has declined to 8.8 billion rubles with a trade surplus of only 1.7 billion rubles. As suggested earlier, the trade surplus with West Europe serves to balance the trade deficit with Japan (as well as pay for grain imports). As a consequence of sharply reduced hard currency revenues, the Soviet Union has had to cut back on its hard currency expenditures, which has even led to the cancellation of some contracts. For example, the Matsushita Panasonic group recently reported the suspension of negotiations on a number of contracts to supply industrial equipment. Matsushita attributes the suspensions to a shortage of foreign currency.[27]

FUTURE: RESTRUCTURING AND SOVIET-JAPANESE TRADE

It is evident from the discussion so far that Soviet-Japanese economic relations are going through difficult times. In discussing the future, it is useful to distinguish between short-term and long-term prospects. In the short term, it seems likely that the Soviet Union will continue to import Japanese industrial technology. A clear indication of this was provided by the "Yaponiya-86" trade exhibition in Moscow.[28] However, there are a number of factors that will limit the Soviet Union's ability to import. First, the reduction of hard currency earnings and the rejection of compensation agreements will limit the Soviet Union's ability to finance trade. Second, the Toshiba affair and the consequent tightening of CoCom regulations will make Japanese companies nervous about selling industrial technology to the Soviet Union. Prior to the "Yaponiya-86" exhibition, the Soviet Union presented the Japanese business mission with a list of fourteen Japanese technologies they were interested in obtaining. Among them were "numerically controlled machine tools."[29] In a more general sense, the Soviet Union's attitude toward imports of western technology may change under Gorbachev. During the 1970s, Brezhnev saw the importation of western technology as a means of injecting innovation into the Soviet

27. "Matsushita's Plants to Make Fridges in Soviet Freeze," *Japan Economic Journal*, 1 August 1987, p. 17.
28. A. Bulatov, "Yaponiya-86," *Vneshnyaya torgovlya*, no. 2, 1987, pp. 48-49.
29. "The Soviet Union Seeking Japanese High Technology in 14 Fields," *Japan Economic Journal*, 4 and 11 January 1986, p. 2.

economy without the use of deep-seated economic reform. The policy failed because the lack of economic reform reduced the effectiveness of the imported technology. Clearly, Gorbachev wishes to instigate the necessary reforms to stimulate domestic innovation. It is too early to tell, but it will be interesting to compare the nature of technology transfer under Gorbachev to that of the Brezhnev period. In some senses, the current cash shortage may be to Gorbachev's advantage, for it will force Soviet producers to confront the failings of the domestic innovation process.

The recent legislation allowing the creation of joint ventures can be seen in part as a response to the hard currency situation and the demise of the compensation agreement. Thus far, the Japanese response to the joint venture legislation has not been very positive. The chairperson of Komatsu Ltd., which was very much involved in the large Siberian development projects, does not think that the joint venture will bring about a sudden increase in Soviet-Japanese trade. The reason for this pessimism is that Japanese business executives cannot see the joint venture working without greater decentralization of decisionmaking to the enterprise level.[30] If the economic reforms introduced by Gorbachev lead to greater flexibility at the plant level, then perhaps the Japanese will be more positive, but they are also unhappy about Soviet majority ownership and the requirement that the chairperson be a Soviet citizen. Despite these problems, there have been a number of proposals for Soviet-Japanese joint ventures in the fisheries, lumber processing, and service sectors. In June 1987, the first Soviet-Japanese joint venture agreement was reached. The Tairiku Trading Company and the Ministry of Timber, Paper/Pulp, and Woodworking Industries agreed to set up a wood processing firm in Irkutsk. With an initial investment of 13.3 million rubles, the firm "Igirma-Tairiku" (51 percent Soviet-owned) will produce 90,000 cubic meters of red pine, 70,000 cubic meters of which will be exported to Japan.[31] While this agreement represents a start, exchanging resources for equipment is still very much within the traditional framework of Soviet-Japanese trade. It remains to be seen if joint ventures promote the development of other sectors of the Siberian economy.

In the long term, Gorbachev's economic policies are seeking to restructure the Soviet economy and promote a more intensive, technologically advanced mode of production. This may lead to a relative decline in the importance of

30. "It's Hard to Invest in the USSR, Exec Says," *Japan Times Weekly,* 6 June 1987, p. 2.
31. "Tairiku Trading Venture 1st Japan-Soviet Tie-Up," *Japan Economic Journal,* 27 June 1987, p. 16.

resource-producing areas such as the Soviet Far East.[32] In the foreign trade arena, the goal is to improve the structure of trade by reducing the role of resource exports and increasing the share of higher value-added goods.[33] Clearly, this strategy cannot work in the case of Japan. Despite the Japanese penchant for foreign cars, the Lada will not be a status symbol in Tokyo. In attempting to reduce the role of natural resources in exports to Japan, the Soviet Union could undermine the fundamental logic of such trade. In sum, if Gorbachev succeeds in restructuring the Soviet economy and improving the structure of Soviet exports, it may further reduce the volume of trade between Japan and the Soviet Union; however, the question then remains: Will a reformed and rejuvenated Soviet economy need to import Komatsu trucks?

32. Theodore Shabad, "The Gorbachev Economic Policy: Is the USSR Turning Away from Siberian Development?" Paper presented at the School of Slavonic and East European Studies' Conference on "The Development of Siberia: Peoples and Human Resources," University of London, 1986.

33. I.D. Ivanov, "Restructuring the Mechanism of Foreign Economic Relations in the USSR," Soviet Economy, vol. 3, no. 3, 1987, pp. 192-218.

INDEX

205

ABOUT THE CONTRIBUTORS

Michael J. Bradshaw is a Research Fellow, Department of Geography, University of Birmingham in Birmingham, England.

Ralph S. Clem is Professor, Department of International Relations, Florida International University, Miami, FL.

Wladyslaw W. Jermakowicz is Associate Professor of Business, Division of Business, Southern Indiana University, Evansville, IN.

Michael Kraus is Associate Professor, Department of Political Science, Middlebury College, Middlebury, VT.

Robert E. Leggett and Robert L. Kellogg are with the Central Intelligence Agency.

Gary G. Meyers is Assistant Professor, Department of Political Science, Middlebury College, Middlebury, VT.

Victor L. Mote is Associate Professor of Geography and Russian Studies, Department of Political Science, University of Houston, Houston, TX.

Lt. General William E. Odom is Director of the National Security Agency.

John E. Parsons is Assistant Professor, Department of Economics, Finance and Accounting, Sloan School of Management, Massachusetts Institute of Technology, Cambridge, MA.

Gertrude E. Schroeder is Professor, Department of Economics, University of Virginia, Charlottesville, VA.

ABOUT THE EDITOR

Ronald D. Liebowitz is Associate Professor of Geography and a member of the Soviet Studies Program at Middlebury College. Since joining the Middlebury faculty in 1984, he has been active in establishing the Soviet Studies program and contributing to the Geography Department. Professor Liebowitz has published articles on Soviet investment policy, the Soviet censuses, regional economic development, and political geography. His current research involves regional economic development policies in multinational socialist states and their relationship to ethno-nationalist movements.